Intelligent Business

Coursebook

Upper Intermediate
Business English

| Tonya Trappe | Graham Tullis |

Pearson Education Limited
Edinburgh Gate
Harlow
Essex CM20 2JE
England
and Associated Companies throughout the world.

www.pearsonelt.com

© Pearson Education Limited 2006

First published 2006
Fourth impression 2013

ISBN: 978-14082-5601-5

Set in Economist Roman 10.5/12.5
Printed in China
GCC/04

Acknowledgements

The authors would like to thank our editors, Tony Garside and Stephen Nicholl, and the following people and their organisations for their assistance: Laurence Baierlein, Gilles Béguin, Gérard Desmarest, Mac MacKenzie, Violaine Fray, Sarah Hamberg, Jennifer Barker, Harvard Business School, Olivier Heller, Insead Fontainebleau, Jean Pierre Masson, Kevin O'Driscoll, Adeline Quesnel and Henriette Tullis. We would also like to thank the students and staff at ESIEA Paris and L'université de Paris XII.

The publishers would like to thank the following people for their helpful comments on the manuscript for this book: Irene Barrall, UK; Louise Bulloch, Intercom Language Services GmbH; Steve Bush, The British Institute, Florence; William Cooley, Open Schools of Languages, Madrid; Peter Dunn, Groupe ESC, Dijon, Bourgogne; Jolanta Korc-Migoñ, Warsaw University of Technology; Louise Pile, UK.

The publishers would like to thank the following people for their help in piloting and developing this course: Richard Booker and Karen Ngeow, University of Hong Kong; Adolfo Escuder, EU Estudios Empresariales, University of Zaragoza; Wendy Farrar, Università Cattolica del Sacro Cuore, Piacenza; Andrew Hopgood, Linguarama, Hamburg; Ann-Marie Hadzima, Dept of Foreign Languages, National Taiwan University, Taiwan; Samuel C. M. Hsieh, English Department, Chinese Culture University, Taipei; Laura Lewis, ABS International, Buenos Aires; Maite Padrós, Universitat de Barcelona; Giuliete Aymard Ramos Siqueira, São Paulo; Richmond Stroupe, World Language Center, Soka University, Tokyo; Michael Thompson, Centro Linguistico Università Commerciale L. Bocconi, Milan; Krisztina Tüll, Európai Nyelvek Stúdiója, Budapest.

The publishers are grateful to The Economist for permission to adapt copyright material on pages 9 (©2004), 17 (©2004), 25 (©2003), 35 (©2002), 44 (©2004), 51 (©2004), 61 (©2001), 77 (©2004), 103 (©2005), 129 (©2004). All articles copyright of The Economist Newspaper Limited. All rights reserved.

We are also grateful to the following for permission to reproduce copyright material:

Brandchannel.com for an extract adapted from 'Gucci – family baggage' by Vivian Manning-Schaffel October 2003 taken from Brandchannel.com produced by Interbrand; Alejandro Eggers Moreno for an extract adapted from 'Fossil-fuel Dependence Do oil reserves foretell bleak future' which first appeared in Pacific News Service April 2004; Copyright Clearance Center Inc. for an extract 'Googling for Courage' by Alan Deutschman taken from Fastcompany.com September 2004 © Mansueto Ventures LLC; and The New York Times Co. for an extract adapted from 'A Path to Helping the Poor, and His Investors' by Harry Hurt III, October 2003 published in The New York Times © The New York Times Co. Reprinted with Permission.

In some instances we have been unable to trace the owners of copyright material and we would appreciate any information that would enable us to do so.

Photograph acknowledgements

The Publishers are grateful to the following for their permission to reproduce copyright photographs:

Advertising Archive 52, 54l and r, 68 (L'Oreal); Alamy/TNT Magazine 13, /Camelot 24, /Pictures Colour Library 29, 129 (inset), Nikreates 50tl, / IML Image Group Ltd 50bl, /mediacolor's 50ct, /Pictor International 91, / Michele Falzone 114; Aston Martin 67; BAA Aviation Photo Library/Andy Wilson 15, /Steve Bates 17; Bechtel Corporation (www.bechtel.com) 19; Blackberry.com 43; Clinique 72l; Corbis/Reuters/Peter Morgan FCtr, 1tr, 95, /Reuters 3bl, 9, 49, 134, /Roy McMahon 12, /Gene Belvins 16t, /Haruyoshi Yamaguchi 16b, /Jose Luis Pelaez Inc 21, /Charles O'Rear 22b, /Reuters/ Paul McErlane 38, /Rob Lewine 55, /Steve Chenn 56, /Sygma/Susana Raab 59, /LWA-Stephen Welstead 60l, /Anne Domdey 60cl, /Michael Prince 60cr, /Jim Craigmyle 60r, / Ariel Skelley 65, /Reuters/Sue Ogrocki 75, / James Leynse 76bl, /Louie Psihoyos 76br, /Owen Franken 82, /Images. com 85, /Roger Ressmeyer 90, /Al Francekevich 100, /Peter Turnley 116, / France Reportage/Muriel Dovic 118, /Patrik Giardino 119, /Keith Wood 126, /Larry Williams 130; Christian Dior 72cb; Empics/Associated Press/ Richard Drew 11, /PA/Chris Young 79, /Associated Press/David Karp 96, Associated Press/Ben Margot 3r, 101, 103; General Electric (www.ge.com) 35 all; Getty Images/AFP 10, /Andrew Yates Productions 25, /Nick Clements 40, /David Buffington 41, /Roy Botterell 64, /Altrendo 80, /Simon Potter 81, Harald Sund 97, /Tinroof 99, /Lonny Kalfus 106, /Ghislain & Marie David de Lossy 107, /Time Life Pictures/John Swope 121, /Neil Emmerson 129 (main), /Robert Daly 133; Google.com 94c and b; Honda FCc, 1c, 105t and b; Image State/Age Fotostock/Pedro Coll 47, 125, /Rob Goldman 73; Kobal Collection 122; Kos Picture Source 23; Lee Stephen 61; Jeff Moore (jeff@ jmal.co.uk) 66, 68 (Sony, Mercedes, Adidas, Pepsi, McDonald's), 115; Nokia 42r; Panos / Mark Henley 8, 92, /Mikkel Ostergaard 5, 111; PetsMobility Networks Inc (www.petsmobility.net) 44; Piboontum, Jay (http://images.airlines.net) 94t; Reuters/Toby Melville 14t; Rex Features/Stuart Clarke 14b, /John Downing 36, /Andre Brutmann 50r, Ulander 69, /Andrew Drysdale 70, /SIPA 72ct, / PB/KMLA 72r, /XWF 74, /Tony Kyriacou 76tr; Science Photo Library/Peter Menzel 46, /Planetary Visions 87; Still Pictures/ Hartmut Schwarzbach FCtl, 1tl, 113, /Paul Quayle/UNEP 88, /Ron Gilling 108; Sony Ericsson 42l, Superstock/Age Fotostock/Stuart Pearce 27, /Dennis MacDonald 30; Topfoto 63, /Image Works/Howard Dratch 68 (IBM), / UPPA/David Wimsett (Shell), /Topham 76tl; Tullis, Graham 22t.

Front cover images supplied by Still Pictures/Hartmut Schwarzbach (left), Honda (centre) and Corbis/Reuters/Peter Morgan (right).

Contents images supplied by Kevin Kallaugher (KAL) (top left), Corbis/ Reuters (bottom left) and Empics/Associated Press/Ben Margot (right). Page 5 supplied by Panos /Mikkel Ostergaard.

Picture Research by Liz Moore.

Every effort has been made to trace the copyright holders and we apologise in advance for any unintentional omissions. We would be pleased to insert the appropriate acknowledgement in any subsequent edition of this publication.

Illustration acknowledgements

All by Kevin Kallaugher (KAL).

Project managed by Tony Garside.

Designed by Wooden Ark

Contents

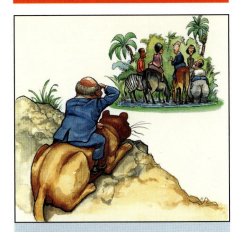

Mergers and acquisitions

Spring in their steps

CEOs are once again on the lookout for global mergers and acquisitions. But are business planners over-optimistic about the chances of success for deals like these? Statistics suggest that three out of four deals have failed to make shareholders richer in the past. So what can leaders do to avoid making the mistakes of their predecessors? **Page 9.**

Targeting the audience

The harder hard sell

The advertising industry is facing more difficult choices than ever. Whether it continues to spend money on traditional media or decides to embrace alternative methods of reaching consumers, one thing is certain: the industry will continue to reinvent itself and meet the creative challenges ahead. **Page 51.**

Competitive advantage

Crunch time for Apple

Steve Jobs, Apple's enigmatic CEO, has already taken the lead in the market for personal music systems and now he's taking aim at PC industry leaders Dell and Microsoft. In the process, he hopes to transform Apple from a niche player to mainstream computer supplier. **Page 103.**

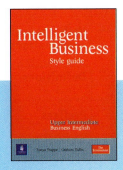

Learning to write well in a foreign language is one of the most difficult challenges facing the language learner. This pocket-sized style guide will help you find the right words, use an appropriate style and write effectively. **See inside the back cover.**

Bookmap

Investing in development

A path to helping the poor

Combating poverty in the developing world has traditionally been the task of governments and voluntary organisations, but a top Swiss investment banker wants to change all that. He encourages private investment through microfinance institutions in potential entrepreneurs in the developing world, which he believes will not only help the fight against poverty but also generate profits for the investors. **Page 113.**

From the authors

As business English teachers, we know how important it is to learn the key business language necessary to participate in an increasingly international work environment. We also recognise the need to learn about business concepts, developments in business and how business works in different cultures. We are therefore delighted to have written *Intelligent Business* in partnership with The Economist magazine, a unique resource of insights into news and business throughout the world.

Key business concepts

When selecting topics we were very aware of the need to include not only general business areas such as advertising and banking but also more complex issues such as consulting and project management. We also chose controversial issues such as energy and technology and topics with a wider economic perspective such as competition and investment. The result, we feel, is a unique overview of business today that gives students both an opportunity to see key language in context and to expand their business knowledge and horizons.

Language development

The exercises developed around the central theme of each unit give ample opportunities to review and practise important grammar and vocabulary in both spoken and written contexts. Furthermore, the career skills syllabus develops the key communicative language and strategies necessary to succeed in today's work environment. All of these are then put to use in the end of unit problem-solving task.

The *Intelligent Business Upper Intermediate* Coursebook is accompanied by a separate Workbook that provides comprehensive self-study language practice along with a complete Cambridge BEC Higher practice exam. There is also the *Intelligent Business Upper Intermediate* Skills Book: a task-driven intensive course that practises key language from the *Intelligent Business* syllabus through authentic business tasks. All of these components are covered by a single Teacher's Book.

Both the Coursebook and the Skills Book can be supplemented with the *Intelligent Business Upper Intermediate* video: a drama illustrating the key language and business skills common to both Coursebook and Skills Book. In addition, there is the www.intelligent-business.org website which contains further information on the course, downloadable resources, teacher support and premium content from the www.economist.com website.

Our intention when writing *Intelligent Business* was to make a truly contemporary world of business accessible to learners of business English – whatever their level of world and business knowledge. We hope you will find that it does so. If it is both enjoyable and beneficial to users, we will have completed our task.

We wish you every success in your future English-speaking working lives!

Tonya Trappe
Graham Tullis

Unit 1
Alliances

www.longman-elt.com www.economist.com

Company bosses on the prowl

Keynotes

Strategic alliances enable companies to share **resources**. This creates **synergies** or advantages and leads to increased **market share** and greater **competitiveness**. Public companies also hope to increase **shareholder value** when they **form** alliances. There are many kinds of corporate alliance. **Corporate partnerships** are formed when two or more companies decide to **co-operate** on one particular project or mission. When companies join together, it is called a **merger**. When one company makes a successful **takeover bid** to buy another one, it is referred to as an **acquisition**.

Preview

Mega mergers

Which of the following companies do you think have formed strategic alliances? Match the ones on the left with the ones on the right.

Disney	Daimler Benz
Starbucks	Miramax
Chrysler	Pepsico

Listening 1

1 Listen to a consultant talking about the alliances and check your answer to the above question.

2 Listen again and answer the questions.

1 Why did each of the pairs of companies want to form an alliance?
2 Which alliances succeeded, and why?
3 Which alliance failed, and why?

Reading

Mergers and acquisitions

1 Read the text on the opposite page and decide if the author is generally optimistic or pessimistic about future strategic alliances.

2 Read the text again. Are the following statements *true* or *false*?

1 In the first paragraph, the author says that CEOs can no longer find targets for mergers and acquisitions.
2 Studying facts and figures from the recent past won't necessarily help CEOs to form a successful alliance.
3 The trend in the 1990s was for companies to build portfolios with diverse investments.
4 The author suggests that media mergers are always likely to improve share value.
5 CEOs need above all to find the right company to acquire.
6 If business planners wish to avoid some of the errors of the 1990s, they should be prudent when taking risks.

3 Read the text again and answer the questions.

1 Why did CEOs reduce their involvement in mergers and acquisitions for a time?
2 Why should CEOs ignore the statistics concerning the success rate of acquisitions?
3 What should CEOs be aware of when venturing into alliances?

Speaking

Do you agree with the author when he suggests that only one in four acquisitions actually creating shareholder value is a good success ratio?

Why do companies find it difficult to make mergers work?

Glossary

dot-com boom rapid growth of internet-based business

protagonists most important people involved in a particular situation

falter weaken

spot identify

herd instinct natural inclination to follow others rather than act alone

Mergers and acquisitions

Spring in their steps

Some notes for company bosses out on the prowl

1 AFTER a long hibernation, company bosses are beginning to rediscover their animal spirits. The $145 billion-worth of global mergers and acquisitions announced last month was the highest for any month in over three years. There are now lots of chief executives thinking about what target they might attack in order to add growth and value to their companies and glory to themselves. Although they slowed down for a while because of the dot-com boom, they are once again on the prowl.

2 What should CEOs do to improve their chances of success in the coming rush to buy? First of all, they should not worry too much about widely-quoted statistics suggesting that as many as three out of every four deals have failed to create shareholder value for the acquiring company. The figures are heavily influenced by the time period chosen and in any case, one out of four is not bad when compared with the chances of getting a new business started. So they should keep looking for good targets.

3 There was a time when top executives considered any type of business to be a good target. But in the 1990s the idea of the conglomerate, the holding company with a diverse portfolio of businesses, went out of fashion as some of its most prominent protagonists – CBS and Hanson Trust, for example – faltered. Companies had found by then that they could add more value by concentrating on their "core competence", although one of the most successful companies of that decade, General Electric, was little more than an old-style conglomerate with a particularly fast-changing portfolio.

4 Brian Roberts, the man who built Comcast into a giant cable company, was always known for concentrating on his core product – until his recent bid for Disney, that is. It is not yet clear whether his bid is an opportunistic attempt to acquire and break up an undervalued firm, or whether he is chasing the media industry's dream of combining entertainment content with distribution, a strategy which has made fortunes for a few but which regularly proves the ruin of many big media takeovers.

5 If vertical integration is Comcast's aim, then it will be imperative for Mr Roberts to have a clear plan of how to achieve that. For in the end, CEOs will be judged less for spotting a good target than for digesting it well, a much more difficult task. The assumption will be that, if they are paying a lot of money for a business, they know exactly what they want to do with it.

6 If CEOs wish to avoid some of the failures of the 1990s, they should not forget that they are subject to the eternal tendency of business planners to be over-confident. It is a near certainty that, if asked, almost 99 per cent of them would describe themselves as "above average" at making mergers and acquisitions work. Sad as it may be, that can never be true.

7 They should also be aware that they will be powerfully influenced by the herd instinct, the feeling that it is better to be wrong in large numbers than to be right alone. In the coming months they will have to watch carefully to be sure that the competitive space into which the predator in front of them is so joyfully leaping does not lie at the edge of a cliff ■

Match the words (1–6) from the text with their meanings (a–f).

1 shareholder value (para 2)
2 conglomerate (para 3)
3 portfolio (para 3)
4 core competence (para 3)
5 bid (para 4)
6 vertical integration (para 5)

a a collection of companies
b an offer to buy
c most important activity
d controlling all stages of one particular type of business
e organisation comprising several companies
f what stocks in a public company are worth

Vocabulary 2   ## Metaphors

The text contains several hunting and animal metaphors, e.g. *on the prowl* (looking for victims). Why do you think the author uses this kind of metaphor?

Find the metaphors in the text which mean:

1 period of sleeping through the winter (para 1)
2 instincts (para 1)
3 something to aim at (para 1)
4 one who hunts another (para 7)

Practice   **Complete the article about mergers with the following words from the text on page 9.**

fortunes	chances	growth	targets	failure	portfolios
shareholder value	acquire				

To merge or not to merge ...

Companies engage in acquisitions and mergers because that is one of the easiest ways to secure fast [1] _growth_ and diversify their investment [2]_____ . As Europe expands and investors increase, the idea of merging appeals to more and more companies. Moreover, the sale of government-owned businesses has meant that large companies are entering the market, aiming to [3]_____ potential rivals but often at the same time becoming possible [4]_____ for other companies on the prowl. However, with all this merger activity the [5]_____ of success are still not good, and statistics show that many fail.

Yet every time two major companies announce a merger, euphoria sweeps the stock markets as dealers and shareholders look forward to making huge [6]_____ . Many alliances are not financially successful, however, and don't succeed in increasing [7]_____ or creating wealth for all involved. Too often, culture conflicts and personality clashes are part of the reason why alliances end in [8]_____ . As Steven Barrett, head of Mergers and Acquisitions at accountants KPMG said, 'When they don't work, the two key management groups do not blend well together.'

Review of tenses

Study the examples taken from the text on page 9 and answer the questions about tenses below.

a   ... company bosses **are beginning** to rediscover their animal spirits. (para 1)

b   ... as many as three out of every four deals **have failed** to create ... (para 2)

c   Companies **had found** by then that they could add ... (para 3)

d   ... a strategy which ... regularly **proves** the ruin of many ... (para 4)

e   ... CEOs **will be judged** less for spotting a good target than for ... (para 5)

1 Which example:

1   refers to unspecified time or a period of time up to the present

2   is making a prediction

3   refers to a situation changing in the present

4   refers to a repeated action in the present

5   gives the background information or an explanation for a past event

2 Which tense is used in each example?

3 Which of the following pairs of time markers are most commonly used with each of the tenses above?

1   by that time, by 2001

2   before long, in the coming weeks

3   recently, since the 1990s

4   generally, these days

5   at the moment, right now

 For more information, see page 157.

Practice

Complete the article with the appropriate tense of the verbs in brackets.

After many weeks of negotiation, William B Harrison, CEO of JP Morgan Chase, and Jamie Dimon, of Bank One, (¹sign) _have signed_ a deal. As part of the deal, Jamie Dimon, who (²be) _____ the CEO at Bank One since he left Citigroup, (³accept) _____ the position of Chief Operating Officer for the next two years after which he (⁴become) _____ the CEO. Mr Harrison has also agreed, on behalf of his shareholders, to pay $7 billion to Dimon for the privilege of keeping the post of CEO for two years.

The situation only became clear after the deal was made and signed: up until then, Dimon, the top man at Citigroup before joining Bank One, (⁵not want) _____ to take a back seat under the new deal and only agreed to a simple merger of equals on the condition that he became CEO. Harrison, who (⁶make) _____ some disastrous acquisitions over the years, wasn't happy because he wanted to finish his career on a high.

Shareholders generally (⁷not get) _____ the chance to negotiate in these situations and now they (⁸ become) _____ increasingly unhappy as a result. Although this particular clash of egos (⁹cost) _____ them $7 billion, at least they know that they (¹⁰see) _____ a significant increase in the share price as a result of the merger.

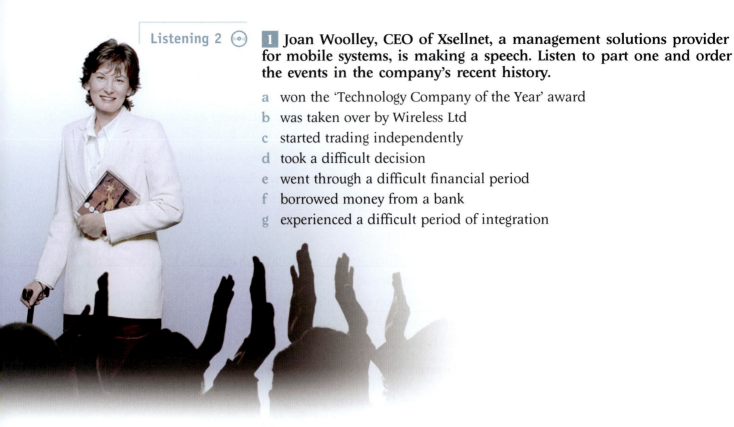

1 Joan Woolley, CEO of Xsellnet, a management solutions provider for mobile systems, is making a speech. Listen to part one and order the events in the company's recent history.

a   won the 'Technology Company of the Year' award
b   was taken over by Wireless Ltd
c   started trading independently
d   took a difficult decision
e   went through a difficult financial period
f   borrowed money from a bank
g   experienced a difficult period of integration

2 Listen again and answer the questions.

1   Which tense does she use when talking about 'the last few years'?
2   Which tense does she use when talking about 2002?
3   Which tense does she use when talking about the alliance?

3 Listen to part two, where Ms Woolley is answering a journalist's question about why the merger failed, and list the four reasons she gives.

1   _____
2   _____
3   _____
4   _____

Which reason does she say contributed most to the failure of the alliance?

Speaking   Work in pairs. Imagine that you work for a small family-run business which has just been bought by a big multinational. Discuss:

–   where the various potential corporate culture clashes might occur
–   how you think you personally would adapt to the new culture, and why
–   what could be done by both companies to ensure a smooth transition from one corporate culture to another

Writing   Write a short press release to announce that your company, Xsellnet, has won the 'Technology Company of the Year' award. Use the answers from Listening 2 above to give a short history of the company. (See *Style guide*, page 30.)

Building relationships

Building good relationships leads to successful business opportunities. Whether networking with people outside the company or striking up a positive working relationship with new colleagues, you will find the following phrases useful.

a *How can I help you? / Is there anything I can do?*

b *How interesting. / I'd love to hear more.*

c *I don't think we've met. I'm …*

d *I'm … I work for Digital France. We offer products and services in …*

e *When can we set up a meeting? Here's my card.*

f *Do you like/enjoy … ? / What do you think of … ?*

1 **Look at the tips for building relationships successfully. Can you think of any more tips?**

1 Be articulate and positive about who you are and what you do.

2 Ask the right questions to find out what you have in common with others.

3 Be willing to share information and help others.

4 Show an interest in what others are saying.

5 Follow up interesting new contacts.

2 **Which of phrases a–f above would you use for the tips (1–5)?**

Speaking **Work with a partner you don't know (well). Introduce yourself and ask questions to find three points you have in common.**

Listening 3 **Listen to two people networking and answer the questions.**

1 What lines of business are the speakers in?

2 What do the companies have in common?

3 How will they both benefit from the possible new business relationship?

Speaking **Work in pairs. Read the extracts of dialogues below and say why the people didn't manage to build a relationship. Change what speaker B said in each case and continue the dialogue.**

1 A Hi, I'm Sandra Hogan. I work for *Marketing Now* magazine. We are looking for successful companies to feature in our May issue.

  B Unfortunately, we've been having a few financial problems recently, but here's my card.

2 A I'm sorry to ask, but as you've finished, could you help me?

  B No, I want to go home early.

3 A Hello, I'm Kevin Hart from Digital Solutions. I see from your badge that we are in the same line of business. Are you enjoying the conference?

  B Not really. I haven't made any useful contacts so far.

Culture at work ## Working relationships

In many cultures, business people will do business only with people they trust and have had time to get to know personally. In other cultures, while it is important to have a good working relationship, it is not essential to know people on a personal level. What is common in your culture? How might this difference cause misunderstanding in multicultural teams?

Dilemma & Decision

Dilemma: Breaking the ice

Brief

When Unilever, one of the world's largest consumer products companies, made a bid to buy Ben & Jerry's, the trendy ice cream maker, Ben and Jerry turned down the offer. The companies were too different, they said. Social responsibility and creative management were the hallmarks of their business philosophy. Unilever was a major multinational with a traditional corporate culture, whose main goal was to make a profit. This, they felt, could never mix with their concept of 'linked prosperity', where the community also profits from business success. The then CEO of Unilever, Niall FitzGerald, felt that if they could get together and talk, they would find common ground. They could then build on that personal relationship and finally make a corporate alliance, which would benefit everyone in spite of what appeared to be corporate culture differences.

Task 1

Work in groups. Read the profiles and make a list of the similarities between the people involved and their companies.

Task 2

Using your list, think of five things Niall FitzGerald could say to Ben and Jerry in order to break the ice. How do you think Ben and Jerry would respond in each case?

Task 3

What concessions or compromises do you think Ben and Jerry would ask for? How do you think Niall FitzGerald would respond? Is it possible for two companies with seemingly different cultures to merge and work together, if the CEOs have a lot in common?

Write it up

Write a memo from Niall FitzGerald to the staff of Unilever informing them of the decision, and why it was taken. (See *Style guide*, page 24.)

CEO profile

Jerry Greenfield and Ben Cohen were born in Brooklyn, New York, in 1951. They met in junior high school and Jerry remembers that he and Ben were two of the wildest students in their school.

They founded their ice cream company in 1978 in a renovated gas station in Burlington, Vermont, with a $12,000 investment ($4,000 of which was borrowed).

Ben and Jerry have been recognised for fostering their company's commitment to social responsibility by the Council on Economic Priorities, as they donate 7.5 per cent of their pre-tax profits to non-profit organisations through the Ben & Jerry's Foundation.

Ben and Jerry are active members of the Social Venture Network and Businesses for Social Responsibility. They also serve on the board of Oxfam America.

Decision:

Turn to page 145 to find out what Ben and Jerry, and Niall FitzGerald said about the proposed merger.

CEO profile

Unilever was created in 1930. It is now one of the world's largest consumer products companies with sales in excess of $50 billion, and operates in 88 countries around the globe.

Niall FitzGerald, the CEO until 2004, was born in 1945 in Ireland. He was a child of the '60s, 'with hair down my back, drawn to the hippy culture of make love not war,' he remembers. At University College Dublin, he joined the Communist Party. 'I'm a practical left-winger,' he says. 'I was taught that to change the world, you must get to the top and do it from within.'

As head of Unilever South Africa, he insisted, against opposition, on unsegregated facilities. Not only aware of the debate on corporate social responsibility but sincerely engaged in it as well, he was behind Unilever's funding of hospitals in Vietnam and schools in Ghana and many other parts of the developing world.

Unit 2 Projects

www.longman-elt.com   www.economist.com

Up, up and away
PAGE 17

Articles
PAGE 20

Career skills: Setting goals
PAGE 21

Dilemma: Test crisis
PAGE 22

Mission to accomplish

Keynotes

A **project** is a complex series of **tasks** that have to be completed within a specific **time period** and with limited financial **resources**. Successfully **managing a project** involves **estimating** and **controlling** the resources, **budget** and **time schedule** necessary for a positive outcome. Starting with the **specifications** of a project, **project managers** put together a **project plan** which will enable them to complete the work **on time** and **on budget**.

Project planning

Projects follow a life cycle which has four phases:

| initiate | | plan | | execute/control | | close |

Which of the following tasks would be included in each of the phases above?

1 review the results
2 evaluate the risk factor
3 forecast costs
4 select the project team
5 deliver the project

6 launch a pilot project
7 obtain status reports
8 validate the project
9 allocate resources
10 prepare a project overview

Listen to Helen Jenssen of MacroPlan talking about project management and answer the questions.

1 Which of the phases does she consider the most important?
2 What two questions should project managers ask themselves at the start?
3 Identify the tasks above that she mentions.

Look at some examples of past and current projects. Choose one of the projects and make a list of the principal difficulties you think might be involved. Discuss the project with another student.

Past projects

– The Burt Rutan X2 spacecraft	(first private sector spacecraft – 2004)
– The Norman Foster Millau viaduct	(completed 2004)
– Airbus A 380	(test flight – April 2005)

Current projects

– Space mission to Mars (Aurora)	(planned for 2026)
– Water-fuelled hydrogen car (Earth 2012)	(planned for 2020)
– Electronic navigation aid for the blind (Noppa project)	(under development)
– Indian Kalpasar Project (world's longest dam 64km)	(planning stage)
– Toyota humanoid robot (human partner robot)	(prototype built)

Managing a project

1 Read the text on the opposite page and answer the question.

How has the T5 agreement facilitated the management of the T5 project?

Glossary

stint period of work

plague (v) cause continual trouble

bump up suddenly increase something

corner-cutting doing things badly or cheaply

spin-off business new company that emerges from a larger enterprise

Managing a project

Up, up and away

Tony Douglas is redefining how to run massive construction projects

1 To the west of London is a vast building site. In the midst of a landscape of mud and men rises a vast glass-fronted box that will soon be Britain's largest free-standing building. This is Heathrow airport's fifth terminal, destined to cater for 30m passengers a year. It will include not just a terminal but also new road and rail links, and connections to the London Transport network.

2 Big construction projects are always tricky, but airports bring special problems: tricky building techniques, and the need to interface with other transport links and to install sophisticated electronics to handle passengers and baggage.

3 The man in charge of this logistical nightmare, Tony Douglas, came to British Airports Authority via stints in the car and the commercial jet industries, and at Kenwood, a domestic appliance firm. For three years, he ran BAA's (British Airports Authority) supply chain. He took over as project manager for T5 (as the project is known) after the last boss left suddenly. The risks attached to this huge project are so great that BAA has been forced to tackle it in novel ways. If this giant endeavour is not completed on time and on budget, it could take the whole company down.

4 First, BAA is unusual in running the project itself. Mr Douglas insists that outsourcing to a big project management group such as Bechtel would cost more, not less. Second, as much as possible of the construction is taking place off-site. This reflects the site's physical constraints: it has only one entry point, through which a 12-metre load must move every 30 seconds for a period of four years. And the site has capacity for no more than two days of storage. The solution, he says, has been some "car industry logistics" – a large investment in computing and training that no individual supplier would have made.

5 But the biggest novelty is the T5 Agreement. This is a contract with the project's main suppliers, companies and subcontractors like Balfour Beatty and Bombardier, which aims to minimise the conflicts and cost-cutting that usually plague big building works.

6 Usually, contractors hold a beauty parade and take on the suppliers who bid lowest. The suppliers rely on glitches and delays to bump up the cost. Every time something goes wrong, legal haggling breaks out among suppliers and between them and the contractor, and work shuts down for weeks on end. With construction behind schedule, time runs short for the final installation and testing of the electronic systems.

7 Under the T5 Agreement, BAA carries the risk, putting a precautionary sum into a fund that will be shared out among all its suppliers if the project finishes on time and budget. The effect, says Mr Douglas, has been to change the whole pace and culture of the project, allowing teams of employees from different suppliers to work together.

8 As one example, he cites the elegant steel air traffic control tower. When the first two sections were engineered, they were out by 9mm. "Normally," says Mr Douglas, "the manufacturers would have blamed the structural engineers, who would have blamed the steel fabricator." At first, they did just that. Then Mr Douglas said, "Guys, this is my problem," and sent them off to find a collective solution.

New departures

9 Passing risk to suppliers chosen by beauty parade increases the risk of corner-cutting. And, as T5's suppliers are partners who will work on future projects, they have an incentive to do a good job. If something goes wrong later, there may be a debate about negligence, but not about which supplier is to blame.

10 If T5 works so well, why isn't BAA building airports elsewhere? A bigger priority, at least for now, is to get permission to build an additional runway at Stansted, London's third airport. But ultimately, success will surely point to a spin-off business that can build other big projects safely and cheaply ■

2 Read the text again and find the information to complete the following lists (1–4).

1 The principal problems related to building airports

a _____

b _____

c _____

2 BAA's options for managing the project

a _____

b _____

3 The specific constraints imposed by the nature of the site

a _____

b _____

4 The major risks usually involved in managing a project like T5 (para 6)

a _____

b _____

c _____

Speaking

1 What are the advantages and disadvantages of the T5 Agreement? Do you think the T5 project will be successful?

2 Look at some of the headlines of news reports about the T5 project and put them in chronological order. What do you think the reports were about?

b **BAA publishes tenders for T5**

a **T5 PROTESTERS OCCUPY CRANE**

c **Planning enquiry clears T5 for take off**

d Tunnel completed on schedule

e Vacon clinches T5 contract

Vocabulary

1 Read the sentences and find synonyms in the text on page 17 for the underlined phrases.

1 The company will be in serious difficulties if they don't complete the project within the time schedule and cost estimates. (para 3)

on time and on budget

2 BAA decided against giving the project to an outside supplier. (para 4)

_____

3 Contractors generally award contracts to the companies that make the least expensive proposals. (para 6)

_____

4 Suppliers who are partners have the motivation to provide quality work. (para 9)

_____

5 Getting permission to build an additional runway is a much more important consideration. (para 10)

_____

2 Find the words and phrases in paragraphs 6 and 9 that are used to refer to problems and match them with their meanings (1–8).

Para 6

1 minor errors   _____

2 situations where something is late   _____

3 disagreement over minor details   _____

4 stops   _____

5 late, overdue   _____

6 expires, is not sufficient   _____

Para 9

7 doesn't happen as planned   _____

8 failure to ensure that work is done correctly   _____

3 The verb *take* is used several times in the text. Which collocations with *take* have the following meanings?

1 assume control or responsibility (para 3)   _____

2 make something fail (para 3)   _____

3 occur (para 4)   _____

4 employ, hire (para 6)   _____

4 Match definitions 1–4 with roles a–d.

1 businesses working under contract on the T5 project

2 the company overseeing the project

3 the company initiating the project

4 organisations directly affected by the project

a project sponsor (BAA)

b contractor (BAA)

c outside stakeholders (e.g. London Transport)

d project partners (e.g. Bombardier)

Practice Complete the article with words from this Vocabulary section.

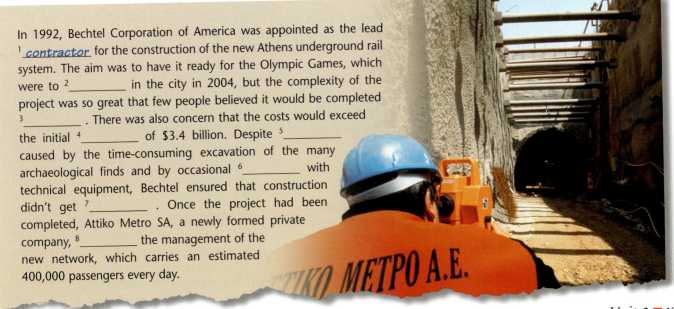

In 1992, Bechtel Corporation of America was appointed as the lead
¹ _contractor_ for the construction of the new Athens underground rail
system. The aim was to have it ready for the Olympic Games, which
were to ² _____ in the city in 2004, but the complexity of the
project was so great that few people believed it would be completed
³ _____ . There was also concern that the costs would exceed
the initial ⁴ _____ of $3.4 billion. Despite ⁵ _____
caused by the time-consuming excavation of the many
archaeological finds and by occasional ⁶ _____ with
technical equipment, Bechtel ensured that construction
didn't get ⁷ _____ . Once the project had been
completed, Attiko Metro SA, a newly formed private
company, ⁸ _____ the management of the
new network, which carries an estimated
400,000 passengers every day.

Articles

1 Complete rules 1–4 with *definite* or *indefinite* to show whether they refer to the definite article *the* or the indefinite articles *a/an*.

1 The _____ article is used with nouns that refer to one unique thing.

2 The _____ article is used before superlative adjectives.

3 The _____ article is used before non-specific singular countable nouns.

4 The _____ article is used when a noun has already been mentioned.

2 Study the examples taken from the text on page 17. Which of the rules 1–4 above are illustrated in each?

a *It will include not just **a terminal** ...* (para 1)

b *It will include ... connections to **the London Transport network**.* (para 1)

c *... BAA is unusual in running **the project** itself.* (para 4)

d *But **the biggest novelty** is the T5 Agreement.* (para 5)

3 Study the text and find two examples to illustrate each of the following rules about using no article.

1 most proper nouns and names

2 uncountable nouns used in a general sense

3 general plural countable nouns

4 abstract nouns used in a general sense

 For more information, see page 157.

Practice Look at the chart of the schedule for the AS 90 project and read the project manager's commentary below. Complete the commentary with a definite article, an indefinite article or no article (Ø).

The AS project management team have drawn up the following schedule for ¹ _**the**_ AS 90 project, which is due to kick off at ² _____ beginning of January. ³ _____ first phase of the project will be carried out by Luke Marshall and Gianni Visconti. They will be organising ⁴ _____ meeting with ⁵ _____ whole team during the first week in January to discuss the needs analysis questionnaire before it is sent out to ⁶ _____ hotel managers in ⁷ _____ United Kingdom, Belgium and ⁸ _____ Netherlands. By ⁹ _____ mid-January, the software specifications and manpower requirements will be submitted for ¹⁰ _____ approval by the project manager and ¹¹ _____ work will start on the pilot programme at the end of February. In April, the B team will take over the implementation phase. This will require ¹² _____ extensive travel for the team members who will be providing training for hotel staff at ¹³ _____ series of one-day workshops. 7 May has been fixed as ¹⁴ _____ deadline for handing over ¹⁵ _____ complete project with all deliverables to our customer.

AS 90 project overview

	Jan				Feb				Mar				Apr				May
	Wk1	Wk2	Wk3	Wk4	Wk5	Wk6	Wk7	Wk8	Wk9	Wk10	Wk11	Wk12	Wk13	Wk14	Wk15	Wk16	Wk17
Finalise questionnaire																	
Send questionnaire																	
Needs analysis																	
Specifications																	
Programming																	
Pilot programme																	
Implementation and training																	
Kickoff																	
Close																	

Career skills

Setting goals

One of the keys to managing a project successfully is to set clear goals for everyone who is involved so that they know exactly what they have to achieve and by what time. Look at some of the phrases that can be useful when setting goals.

a *What's the schedule for this?*
b *How much are you budgeting for ... ?*
c *I think we should aim to ...*
d *What will you need in the way of resources?*

e *So what exactly would be involved?*
f *When do I have to get this in by?*
g *Is that feasible?*
h *Does that sound reasonable/doable?*

Listening 2

1 Listen to two dialogues between a project manager and members of her team. Does she respect the following advice?

> When you set goals you should always make sure that they are realistic, precise and timed.

2 Listen again and make notes about the dialogues. What is the role of each person the project manager talks to? What goal is set in each case?

3 Which of phrases a–h above do the speakers use?

Speaking

1 Work in pairs. Take turns to play the roles of senior manager and project leader. Set goals (time, resources and budget) together for each of the projects below.

The senior manager has asked the project leader to:

1 take responsibility for organising the transfer of the company's headquarters to a new location
2 prepare a one-week training course for senior executives
3 create a new company website
4 organise the company's annual sales conference

2 Work in pairs. Brainstorm ideas for a project that you would like to initiate. Draw up a brief outline and discuss your project with another pair.

Writing

Choose one of the projects in Speaking exercise 1 and write an email to your team, summarising the goals that you agreed on with your manager. (See *Style guide*, page 20.)

Culture at work

Respecting deadlines

In some cultures, attitudes to time are different and it is not always considered essential to respect a deadline. What is the case in your culture? Do people try to complete work on time or do they consider it normal for deadlines to be extended?

Unit 2 ■ 21

Dilemma & Decision

Dilemma: Test crisis

Brief

Infineon is an international semiconductor manufacturer which manufactures semiconductor chips at its five factories in Europe and at its plant in Asia. Each Infineon plant traces incoming orders and then plans its production. All the chips are then tested internally at each site before delivery.

At the monthly production meeting at the plant in France, managers are worried. It looks as if they have identified a serious problem that could impact on deliveries. Production levels will have to be increased during the coming months to deal with an increase in orders, but that is not where the problem lies. It is with the testing equipment. The planning and supply chain managers and quality controllers can see quite clearly that they will not have the capacity to test the increased production with their existing machines. They have five months before the situation becomes critical. During that time they must find and implement an effective solution.

An emergency meeting has been called to decide what action to take and to set up a project group to deal with the implementation. The four managers who will be attending the meeting are each going to propose a solution and they will then decide together on which solution should be adopted. They will then set up a project team and fix the objectives.

Task 1

Work in groups of four. Student A turn to page 137. Student B turn to page 138. Student C turn to page 140. Student D turn to page 142. Prepare the arguments that you will use in favour of your solution. Assume similar costings for each solution.

Task 2

Attend the meeting with your colleagues. Take turns to present your solution. Then, as a group, agree on the course of action that you would choose and appoint a project manager to implement the solution.

Task 3

Present the solution to another group. Did they choose the same solution?

Write it up

Write the minutes of your meeting to circulate to senior management. (See *Style guide* page 26.)

Decision:

- Listen to Oliver Heller explaining how the engineers and planners at Infineon approached the problem.

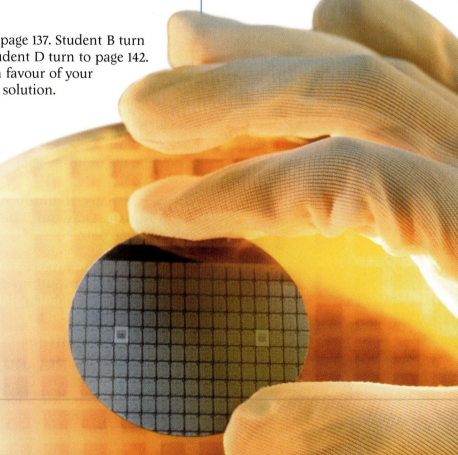

Unit 3
Teamworking

www.longman-elt.com   www.economist.com

The stuff teams are made of

Keynotes

Teamwork, or the ability of a group of people to work well together to **accomplish** a **common goal**, is one of the fundamentals of the world of work. Professionalism and efficiency are often measured in terms of how good one is as a **team player** or how much one contributes to **team spirit**. Successful teams accomplish their objectives because they are **committed**, respect the various **roles** within the team and meet their **deadlines**. Teams spend a large part of their working lives in **meetings**. It is therefore important to make sure that every meeting is positive, **informative** and a necessary use of the team's time. The **chairperson** or **facilitator** plays a key role in **co-ordinating** the team's work and keeping everyone focused at meetings.

Team meetings

1 Look at the list of teamworking tasks (a–j) which are often given as reasons for holding meetings and answer the questions.

1 Which tasks are not good reasons to hold a meeting?
2 Which tasks could be easily completed by email, memo or telephone?
3 Which tasks are best achieved in a meeting?

Meetings are held to ...

a explain new projects
b establish common goals
c make team decisions
d allow members to socialise
e create policies

f share information
g announce minor decisions
h co-ordinate team activities
i get weekly progress updates
j solve problems

2 Alternative types of meeting can save time and reduce the number of people present. Read the descriptions and decide which one is best for situations a–d below.

1 The café meeting
If sessions in the meeting room tend to last too long, brainstorming in particular can take place elsewhere, for example over coffee or a snack, to provide a relaxed and creative atmosphere.

2 The stand-up meeting
Everyone in the team stands in a circle and gives updates on work, conveys solutions to problems and asks for help if necessary. Because people are standing up, they are more concise and to the point.

3 The egg-timer meeting
When it is preferable to have people sitting comfortably, as they may need to refer to notes etc., use an egg-timer to make sure nobody speaks for too long. Participants conduct the meeting in a precise and time-efficient manner.

4 The walking meeting
This is when two or three members of the team take a 10–15 minute walk outside the office complex to discuss confidential matters in an informal context.

a You want an alternative to the lengthy Monday morning meeting, in which team members report back on the previous week's work.
b You need to talk to three project leaders so that they come up with ideas about how to get their teams on board a new project.
c You are concerned about the quality of one of the team's work. You wish to get the opinion of two of the other project managers.
d You want precise feedback from all the team managers on current projects.

Which type of meeting do/would you prefer? Are there other situations they could be suitable for?

Meeting techniques

1 Read the text on the opposite page and say why the author thinks meetings can be a waste of time.

Glossary

tedious boring

hog the floor dominate the discussion

scepticism doubting the truth of what other people say

mould form

Meeting techniques

Think before you meet

Too many meetings are a waste of time

1 WHAT do corporate leaders do all day? Much of their time is spent in meetings. No wonder: the rules of team-working are established in meetings, which in turn are the basic building blocks of corporate existence. However, meetings might not always be the best use of the team's time.

2 Meetings, like teams, do not necessarily achieve what they set out to do. One recent study in America by consultants Synectics found that senior and middle managers spent more than three-quarters of their time in meetings. On average, only 12 per cent of managers thought their meetings were productive. In high-performing companies, that figure rose to 25 per cent and in the lower performers it dropped to 2 per cent.

3 "Despite IT, we all go to more and more of them," reflects Jonathan Day of McKinsey. But there must be a way to make them work. They can't all be a waste of time. Perhaps team leaders should do everything they can to make sure they organise them properly. Indeed, running meetings well is clearly an art, and a growing number of

companies (including Synectics, which modestly claims to run the best meetings in the world) are offering help. Lots of meetings, of course, happen in the corridor or around the coffee machine, and those are probably the most efficient sort, because they tend to be spontaneous, small and quick. Bigger ones are usually more problematic, and team members have to put up with meetings where too little thought goes into the agenda, the location, the people asked to attend and the outcome, say those who try to improve them. That allows unimportant ideas or tedious individuals to hog the floor, with the result that a lot of team members find it hard to look forward to the next meeting.

4 Meetings tend to be held either to share information or to solve problems. For the first sort, Roger Neill of Synectics advocates asking all the participants to say at the end what they think they have heard, and correcting their accounts if they are wrong. With problem-solving, the aim ought not to be just brainstorming and coming up with ideas but also paying proper

attention to putting solutions into practice. He also thinks it is wise to ask people what they liked about the things they heard; criticism usually comes unasked. Pessimism, scepticism and challenge all cause trouble.

5 What makes meetings especially important to companies, though, is that this is where teams are moulded. That is why companies must learn how to run them. David Bradford, a professor at Stanford Business School, who specialises in studying teams, argues that meetings often waste huge amounts of time: in one business, the executive team spent three meetings designing business cards. Of course, one person should have done this before the team started working together. The way to get a good decision is to frame the question carefully. If you want to invest in China, do not announce that you are planning to do this, or ask the meeting whether you should. Instead, enlist your colleagues' help by saying: "We want to be in the Chinese market: how do we get there?" ■

2 Read the text again and answer the questions.

1 Why are corridor and coffee machine meetings often efficient?
2 What are the two main reasons for holding meetings?
3 What kind of feedback do people give easily?
4 Why do companies consider meetings to be very important?
5 What happens when meetings are not properly organised?

Speaking

Teams can be moulded in meetings. Some companies organise other team-moulding activities like paintballing, away days and bungee jumping. How do you feel about these activities? What other activities can help to build a team? Which ones would you personally like / not like?

Vocabulary

1 Use the following words to form collocations beginning with *team*. Put them into three groups: People, Things to do, Concepts.

| project morale leader spirit player task goal member building |

2 Find the multi-part verbs in paragraphs 3 and 4 of the text on page 25 which mean the following.

1 tolerate
2 be excited about
3 think of

Practice

Complete the article below with the appropriate form of words from this Vocabulary section, and the following words taken from the text on page 25.

| brainstorming   attend   agenda   participants |

When three people from our department left to join another company, ¹ _team morale_ was very low. We knew we had to recruit new ² _____ and that a long integration process would slow our work down considerably. We were worried that the positive atmosphere and ³ _____ that had taken us a while to build would be affected by this setback. It was decided to have a meeting, and the first item on the ⁴ _____ was a(n) ⁵ _____ session to ⁶ _____ ideas on the best way of organising a(n) ⁷ _____ activity that would help the new recruits to fit into the structure as quickly as possible. All the ⁸ _____ at the meeting put their ideas forward and finally we agreed that we should all ⁹ _____ a day's training session organised by a specialist consultant. The day will be spent socialising and completing simple ¹⁰ _____ set by the consultant. We hope to have the new team operating as efficiently as ever in the next couple of weeks.

Writing

You are the managing director of a company that organises paintballing activities. Fax an answer to an inquiry about your product, prices, terms and schedules. (See *Style guide*, page 22.)

Team roles

1 Read the article below about team roles. Which role (1–5) is being referred to in each of the following statements?

a They make sure everyone has the chance to give their input in meetings.

b They are focused mainly on task not process.

c They are focused mainly on process not task.

d They can describe what was said during meetings.

e They can play any role on the team.

f They tell the facilitator if the meeting is going on for too long.

g They discuss progress with people outside the team.

Team roles are specific and interdependent

1 Team leader

The team leader may or may not be part of the managerial staff. It is his/her job to provide an environment that helps teams to get their work done. The leader organises locations and times for meetings and is responsible for providing resources required by the team to carry out their tasks. It is the job of the leader to remind the team what result the organisation expects of them and how their tasks fit in with the overall goals and mission of the company. He/She works closely with the facilitator in planning the agenda of a meeting, setting outcomes and ensuring next steps are assigned, as well as communicating on the team's progress with other members of the organisation.

2 Team facilitator

The team facilitator helps develop and apply the procedure for teamwork. He/She establishes the ground rules and then makes sure that they are respected. If, for example, it is agreed at the outset that all members should give their input, it is the role of the facilitator to make sure decision-making is not dominated by strong personalities in the team. As the role of the facilitator in decision-making is neutral, it is a good idea to rotate from team member to team member.

3 Team recorder

The team recorder is responsible for writing down key points, ideas and decisions at meetings. Recorders need to prepare for meetings by reviewing the agenda carefully. Recording ideas is particularly important, and the recorded text should be as close to the actual words used as possible. The recorder's notes are very different from the minutes of a meeting, which are a summary of what was said at a meeting.

4 Timekeeper

The timekeeper's job is to monitor how long the team is taking to accomplish its tasks and provide regular updates to the team on how well or poorly they are using their time. He/She also collaborates with the team leader and facilitator and other team members to determine new time schedules if these are necessary.

5 Team members

All team members must be enthusiastic and committed to the team's purpose. They should be willing to share responsibility and to accept different roles such as facilitator or leader. They must share knowledge and expertise and never keep information to themselves. They should respect the opinions and positions of others in the team.

2 Read the article again. Whose role (1–5 above) is it to do the following?

a review the agenda

b remain neutral

c provide resources

d provide updates

e write down key points

f establish ground rules

Work in groups of four. Discuss roles 1–4 above and decide which of them would be most suitable for each person in your group. (Try to agree on one role per person.)

Modal forms

1 Study examples a–f taken from the text on page 25. Match 1–6 with a–f.

1 obligation about a present situation
2 advice about a present situation
3 a possibility

4 advice about a past situation
5 positive deduction
6 negative deduction

a *However, meetings **might** not always **be** the best use of the team's time. (para 1)*

b *But there **must be** a way to make them work. (para 3)*

c *They **can't** all **be** a waste of time. (para 3)*

d *... team leaders **should do** everything they can to make sure they organise them properly. (para 3)*

e *That is why companies **must learn** how to run them. (para 5)*

f *Of course, one person **should have done** this before the team started working together. (para 5)*

 For more information, see page 158.

2 Read the sentences about a team leader. Use the words in brackets and *might / might not be* or *must / can't be* to make more sentences about her.

1 She has worked from 7:00am to 9:00pm. (tired) *She must be very tired.*

2 She hasn't achieved very much. (an efficient worker)

3 The members of her team haven't been helpful. (pleased with them)

4 They haven't respected the deadlines. (satisfied with their work)

5 Her boss wants to speak to her tomorrow. (worried about this)

Past modals

3 Study examples d and f above and notice how modals are used to refer to the present and past. What are the past forms of the following?

must be   can't work   might know

 For more information, see page 158.

4 Make deductions about the following past situations.

1 He was busy when he set the deadline. (time to plan things properly)
He can't have had time to plan things properly.

2 The team didn't meet the deadline. (not enough time)

3 The instructions weren't clear. (the team/confused)

4 The team had to work overtime every day last week. (not happy)

5 All the other teams were waiting for the results of our work. (they/frustrated)

Work in pairs. Discuss past situations where you made mistakes or could have done something better. Say what you should have done but didn't.

Team building

Team building involves individual members being positive and putting the team's interests ahead of their own. Look at the following useful sentences.

a *We're definitely moving in the right direction.*
b *Go on, I'm listening.*
c *That's a great idea.*
d *Let's look at ways of getting round this problem.*
e *I'm confident you'll get it done on time.*
f *Tell me more.*

Good team members generally have qualities 1–3 below. Match the qualities with sentences a–f above.

1 They are active listeners.
2 They praise and encourage other team members' work.
3 They have an optimistic and positive attitude.

Listening 🔘 **Listen to two members of a team in a meeting. Identify five more sentences to add to the list (a–f) above and indicate which qualities they correspond to.**

Speaking ## Team players

1 Work in groups. Discuss what you, as a positive team player, would say in each of the following situations. How do you think negative team members would respond?

2 Role-play the situations.

2 One of your colleagues, who is usually a hard worker and positive team member, seems depressed and tired. He doesn't seem to be concentrating on his work and he is slowing down the team's progress. You feel sure he has personal problems at the moment and that it would help to talk things over.

1 The team is working to a very tight deadline. Everything could be late and team morale is very low. You've spoken to management and they've refused to extend the deadline, but they've agreed to assign two new people to the project and to pay overtime. Talk to the team.

3 You have been assigned the task of collating the team's work and putting forward the best proposals they've come up with. Two solutions appear to be potentially good. One was suggested by you and would be a quick and easy solution. The other, a little more complicated, was suggested by a team member who had very negative feedback on her last project and whose morale needs boosting. Present the best proposals.

Culture at work ## Exchanging information

Some cultures find teamworking easier than others. In individualistic cultures, 'information is power' and people prefer to retain it in order to advance their personal careers. In collectivist cultures, the greater good of the company is the main concern of all employees. Which is closest to your culture? How might a difference in attitude cause conflict in multicultural teams?

Dilemma & Decision

Dilemma: Leading the team

Brief

Peter Drumand is the team leader of a group who were briefed to come up with ways of improving customer communications at Walton's department store. After three weeks of information gathering and meetings the team made the following recommendations:

- extend telephone coverage by one hour per week, to answer more enquiries
- update webpage at least once a week
- research further the idea of holding store meetings to answer customer questions directly

Peter feels sure that these are good ideas but fears the management will not approve them because they are costly. He cannot decide whether to present the ideas to management or not.

Task 1

Work in pairs. Discuss the following arguments. Which ones do you agree/disagree with?

- Peter should not present the team's recommendations to the board as final. A team leader should never let his/her team make an obviously bad decision. He should protect the team and the department's reputation by asking for more time.

- If cost was a concern, the team ought to have been told at the beginning. It is Peter's responsibility to admit that he is at fault for not briefing the team properly, and he should ask for a new deadline so they can find other, less expensive proposals.

- On the basis of shared information, the team developed reasonable, specific recommendations for improving customer communications. Peter should present these recommendations and suggest developing a budget for them.

Task 2

Decide what you think Peter should do.

Task 3

Discuss the conclusions you have reached with another pair. Work together as a team to make a joint decision about what Peter should do and say. How do you think management will react?

Write it up

Write a memo from Peter to the management explaining what he has decided to do, and why. (See *Style guide*, page 24.)

Decision:

⊙ Listen to a business consultant saying what he thinks Peter Drumand should have done.

Review 1

Language check

Review of tenses

Complete the sentences with the appropriate form of the verbs in brackets.

1 The team regularly (meet) _____ to discuss progress.

2 We got the figures late and by that time we (already go) _____ over budget!

3 They (have) _____ the results of the research in the next few weeks.

4 Right now we (work) _____ on the planning phase of the project.

5 We (look) _____ for a strategic partner for months, but we just can't find one.

6 The team generally (respect) _____ deadlines.

Articles

Complete the article with either a definite or indefinite article or no article at all (ø).

One of [1]_____ most common arguments for mergers and acquisitions is the belief that [2]_____ 'synergies' exist. Unfortunately, research shows that [3]_____ predicted efficiency gains often fail to materialise following [4]_____ merger. 'Horizontal' mergers (between companies operating at the same level of production in the same industry) may also be motivated by [5]_____ desire for greater market power. In theory, authorities such as [6]_____ Britain's Competition Commission should obstruct any merger that could create a monopoly, as that would result in an abuse of [7]_____ power. However, some experts have argued that mergers are unlikely to create monopolies even in [8]_____ absence of regulations, since there is no evidence that mergers in the past have generally led to [9]_____ increase in the concentration of [10]_____ market power.

Modal forms

Choose the correct forms of the words in italics.

1 All meetings *can't be / mustn't be* a waste of time, surely!

2 You really *should have completed / must have completed* the planning phase before you started executing the project.

3 We still *might come / must come* in under budget, but it looks unlikely.

4 There *must have been / should have been* some mistake; those are not the plans.

5 He *might have been / must have been* there but there were so many people that I can't say for sure.

Consolidation

Choose the correct forms of the words in italics in the team-building course description. (ø = no article)

Building a successful team

Your team [1]*must be / might be* just [2]*forming / formed*, or you may be [3]*will renew / renewing* your goals for the coming year. Perhaps you [4]*have lost / were lost* some members recently or [5]*had recruited / recruited* new ones. This course [6]*is taking / will take* you through the various stages of a team's development.

Becoming an effective team member

The key to [7]*a / ø* team's success is [8]*the / an* effort that each team member makes. This course [9]*teaches / is teaching* key points for developing [10]*a / the* team-oriented attitude, and by the end you [11]*must have learned / should have learned* how best to work with [12]*the / ø* colleagues and other team members. Very quickly, you [13]*will see / will be seeing* better team results as you develop [14]*the / ø* communication skills and as you fulfil your specific role and encourage other team members to do [15]*the / ø* same.

Vocabulary check

1 Choose the best options (A–C) to complete the text.

Europe's bridge projects

In Greece, the Rion-Antirion bridge opened four months ahead of ¹_____ and, even more surprisingly, within its $930m ²_____ . Vinci, a leading French ³_____ company, formed a strategic ⁴_____ with a local ⁵_____ to build the bridge. This successful ⁶_____ managed to meet the strict ⁷_____ and be on time at every ⁸_____ of the project.

Bridges are often designed by engineers, but the Millau Viaduct project in France was designed by the British architect Norman Foster, who worked in collaboration with a team of engineers to ⁹_____ the team's common ¹⁰_____ of building the world's highest bridge.

The next big ¹¹_____ may be the planned project to build a bridge from Sicily to the Italian mainland. Industry ¹²_____ believe, however, that the project may not be ¹³_____ : the experts and project sponsors are making ¹⁴_____ of 11,000 vehicles a day – only 1,000 more than now go by ferry.

	A	B	C
1	timetable	schedule	agenda
2	budget	figure	expenses
3	creation	structure	construction
4	alliance	grouping	commitment
5	contractor	licensee	manufacturer
6	integration	conglomerate	partnership
7	delays	rules	deadlines
8	aspect	phase	factor
9	accomplish	succeed	make
10	idea	goal	proposal
11	interest	subject	challenge
12	analysts	judges	referees
13	sufficient	feasible	enough
14	forecasts	plans	figures

2 Replace the words in *italics* with the appropriate form of a multi-part verb.

1 Pressure is on the team to *invent* new ways of working on each project.

2 The new project leader will not *tolerate* lateness.

3 The project will soon be behind schedule if we don't *employ* more workers.

4 The merger has been successful and shareholders can *get excited about* higher dividends this year.

5 As the team leader was away for a few days, the facilitator *assumed responsibility for* the organisation of the tasks.

Career skills

Building relationships

Put the dialogue in the correct order.

☐ a We're interested in featuring your company in our June issue.

☐ a Hello, I don't think we've met before. I'm Sarah Beckford from *Management Issues* magazine.

☐ a Thank you. Here's my card.

☐ b Why don't you contact me next week and we can discuss it further?

☐ b Pleased to meet you. How can I help you?

Setting goals

Find and correct the mistake in each sentence.

1 I'd like you to take up responsibility for the market research.

2 How many is the budget on this one?

3 We should aim to must finish on time.

4 They gave to us a provisional budget.

5 Tell me what you need in the way from resources.

6 Does the deadline sound you reasonable?

Team building

Match the sentence halves (1–6 with a–f).

1 We're definitely moving in the right direction, but

2 Go on, I'm listening –

3 That's a great idea, and

4 Let's look at ways of getting round this problem

5 I'm confident you will get it done on time –

6 Tell me more

a it's better to say what you have on your mind.

b I think we should act on it straightaway.

c about the project; I'm really interested.

d you've never been late before.

e we just need to move a bit faster.

f rather than just worrying about it.

Unit 4
Information

www.longman-elt.com   www.economist.com

The real-time economy

Keynotes

Information is a key resource for modern businesses, and **information management** has a direct impact on efficiency and performance. Information **flows** between the different parts of a business's **information system (people, procedures, resources)** in the form of data, voice, text and images. **Information technology, hardware** and **software**, allows this information to be **gathered, processed, exchanged** and **stored**. Managers are thus able to analyse developments in their business in **real time**, i.e. instantaneously, in order to solve problems and exploit opportunities. Information systems are connected to **internal** and/or **external networks (internet / intranets / extranets)** and must be secured against attack.

Information flows

Look at the graph and answer the questions.

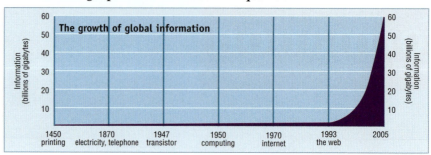

1 Why do you think the amount of information increased so sharply?
2 Do you think it will continue to increase like this?
3 How has this changed the way that people live?

How many emails do you receive/answer every day? What are the main ways that you communicate information?

1 Listen to an interview with Jennifer Barker, an information manager, and focus on the interviewer's questions. Some of the questions below are not exactly the same as the actual questions she is asked. Replace these with the exact questions that the interviewer asks.

1 What is an intranet?
2 How many employees regularly connect to the intranet?
3 What are the most popular parts of the intranet?
4 How difficult is it to manage an intranet?
5 What are the main security issues for the intranet?
6 Who supplies the content for the intranet?
7 How has the intranet changed since it was introduced?

2 Listen again and give the following information.

1 the number of users
2 the four most popular parts
3 two challenges for intranet managers
4 one thing that's impossible and one that's possible
5 the people who contribute content

Do you think intranets are a good idea, or do they just contribute to excessive amounts of information? How do you deal with excessive amounts of information? Do you think that having a lot of information makes it easier for managers to do their jobs?

Automating management

1 Read the text on the opposite page and answer the questions.

1 What is Gary Reiner's position at General Electric?
2 What is the principal objective of the company's plan to improve its information system?
3 What is a real-time enterprise?
4 What are the three main benefits of a real-time enterprise?

Glossary

verbose using more words than necessary

quest search

shoot in the dark guess

spell the death of announce the end of something

Automating management

How about now?

Information technology is speeding up business decision-making and creating a real-time economy, says Ludwig Siegele

1 YOU can't accuse Gary Reiner of being verbose. Ask General Electric's chief information officer a question, and you get an answer that is right to the point. And he regularly checks whether his listeners are still following: "Are you getting what you need?"

2 Anything else would be a disappointment. After all, America's GE is known for its obsessive quest for perfection. And Mr Reiner heads the company's most important initiative: computerising, or "digitising", as much of its business as possible. That not only means buying and selling things online but, more importantly, setting up a digital nervous information system that connects everything involved in the company's business: IT systems, factories, employees, suppliers, customers and products.

3 GE's aim is to monitor everything in real time, Mr Reiner explains, calling up a special spreadsheet on his PC: a "digital dashboard" with green, yellow and red colours that signal the status of programs that are critical to GE's business. If one of them stays red or even yellow for too long, Mr Reiner gets the system to email the people in charge via the network. He can also see when he had to intervene the last time, or how individual applications — such as programs to manage book-keeping or orders — have performed.

4 As chief information officer, Mr Reiner was the first in the firm to get a dashboard. Now all GE's senior managers have them. The principle is always the same: the dashboard compares how certain measurements, such as response times or sales or margins, perform against goals, and alerts managers (in real time) if they need to take action.

5 GE, which estimates that its digitisation efforts saved it $1.6 billion in just one year, has a long history of innovative business management. In years to come, experts predict, many companies will use information technology to become a "real-time enterprise" — an organisation that is able to react instantaneously to changes in its business. And as firms wire up and connect to form networks with their business partners, they make the entire economy more and more real time, creating not so much a "new" but a "now" economy.

Instant gratification

6 But the real-time enterprise is not simply about speeding up information flow. It is also about being able to monitor a business continuously and react when conditions change. Today, businesses "are mostly shooting in the dark", says Michael Maoz, of Gartner, an IT consultancy. Real-time technology, he predicts, will give firms a window into their business they never had before.

7 Mr Maoz also emphasises the third main benefit of a real-time enterprise: using newly available information to offer new products and services. New hardware, such as wireless sensors, makes it possible to gather ever more information and enter it into a company's computer systems. By themselves, these data would just contribute to the increasing information overload. But they also present a new business opportunity: to develop software that analyses them and suggests ways of optimising the supply chain, or even automates the response to certain kinds of new information.

8 How much will all this change the company and the economy as we know it? IT will probably not spell the death of big firms. But real-time technology will have an impact on the workings of companies. It is also likely to make economies more fluid, and perhaps more volatile. The financial markets have already shown that putting even parts of the economy on autopilot can lead to accidents. The stock market crash of 1987 was caused in large part by automated program trading. Perhaps, one day, the "now economy" will have to have circuit breakers installed ■

2 Read the text again. Three of the following questions cannot be answered using information from the text. Identify those questions and answer the other five.

1 What reputation has GE acquired as a company?
2 How many people work in Gary Reiner's department?
3 Which groups of people are connected through GE's information network?
4 Why are some managers reluctant to use the new system?
5 How does the digital dashboard help managers to make decisions?
6 When will the digitisation of GE be completed?
7 What are the two main benefits that Mr Maoz foresees for real-time enterprises?
8 What was one of the causes of the stock market crash of 1987?

Speaking

1 Do you think that developments like those at GE will make the lives of managers easier or more stressful?

2 How will the businesses of the future be affected by the development of IT? What do you think are some of the risks if business becomes more and more computerised?

Vocabulary

Read the sentences and find synonyms in the text for the underlined words and phrases.

1 The new system will a link together b all the component parts of the company's business. (para 2)
2 Gary Reiner uses a colour-coding system to check the a condition of key b software applications. He can then use the c interconnected computers to alert managers. (para 3)
3 Using their a monitoring software, managers have access to certain b indicators of performance and can see how they c match the d objectives that have been fixed. (para 4)
4 The firm a calculates that b adopting automated computer systems helped to c reduce spending by more than one billion dollars. (para 5)
5 The new networked companies will be able to a accelerate the b movement of data and gain greater understanding of their operations. (para 6)
6 New a electronic devices will enable companies to b collect additional c data. (para 7)

Practice

Complete the article with words from this Vocabulary section.

General Electric was one of the first companies to champion 'Six Sigma', a revolutionary approach to quality management that was pioneered by Motorola. Six Sigma uses statistics to produce exact [1] _measurements_ of key business indicators in order to calculate the efficiency of business operations. To do this, [2] _____ about specific [3] _____ that the company wishes to achieve is first [4] _____ and then entered into a computer [5] _____ . This is then matched with the operational results that are actually obtained, which allows managers to see how an operation [6] _____ its original objectives. Six Sigma not only [7] _____ the whole process of quality management, it also allows businesses to make continuous improvements and [8] _____ large amounts of money.

Question forms

Read about the three main types of questions and study the examples from the text on page 35.

Open questions are used when we want to ask someone to provide specific information about something.

*How **much** will all this change the company and the economy as we know it?* (para 8)

How do the verb forms in the following questions differ? Why is this?

*Who **did** you contact about the new software?*

*Who **contacted** you about the new software?*

Closed questions, which can always be answered by either *Yes* or *No*, are used when we want to obtain confirmation or clarification about something.

Are you getting what you need? (para 1)

Tag questions are in two parts. If the main verb is in the affirmative, the tag question is usually in the negative, and vice versa, for example:

*You **don't know** what caused the system to crash, **do you**?*

 For more information, see page 158.

Practice Complete the questionnaire for executives returning from overseas assignments with the appropriate open or closed question words and verb forms.

---

1   _What was_   the agreed duration of your assignment? *2 / 4 / 6 months*

2   _____ you terminate your assignment before the agreed date? *Y/N*

If your answer to the above question is 'yes', please answer question 2.1.

2.1 _____ reasons _____ you terminate before the agreed date? *(please specify)*

3   _____ you satisfied with the remuneration package that you received? *Y/N*

4   _____ you be prepared to accept a similar assignment elsewhere if offered one? *Y/N*

5   _____ you received career counselling since your return? *Y/N*

6   _____ briefed you about your assignment?

7   _____ the members of your family take advantage of cultural training before departure? *Y/N*

8   In your view, _____ qualities _____ a manager possess in order to succeed on an overseas assignment? *(please specify)*

9   _____ the management of overseas assignments be improved? *(please specify)*

10   _____ you report to in the host country?

11   _____ you agree that your career has been enhanced by this experience? *Y/N*

12   _____ you found it difficult to readjust to working back at the parent company? *Y/N*

Writing You are a member of the Human Resources department. Write a letter to accompany the questionnaire that is sent out to executives. Explain the reasons for the survey and give details of when to return the completed questionnaires. (See *Style guide*, page 16.)

Complete the tag questions. There is more than one possible answer.

1   Last week's meeting (be) _____ very productive, _____ it?
2   You (be able) _____ to help me with these calculations, _____ you?
3   You (suggest) _____ that we didn't give you all the information you needed, _____ you?
4   But that (mean) _____ that the project won't be successful in the long term, _____ it?
5   I'd love to have a copy of that chart you showed us. You (give) _____ me one, _____ you?

Listening 2 **Practise saying each of the questions with the correct intonation. Then listen and check.**

Speaking **Work with a partner. Prepare tag questions for situations 1–5. Take turns to read and respond to the questions.**

1   You are very surprised to hear that one of your colleagues, Jeff, has been promoted. Make a comment to another colleague.
    You're not telling me he got that job, are you?
2   An important file has gone missing from your office. Talk to the person you share your office with.
3   You'd like to take part in a training seminar but you think it may be too late to apply. Ask the HR manager.
4   You need to know if your colleague can take you home by car, as promised, after work.
5   You've heard a rumour that one of your best members of staff is thinking of leaving. Confront him/her.

Listening 3 **1 Listen to an interview with Gérard Desmarest, an intelligence and security consultant and author. In what order does he talk about the following?**

a   the main security weakness of business organisations
b   the difference between two key terms/concepts
c   what he did when he was hired to assist a company
d   how to make staff more aware of security risks

2 Listen again and answer the questions.

1   a   What sources of 'business intelligence' are mentioned?
    b   What forms can 'industrial espionage' take?
2   a   How should companies protect their information systems?
    b   How can competitors obtain information from employees?
3   a   What is the best way to make staff more aware of security risks?
    b   What do most companies fail to do? Why?
4   a   Why did the consultant visit the company at the weekend?
    b   Why does he refuse to give details about exactly what he did?

Questioning techniques

Questions are used in a variety of different ways and not always just to obtain information. Asking the right type of question at the right time can make the difference between a successful exchange and an unsuccessful one. Look at the following examples of different question types.

a *If you were in my position, how would you approach this?*

b *Why didn't you follow my instructions?*

c *Do you know who I could ask for some advice about this?*

d *Shall we move on to the next question?*

1 Match the different types of question with a–d above.

1 Invitation questions are used either to invite someone to do something or to make a suggestion about what you think should be done.

2 Hypothetical questions are often phrased using a conditional form. This reassures the listener and makes the question easier to answer.

3 Negative questions are often used to criticise other people. They can also express annoyance or surprise.

4 Embedded questions are in two parts: an introductory question + affirmative verb. This makes the question more indirect and polite.

2 Look at the following questions. Which types of question are they?

1 What would you do if you were asked?

2 How about taking a break?

3 Don't you realise how important this is?

4 Could you tell me where I can get a copy of that?

5 Do you have any idea when the modifications will be made?

6 Why didn't you tell me?

Listening 4 ⊙ Listen to four short dialogues. Which two types of question above are used in each dialogue?

Practice Choose one of the situations below and prepare the questions that the supervisor would ask. Take turns to play the roles of the supervisor and the employee.

1 An employee in your department has been using the company's computer to update his/her weblog (internet diary). You suspect that he/she may have given away confidential information.

2 The report that you asked an employee to prepare contains a number of mistakes. Information about sales figures is inaccurate and there are a lot of spelling and grammar mistakes.

3 You need to ask an employee to replace you for one day at a trade show. You know that this is a difficult thing to ask as he/she has a lot of work at the moment.

Culture at work ## Asking appropriate questions

In some cultures it is not considered polite to ask direct questions, which may cause conflict or embarrassment. Instead, questions are phrased in an indirect manner and allude to things rather than explicitly state them. What is the normal way of asking questions in your culture? Are some types of question avoided?

Dilemma & Decision

Dilemma: Spying on staff

Brief

DigitalVisions is a US multinational corporation that has subsidiaries in different parts of the world. New US legislation makes it obligatory for public companies like DigitalVisions to give their employees access to an internal financial hotline. Employees can use the hotline to communicate information anonymously if they suspect or are aware of financial misconduct. However, some companies may be encouraging use of the hotline to obtain more general information about their employees.

The European subsidiary of DigitalVisions has just received an email copy of the document which outlines how the proposed hotline will be used. One part of the document reads as follows:

'All members of staff who wish to communicate sensitive information via the new hotline can do so anonymously. However, the company reserves the right to use this information as the basis for further investigation where and when this is considered necessary.'

A copy of this email has been communicated to the press, and employees and trade union representatives are calling for a demonstration against the proposed hotline. The company has decided to organise an emergency meeting to discuss the situation and to try to resolve the crisis before it leads to a further deterioration of the company's image in the local and national press. Attending the meeting will be the:

- Director of Information and Public Policy (USA)
- Director of the European subsidiary
- Representative of the Trade Union movement

Task 1

Work in groups. Group A, you represent the Director of Information and Public Policy. Turn to page 137. Group B, you represent the European Director. Turn to page 138. Group C, you represent the Trade Union. Turn to page 140. Read the arguments you will present during the meeting. You should also prepare a short list of questions to ask the other participants about their positions in relation to the hotline.

Task 2

Work in different groups of three, so that each of the three roles is represented in each group. Hold the meeting and present your arguments. Ask the questions that you have prepared.

Task 3

Reach an agreement about the best way to deal with the problems that the hotline is causing.

Write it up

Write a short report, summarising the situation and outlining the conclusions reached by your group. (See *Style guide*, page 28.)

Decision:

- Listen to what Paolo Orsolani, a legal specialist, has to say about the dilemma facing DigitalVisions.

Unit 5
Technology

www.longman-elt.com   www.economist.com

The march of the mobiles
PAGE 44

Relative clauses
PAGE 46

Career skills: Briefing
PAGE 47

Dilemma: Turning ideas into reality
PAGE 48

The pace of change

Keynotes

The rapid pace of **technological development** is affecting every aspect of our personal and professional lives. **Consumer electronics products** are making our lives more comfortable and entertaining. New and more innovative **models** are coming onto this almost **saturated market** all the time. The facility of **browsing** and **uploading** onto or **downloading** from the internet has changed forever the way we work and view the world. **Nanotechnology** is a new **growth market**, which promises to bring smaller, lighter, more portable technological **devices**. But nowhere has technology more deeply changed our **lifestyle** than in the field of **mobile telecommunications**

Unique selling features

1 Read the descriptions of some of the latest hi-tech products. Which ones would you like to own or use, and why?

eMusic-live is installing machines at concerts that dispense cigarette lighter-sized hard drives which contain digital recordings of performances, which are easy to upload onto a computer.

Adidas is designing a new shoe containing a battery-powered microprocessor and electric motor to help the shoe respond to changing weather conditions.

Microsoft labs in China are developing a digital pen that people can use to write on paper as well as electronic documents. Users can also upload pen-written documents onto their computers.

A wireless portable internet radio developed by Reciva uses a special browser to capture stations on the web.

DaimlerChrysler has designed a vibrating accelerator pedal that alerts motorists to slow down when it is economically wise. The system tells the driver when an intersection is approaching to avoid sudden stops that waste fuel.

2 Look at the different mobile phones below and on the opposite page. Which one do you like most, and why?

1 Clamshell

2 Jackknife

3 Clip-on

4 Gaming console

Describing features and functions

1 Listen and match the descriptions you hear with the phones above.

2 Listen again and complete the information.

a

Manufacturer: _____

Features:
It has two _____ : it is
not only a mobile phone but can also be
attached to a _____ or an
_____ .

b

Manufacturer: _____

Features:
It has a protective device for the
_____ and has room
for both a _____ and
a _____ .

c

Manufacturer: _____

Features:
The phone is a _____
feature. This suggests mobile phones could be
designed to perform _____
in the future.

d

Manufacturer: _____

Features:
When open, it has a _____
mobile phone keypad. They modelled its
_____ on a digital
camera.

Speaking   Work in pairs. Take turns to describe the Blackberry mobile phone. If either or both of you own mobile phones, talk about how they compare with the Blackberry.

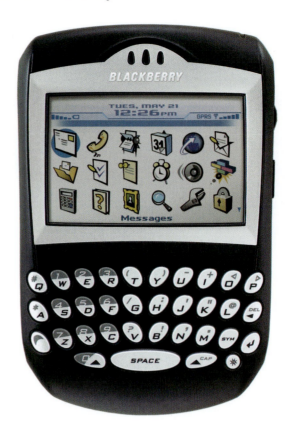

Reading   ## Continuous improvement

1 Read the text on the following page. What are the different ways in which mobile phone companies can boost revenues by
a) increasing sales and b) encouraging people to use their phones more?

2 Read the text again and answer the questions.

1   What are the features of the new mobile phone for dogs?
2   What does the writer mean when he says the mobile phone industry is a *victim of its own success*?
3   How are some countries allowing poor people to use mobile phones?
4   How can the potential market for mobile phones in Japan be at least five times greater than the population?
5   Why is it good to make use of people's phones when they are asleep?

Speaking   What reasons can you think of for installing phones on dogs, and in cars, laptop computers, household appliances and industrial machinery? Can you think of other useful places where phones could be installed?

Are mobile phones a good thing for society in general?

Are there any disadvantages to having 24-hour phone communication?

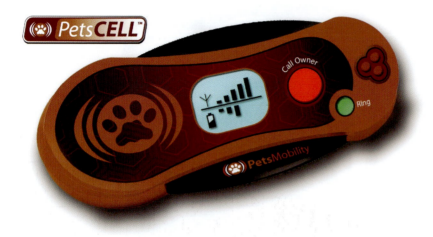

Glossary

start-up new, recently formed company

untapped market potential market which hasn't yet been exploited

saturated (market) where there are more goods than people who want to buy them

Continuous improvement
The march of the mobiles

Is there no limit to the potential market for mobile communications?

[1] WHEN it comes to new designs for mobile phones, the model that was announced last week by a start-up based in Arizona really goes to the limit. Shaped like a bone, it operates only as a speakerphone, picks up automatically when called, is mounted on a red strap for wearing around the neck, and is labelled with a large paw – because the PetsCell, as it is called, is a mobile phone for dogs. Pets Mobility, the firm behind this astounding device, boasts of "connecting every member of your family – even your pet".

[2] This is not quite as ridiculous as it sounds. Indeed, you can expect more examples of this kind of thing. The reason is that the mobile-telecoms industry has become a victim of its own success. With sales of 600m units a year, mobile phones are simultaneously the world's most widespread communications devices, computing devices and consumer electronics products. Almost everybody in the developed world now has one, and growth is booming in the developing world, too. China is the world's largest market for mobile phones, and Africa is the fastest-growing. In the least developed parts of the world, entrepreneurs such as Bangladesh's "telephone ladies" rent out mobiles by the minute, putting phones into the hands of even the poorest. The much quoted statistic that two-thirds of the world's population has never made a phone call is no longer true.

[3] As a result, the industry is frantically looking for new sources of growth, since it will not be able to rely on subscriber growth for much longer. And in the developed world, it cannot rely on subscriber growth even now. Hence the logic of selling phones for dogs. Another untapped market is phones for infants: Communic8, a British firm, has launched the MyMo, a simple phone aimed at four- to eight-year-olds, while SK Telecom in South Korea offers a similar device, i-Kids, with built-in satellite tracking. And even when every human, cat and dog has a phone, there are always cars, laptop computers, household appliances and industrial machinery. Install a phone and some sensors inside a bulldozer, and it can call a mechanic before it goes wrong. DoCoMo, Japan's leading mobile operator, estimates that the potential market for mobile phones in Japan is at least five times the number of people.

[4] Another approach is to encourage people to use their existing phones more than they do at the moment. Third-generation networks, which will offer lots of extra capacity, will lead to lower prices and, the industry hopes, more phone calls. Similarly, there is much excitement about "fixed-mobile convergence", a technology that allows people to use their mobile handsets to make cheap calls at home over fixed-line networks – again, it is hoped, boosting usage. Extending mobile coverage, so that subscribers can make calls wherever they are, is another tactic. Coverage is already available in underground railway networks in many cities, and within two years it will be extended into what is many people's last remaining phone-free environment: aeroplanes.

[5] When everyone on earth is on the phone all day long – calling their dogs, cars or washing machines, if not each other – will the market finally be saturated? No. There are already plans to stream music, video and other downloads to mobile phones in the dead of night, when networks are almost empty. Even being asleep, it seems, need not prevent you from using your phone. Evidently, the industry has far to go before it reaches the limits of mankind's desire to communicate ■

Match the nouns (1–9) from the text with their meanings (a–i).

1	design (para 1)	a	a piece of equipment used for a specific task
2	model (para 1)	b	an area where mobile technology can operate
3	subscriber (para 3)	c	a particular type of machine
4	laptop (para 3)	d	software or information that can be moved from one electronic device to another
5	appliance (para 3)	e	a device to read information
6	sensor (para 3)	f	a portable computer
7	network (para 4)	g	a person paying to hire a telephone line
8	coverage (para 4)	h	a set of connected technologies or systems
9	download (para 5)	i	the appearance of something because of the way it has been planned and made

Vocabulary 2 ## Compound nouns

In the text there are examples of compound nouns such as *subscriber growth* and *household appliances* (para 3). Join the nouns in box 1 to the nouns in box 2 to form compound nouns. Some words in box 1 can go with more than one word in box 2.

1	
internet	
mass	
market	
information	
computer	
profit	
consumer	

2	
product	
market	
technology	
margin	
programmer	
access	
share	
leader	

Practice **Complete the article about Motorola's new strategy with the appropriate form of words from Vocabulary 1 and 2.**

Padmasree Warrior, Motorola's chief technology officer, is launching a new strategy, which, she says, will lead to more mobility. This, she hopes, will increase the number of ¹ _subscribers_ in the almost saturated mobile phone market. Nokia is the mobile phone ² _____ out in front of Motorola, which is number two in this highly competitive industry. With an increasing number of competitors trying to attract fewer and fewer customers, all telecommunications companies have seen their ³ _____ shrink lately. Many big telecom companies are facing

pressure from shareholders to find new growth markets and original strategies in an effort to boost falling revenues and increase ⁴ _____.
Ms Warrior leads an army of 4,600 technologists and researchers who have come up with plans to do just that. They intend to start by connecting their technology ⁵ _____ into one, for example combining wireless and multimedia technologies in their new mobile phones. Their latest ⁶ _____ , the Razr V3, has been described as a triumph of engineering,

marketing and innovative ⁷ _____ . Motorola also plans to smooth the transition between home, work, automotive and mobile environments by providing easy and high-speed ⁸ _____ on trains and email in cars, and their customers will be able to get video ⁹ _____ onto their phones. The company even intends to extend ¹⁰ _____ so that mobiles can be used on planes. Phones let you talk everywhere; Motorola will let you do everything everywhere!

Writing **Write a formal email from Padmasree Warrior to the Motorola staff, outlining her plans for the company's future. (See *Style guide*, page 20.)**

Relative clauses

Study the examples of relative clauses from the text on page 44.

Defining ... *the model* **that was announced last week by a start-up based in Arizona** ... (para 1)

Non-defining *Third-generation networks*, **which will offer lots of extra capacity**, *will* ... (para 4)

Shortened relative clauses Some relative clauses can be shortened by using the present or past participle if the pronoun is the subject of the clause. In the case of past participles, the verb has to be used in a passive sense.

... *the model* **announced last week by a start-up based in Arizona** *really goes to the limit.*

Third-generation networks, **offering lots of extra capacity**, *will lead to* ...

For more information, see page 159.

Practice **1** **Shorten the relative clauses in the following sentences. Check your answers by finding the sentences in Preview on page 42 and the text on page 44.**

1 A radio which was developed by Reciva uses a special browser.

   A radio developed by Reciva uses a special browser.

2 Adidas is designing a new shoe which contains a battery-powered microprocessor.

3 Bangladesh's 'telephone ladies' rent out mobiles by the minute, which puts phones into the hands of even the poorest.

4 Communic8 has launched a simple phone which is aimed at four- to eight-year-olds.

2 **Read the article below, in which the relative clauses are in *italics*, and do the following.**

− Complete the article with the appropriate relative pronoun.
− Put brackets round the relative pronoun if it can be omitted.
− Add commas where they are needed.
− Rewrite 5 and 8 using shortened relative clauses.
− Decide which two clauses could be either defining or non-defining.

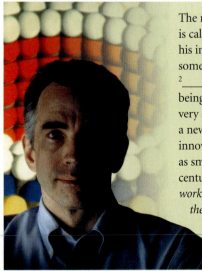

The man [1] **who/that** *invented nanotechnology* is called Eric Drexler. He believes that the name of his invention has been stolen and applied to something else. For the term nanotechnology [2]_____ *once had a precise meaning* is now being used by anyone with half a plan for making very small things. Miniaturisation is not, of course, a new idea. One of the consistent aims of innovation in technology has been to make things as small as possible. It was the famous twentieth-century physicist Richard Feynman [3]_____ *work first suggested that miniaturisation might go all the way down to the molecular level.* Eric Drexler [4]_____ *went to the Massachusetts Institute of Technology in the late 1970s* turned these ideas into a PhD thesis and a book called 'Engines of Creation' [5]_____ *was published in 1986.* His vision was of a revolution [6]_____ *would change manufacturing technology forever.* Although there are few commercial products yet, some are clearly on the horizon. Molecule-sized transistors and other electronic components [7]_____ *have already been developed* are being studied by researchers [8]_____ *are trying to work out how to fit them together.* In spite of the huge budgets [9]_____ *nanotechnology requires* and the slow technical progress, nanotechnology is believed to be the technology [10]_____ *will bring us lighter, stronger, cleaner and more precise technological products in the future.*

Briefing

When briefing people on what their projects or assignments will involve, it is important to be clear and thorough as briefs are the starting point for putting strategies into action. Look at the following useful phrases.

a *The project will involve ...*
b *Let's look at this diagram to get a better picture of ...*
c *To get results, we need to ...*
d *Jill, can you make that a priority?*
e *What we need to achieve is ...*
f *I want the IT department to get on to that.*
g *Probably the best way to do this is to ...*
h *As this chart shows ...*

Match phrases a–h with stages 1–4.

When briefing it is important to:

1 outline objectives
2 describe methods
3 assign roles to people/departments
4 use visual aids to clarify points

Listening 2 ⊙

1 **Listen to an extract from a briefing session about setting up a corporate website and answer the questions.**

1 What is the main objective of the website?
2 What areas do the IT experts need to answer questions about?
3 What will recent questionnaires be used for?
4 Which two departments are roles assigned to?
5 What does each of these departments have to do?

2 **Listen again. What language is used to do the following?**

1 outline objectives
2 describe methods
3 assign roles
4 refer to visuals

Speaking **Work in pairs. Prepare a briefing session from the following notes. Take turns to give the briefing.**

> Task: update the design of our DVD recorder
> Engineers: improve picture and sound quality
> Designers: come up with new colours and designs; look at competition (show slides of competitors' latest models)
> Marketing team: get market feedback on prototype – organise focus groups / questionnaires.

Culture at work ## Assigning tasks

In some cultures, hierarchy is very clearly defined and respected. Senior staff members make all the major decisions and initiative is neither expected nor rewarded. Briefing sessions have a dictatorial style and orders are expected to be carried out to the letter. In other cultures, briefing sessions can be more flexible, and working methods can vary as long as objectives are achieved. Which corresponds best to your culture? Which of the above culture types would you be most comfortable in, and why?

Dilemma & Decision

Dilemma: Turning ideas into reality

Brief

The National Endowment for Science and Technology (NESTA) was set up to maximise creativity and innovative potential. They give financial backing in the form of grants and loans as well as advice on production and marketing strategies to organisations with new technological inventions. They are less interested in short-term results than other providers of capital and they consider the social and cultural value of products to be as important as the long-term commercial value.

Task 1

Work in small groups. Read the descriptions of the applicants for a NESTA grant below. Discuss the merits of each product in terms of: innovative potential, long-term returns and the social and cultural impact of the technology.

Task 2

As members of the NESTA committee that awards grants, decide which product your group would choose to back, and develop your own arguments as to why this technology is of particular importance. Prepare to present your views to the committee.

Task 3

Each group should present their chosen product and say why it is the most worthy. As a class, decide on the winning product.

Decision:

Now turn to page 145 and read what NESTA decided.

Point and click for learning on the move

Hypertag Ltd wants to produce interactive mobile multimedia technology. Their technology uses hand-held computers which, when pointed at an electronic device near an exhibit at a museum or art gallery, can offer lots of relevant information including text, video, pictures and sound.

Working tyrelessly for the environment

UTDR Research has developed a machine which can recycle tyres in an environmentally-friendly fashion. It also converts the waste into marketable by-products, which can produce revenue for the business. At present, 190,000 tonnes of waste tyres in landfill sites or official dumping grounds are, among other disadvantages, under constant threat of unmanageable fires.

Nanotechnology to fight bioterrorism

Nanosight has developed a way of synthetically reproducing a version of what happens when the body first detects a virus, using computer and microelectronic technology. This technique is not limited to detecting biowarfare viruses but can speed up drug development and dramatically reduce costs for pharmaceutical companies.

VISION OF THE FUTURE

Camfed have come up with a revolutionary invention in optics, which will lead to the production of energy-efficient, low-cost, high-performance displays and ultimately home cinemas and TV. To date, displays have been either thin and expensive or space-consuming and cheap.

Write it up

Write a press release announcing the winning product. (See *Style guide*, page 30.)

Unit 6
Advertising

www.longman-elt.com   www.economist.com

The power of persuasion

Keynotes

Advertising is a means of communication between an organisation and its **target audience** using space or time purchased in the **media** (TV, radio, magazines, newspapers, websites, **billboards**, etc.). Businesses generally use the services of **advertising agencies** to create **advertising campaigns** that use combinations of **commercials**, **posters**, **print adverts** or internet **pop-ups** in order to **publicise** their products or services and persuade consumers to buy. Increasingly, **advertisers** are using other forms of **promotion** such as **in-store displays**, **product placements** and **product demonstrations** to draw attention to what they want to sell.

Advertising media

1 Look at the examples of adverts that have appeared in unusual places and discuss the following questions.

1 What are the target audiences for each of the adverts?
2 How successful do you think these adverts are?
3 Can you think of other unusual places to advertise these products?

2 Where would be the best place to advertise the following?

1 golf equipment
2 medical insurance
3 discount travel for students
4 hotel accommodation
5 a second-hand car
6 a new movie

Speaking Can you think of any more new, unusual places where it would be possible to place advertisements?

How many adverts do you see every day? Where are they placed? Which three media do you think are used the most for advertising?

Reading ## Targeting the audience

1 Read the text on the opposite page. Choose the best subheading for the beginning of the text.

1 The advertising industry is going through a crisis period – sales are down and times are hard.
2 The traditional media are finally attracting a new younger audience and more advertisers as a result.
3 More people are rejecting traditional sales messages, presenting the ad industry with big challenges.

2 The following questions refer to information given in paragraphs 1–6. Which paragraphs are referred to in each?

1 Why have some forms of advertising become ineffective? *para 2*
2 What are the two weaknesses of the internet as an advertising medium?
3 What new services have advertising agencies started to offer?
4 What happened in the past when new advertising media appeared?
5 How much does it cost to advertise at peak viewing times in the USA?
6 What proportion of the money spent on advertising may be wasted?

3 Answer the questions above.

Targeting the audience
The harder hard sell

Glossary

go down the drain be wasted

splurge spend a lot of money

relentlessly continuously, without stopping

1 It was Lord Leverhulme, the British soap pioneer, who is said to have complained that he knew half of his advertising budget was wasted, but didn't know which half. The real effects of advertising have become more measurable, exposing another, potentially more horrible, truth for the industry: in some cases, it can be a lot more than half of the budget that is going down the drain.

2 The advertising industry is passing through one of the most disorienting periods in its history. This is due to a combination of long-term changes, such as the growing diversity of media and the arrival of new technologies, notably the internet. With better-informed consumers, the result is that some of the traditional methods of advertising and marketing simply no longer work.

The media are the message

3 But spending on advertising is up again and is expected to grow this year by 4.7 per cent to $343 billion. How will the money be spent? There are plenty of alternatives to straightforward advertising. They range from public relations to direct mail and include consumer promotions (such as special offers), in-store displays, business-to-business promotions (like paying a retailer for shelf space), telemarketing, exhibitions, sponsoring events, product placements and more. These have become such an inseparable part of the industry that big agencies are now willing to provide most of them.

4 As ever, the debate in the industry centres on the best way to achieve results. Is it more cost-effective, for instance, to use a public relations agency to invite a journalist out to lunch and persuade him to write about a product than to pay for a display ad in that journalist's newspaper? Should you launch a new car with glossy magazine ads, or – as some car makers now do – simply park demonstration models in shopping malls and motorway service stations? And is it better to buy a series of ads on a specialist cable TV channel or splurge $2.2m on a single 30-second commercial during this year's Super Bowl?

Net sales

5 Such decisions are ever harder to make. For a start, people are spending less time reading newspapers and magazines, but are going to the cinema more, listening to more radio and turning in ever-increasing numbers to a new medium, the internet (see chart 1). No one knows just how important the internet will eventually be as an advertising medium. Some advertisers think it will be a highly cost-effective way of reaching certain groups of consumers. But not everyone uses the internet, and nor is it seen as being particularly good at building brands. So far, the internet accounts for only a tiny slice of the overall advertising pie (see chart 2), although its share has begun to grow rapidly.

6 Despite all of these new developments, many in the advertising business remain confident. Rupert Howell, chairman of the London arm of McCann Erickson, points out that TV never killed radio, which in turn never killed newspapers. They did pose huge creative challenges, but that's OK, he maintains: "The advertising industry is relentlessly inventive; that's what we do." ■

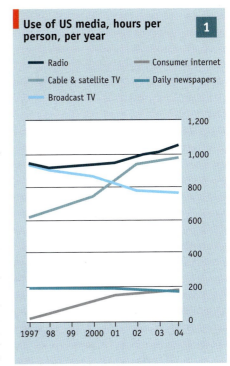

Use of US media, hours per person, per year — 1

- Radio
- Cable & satellite TV
- Broadcast TV
- Consumer internet
- Daily newspapers

(1997, 98, 99, 2000, 01, 02, 03, 04; scale 0–1,200)

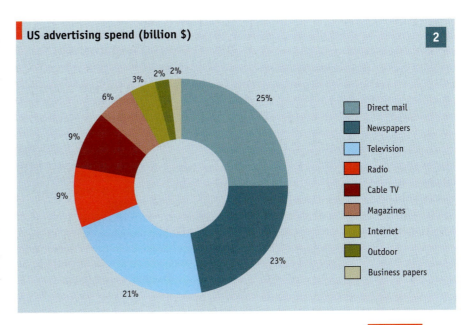

US advertising spend (billion $) — 2

- Direct mail — 25%
- Newspapers — 23%
- Television — 21%
- Radio — 9%
- Cable TV — 9%
- Magazines — 6%
- Internet — 3%
- Outdoor — 2%
- Business papers — 2%

4 Are the following statements about chart 1 *true* or *false*?

1 Americans are spending more time reading newspapers.
2 Broadcast television is more popular than satellite and cable TV.
3 The number of radio listeners has increased significantly.
4 Internet usage doubled during the period from 2000 to 2003.

5 Complete the sentences about chart 2.

1 _____ and _____ were the two media on which advertisers spent the most.
2 In the print media, _____ was the least popular medium with advertisers.
3 In broadcasting, _____ accounted for a little over double the amount spent on radio.

Vocabulary

1 Find words and phrases in paragraph 3 and match them with their meanings (1–6).

1 trade fairs and shows _____
2 promotional price reductions _____
3 featuring a product in a film or TV programme _____
4 publicity material delivered to homes _____
5 communicating with the press _____
6 selling to customers over the phone _____

2 Look at the examples of verb + noun collocations from the text.

to achieve results (para 4)   *to pose a challenge* (para 6)

Complete the collocations below with the following verbs and nouns.

Verbs run launch make sponsor	**Nouns** brand audience image

1 to target an   5 to project an
2 to _____ a new campaign   6 to endorse a _____
3 to   an advert in the press 7 to   a commercial
4 to   a sports event

Practice

Complete the text with the appropriate form of the collocations above.

Signing a celebrity and using their star status to ¹ *endorse a brand* is one of the standard advertising techniques. Tag Heuer, the watchmaker which ² _____ a number of _____ , currently has Tiger Woods under contract. Nicole Kidman has ³ _____ for Chanel No. 5, which has been shown around the world. But choosing the celebrity who will ⁴ _____ exactly the right _____ is not always so easy, as several companies have found out. What happens when a company is about to ⁵ _____ a new _____ featuring a celebrity and it suddenly finds out that he or she is accused of a criminal offence? While there is no doubt that most celebrity endorsements do increase sales, more and more advertisers are turning to other, less risky ways of ⁶ _____ the _____ that they want to reach.

Speaking

What examples of product placement in films, video games or on TV can you think of? Do you think this is an effective form of advertising?

Gerunds and infinitives

1 Study the examples taken from the text on page 51. Which of the examples contain a gerund and which contain an infinitive?

a *The real effects of advertising have become more measurable,* **exposing** *another, potentially more horrible, truth for the industry.* (para 1)

b *But* **spending** *on advertising is up again ...* (para 3)

c *... and is expected* **to grow** *this year by 4.7 per cent ...* (para 3)

d *... big agencies are now willing* **to provide** *most of them.* (para 3)

e *... it will be a highly cost-effective way of* **reaching** *...* (para 5)

f *... although its share has begun* **to grow** *rapidly.* (para 5)

2 Which of the following rules apply to gerunds and which to infinitives? One rule applies to both – which is it?

1 _____ : used after prepositions (*without, of,* etc.)

2 _____ : used as nouns

3 _____ : used to form a shortened relative clause

4 _____ : used after the verbs *intend, plan, decide, expect,* etc.

5 _____ : used after the verbs *like, hate, start, continue,* etc.

6 _____ : used after adjectives (*liable, willing, best,* etc.)

3 Match rules 1–6 with examples a–f above.

For more information, see page 159.

For more information, see page 159.

Practice Complete the article with the gerund or infinitive form of the verbs in brackets.

(¹advertise) _Advertising_ dates back to early history and initially consisted simply of people (²communicate) _____ messages orally about where certain items could be found. It was the invention of (³print) _____ that really launched written messages as a vehicle for (⁴promote) _____ the sale of products. In London, the first print ads (⁵appear) _____ were posted on the doors of churches, (⁶announce) _____ that prayer books were available from a local printer.

Newspapers accelerated the growth of advertising, and with more and more people able (⁷read) _____ , businesses began (⁸take out) _____ adverts to sell imported goods like tea and coffee. However, it was in the USA that advertising really became an industry in itself. Some of the key moments in this process were:

1882 Procter and Gamble launch their Ivory Soap ad, (⁹spend) _____ a record sum of $11,000 on the campaign.

1922 AT&T's New York radio station introduces broadcast advertising by (¹⁰invite) _____ listeners (¹¹buy) _____ ten minutes of radio time for $100.

1957 The first broadcast television commercials are made, (¹²open up) _____ a new medium for advertisers.

1995 MTV's new style of video images starts (¹³revolutionise) _____ the way that TV commercials are made.

1995 The amount of money spent on internet advertising continues (¹⁴rise) _____ and reaches $2 billion for the first time.

2004 Procter and Gamble manages (¹⁵attract) _____ more than four million consumers to its website for the launch of its new toothpaste.

Speaking Prepare brief notes about your plans (professional or personal) for the coming year. What do you hope to achieve? What are you looking forward to doing? What decisions do you think you will have to make?

Discuss your notes with a partner. How are your plans different? Do you share the same goals?

Talking about adverts

Look at the two adverts. Who is being targeted in each advert? Which advert do you prefer, and why? Which advert do you think is more effective?

1

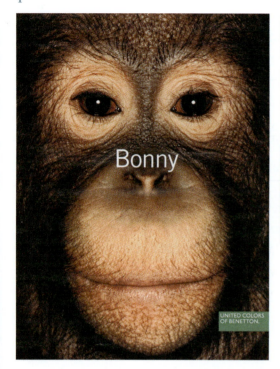

2

FREELANDER MAASAI £14,995

Listening 1 **1** Listen to Naomi Johnson of the Institute of Advertising and Design talking about the two adverts. Complete the table.

	1	2
Advertiser	_____	_____
Product	_____	_____
Key words used to describe the advert	*emotional impact*	*straightforward*
	_____	_____
	_____	_____

2 How do Naomi's opinions of the adverts differ from yours?

Speaking What are your most/least favourite adverts?

Which current adverts do you think are the most creative in your country?

How is the advertising industry regulated in your country? What sorts of products or services cannot be advertised?

Writing Choose a poster advertisement from your country that you find distasteful. Write a letter to the government authority responsible for advertising, outlining the reasons why you think it should be banned. (See *Style guide*, page 16.)

Storytelling

When we communicate with other people at work, we spend much of our time telling stories about things that have happened. Telling a good story can leave a strong impression and can help your listener to visualise a situation. Look at the following phrases, which can be used when telling a story.

a *It turned out ...*
b *You'll never believe this ...*
c *To cut a long story short ...*
d *Just then ...*

e *In the end ...*
f *At that very moment ...*
g *To get to the point ...*
h *Guess what happened next?*

Which of phrases a–h would you use if you wanted to do the following?

1 give a shortened version
2 talk about the outcome
3 get your audience to anticipate
4 focus on a critical moment

When you tell a story, remember to do the following.

– Set the scene: describe where and when the story took place.
– Describe the people who are involved.
– Describe the sequence of events.
– Explain how the story ended.
– Not speak too fast, and pause at critical moments in your story.

Listening 2

1 **Listen to a person telling a story. Does he follow the advice above?**

2 **Now listen to another version of the same story. How is it different?**

3 **Listen to another speaker telling a different story and answer the questions.**

1 Who is the main character in the story?
2 Where/When does the story take place?
3 What is the sequence of events?
4 What happens at the end?

Which of phrases a–h above does the speaker use?

Speaking

Work in groups. Think of something unusual that happened to you or to someone you know, or think of a film or book. Prepare a two-minute story about it. Join a student from another group and tell each other your stories.

Culture at work ## Personal narratives

The types of stories that people tell vary from one culture to another. In some cultures, people avoid telling first person narratives and prefer to tell stories that do not involve them personally. In some western cultures, however, it is considered acceptable to tell a story about your own experience. What types of stories do people tell in your culture? What sorts of subjects should you avoid if you are telling a story in a business context?

Dilemma &Decision

Dilemma: Danger Zone

Brief

The marketing team of Wonder Image Inc are about to launch their latest action video game, Danger Zone, using a series of striking TV commercials with real actors.

The first commercial takes place in an underground car park, where we can see the silhouettes of three people moving in semi-darkness. Then there is a sudden blinding flash as a gun goes off and a young man is heard saying, 'This is where I met the two strangers – and I didn't want to meet them again.' The storyboard for this commercial has been shown to two sample groups – a group of target consumers (12–25-year-old males) and a representative group of older viewers. The reactions of the first group have been extremely positive, but in the second group several people have expressed concerns that the commercial will be too extreme. The marketing team are worried: if viewers complain to the government's Advertising Standards Committee, there is a chance that the commercial could be banned and the launch would be endangered.

Task 1

Work in groups. You are members of the marketing team and you now have to decide what to do about the launch of Danger Zone. Among the options that you can consider are the following:

• cancel the first commercial and delay the launch until a new storyline can be developed (you can suggest ideas for this)

• contact the ASC to see if the commercials can be shown after 10:00pm

• go ahead with the launch of the campaign without changing anything

• radically alter the campaign and/or choose an alternative method of advertising the game

Task 2

Meet with another group and present your decision about the launch.

Task 3

As a class, review the solutions proposed by each group and agree on the one that the class thinks would work best.

Write it up

Write a fax to send to the advertising agency informing them of your decision. (See *Style guide*, page 22.)

Decision:

Turn to page 146 to find out what happened with the launch of Danger Zone.

Review 2

Language check

Question forms

Complete the frequently asked questions about the Advertising Standards Commission (ASC).

1 _____ does the ASC come to the conclusion that an ad is making false claims?

2 _____ kind of evidence does a company need in order to support the claims in its ads?

3 _____ letters from satisfied customers considered to be sufficient support?

4 _____ the ASC review my ads before I run them to check they comply with the law?

5 _____ I easily find out if the ASC already had an investigation into my company?

6 We offer a money back guarantee, so we don't need to support our claims, _____ ?

Relative clauses

Read the following sentences about industrial espionage. Are the relative clauses more likely to be defining or non-defining? Add commas where necessary.

1 The office that the team of US and Chinese scientists were working in was broken into last night.

2 The thieves who tried to make it look like a simple burglary stole computers containing plans, diagrams and specifications for a technology named Butler.

3 Butler which will allow anyone who has a TV to access the internet was top-secret because of its commercial potential.

4 The research was being done in conjunction with the University of Buffalo and the visiting professors who recently arrived from China.

5 The American Society for Industrial Security whom they commissioned to do a study said the potential losses for all industry could amount to as much as $63 billion.

Gerunds and infinitives

Complete the text with the appropriate form of the verbs in brackets.

For many years, scientists have had visions of (¹build) _____ the smart, fully automated home, which contains fridges that are able (²suggest) _____ recipes for the ingredients inside them and cupboards that have no difficulty in (³order) _____ groceries before they run out.

People have dreamed that one day they could afford (⁴buy) _____ internet-capable kitchen appliances. So why haven't we managed (⁵make) _____ the dream a reality yet? (⁶have) _____ wireless networks would seem to be the answer, and now Nokia hopes (⁷turn) _____ its phones into universal remote control devices, (⁸mean) _____ the dream may come true sooner than we think.

Consolidation

Choose the correct forms of the words in *italics*.

The customer is finally king

The latest dilemma ¹*who/which* TV advertisers have to face is how to attract cynical consumers ²*which/who* have found ways to avoid ³*to watch / watching* TV commercials. A recent survey, ⁴*organised / organising* by 'The Economist', showed that consumers are more interested in ⁵*getting / to get* information themselves than simply ⁶*to listen / listening* to what advertisers have to say. It is becoming increasingly important for advertisers ⁷*asking / to ask* themselves how they should adapt and ⁸*how / what* it means for organisations ⁹*who/that* can't afford ¹⁰*to lose/losing* any more business. 'For the first time, the consumer is boss, ¹¹*who / which* is fascinatingly frightening, because what we were good at ¹²*to do / doing* will no longer work!' says Kevin Roberts, chief executive of Saatchi and Saatchi.

Vocabulary check

1 Join the nouns in box A to the nouns in box B to form compound nouns. Some words in box A can go with more than one word in box B

A	B
mass	development
information	access
product	programmer
consumer	electronics
growth	technology
internet	demonstration
computer	market

2 Complete the article with the following words and five words from above.

campaign	events	publicity
phones	advertisement	

Humanoid robots are becoming ever more like humans, thanks to the rapid advances in computer [1]_____ and the creativity of their designers. But why have robots taken on a human form? Is it to make the [2]_____ feel more comfortable with them or is it because of the [3]_____ they generate for the firms that make them?

It is certainly true that humanoid robots are a wonderful [4]_____ for the likes of Honda and Sony. Asimo, the humanoid robot from Honda, is capable of a perfect product [5]_____ , showing what it can do by walking on stage at all the industry's major [6]_____ to collect awards for the company. Toyota organised a huge media [7]_____ to inform the world about Partner, their robot who plays the trumpet. Sony's QRIO understands a small number of voice commands, and with its wireless connection to the [8]_____ it can broadcast what its camera eyes see.

But it is also true that these companies see their robots becoming mass [9]_____ products. Hideki Komiyama of Sony has no doubts. 'Robots are going to be a part of everyday life,' he says, 'and will become as common in the future as mobile [10]_____ are today.'

Career skills

Questioning techniques

Match the questions with the answers.

1 What would you do if you were me?
2 I think we should leave the report as it is. Do you agree?
3 Would you like a break now?
4 Why weren't you here yesterday?
5 Don't you understand how urgent this is?

a Well, I'm sorry, I didn't, but I do now.
b I took a lot of work home with me to do there.
c Yes, I do. It looks fine to me.
d Oh, yes, I should think we all need one.
e I'd tell the truth.

Briefing

Match the sentence halves (1–5 with a–e).

1 This project will involve
2 As this chart shows,
3 To get quick results, we need to
4 I want the Human Resources department
5 Finally, I want you to make this

a a priority – we have no time to lose.
b organise retraining programmes for all the staff as soon as possible.
c to find trainers and schedule training sessions.
d we are far behind our competitors in software terms.
e a complete change in software systems.

Storytelling

Complete the story with the following expressions.

you'll never believe this   to cut a long story short
guess what happened   it turned out   in the end

[1]_____ to me at the weekend. I met this guy at the conference who I thought was really boring at first, but we got talking and [2]_____ I realised he was the very man I needed to meet. The thing is that his company has been the victim of industrial espionage, too, and has had all sorts of problems. Anyway, [3]_____ , he explained how information gets out of an organisation. [4]_____ , but in their company they did everything to discover how it happened, spent a lot of time and money, and so on, and [5]_____ that the problem was … mobile phones – because, of course, modern ones have cameras in them, and no one had thought of that!

Unit 7
Law

www.longman-elt.com   www.economist.com

In the name of the law

Keynotes

The activities of all companies are subject to national and **international laws**, which lay down the conditions under which they can operate in their home markets and abroad. Companies and individuals use the services of a **law firm** or of a corporate **legal department** to take **legal action** or **to litigate** in order to obtain **compensation** for harm they have suffered. Both sides in a **lawsuit** are represented by their **lawyers** (US *attorneys*); the **plaintiff** or **litigant** brings the lawsuit against the **defendant**. Businesses can be **sued** if they fail to respect their obligations under the law. Most **lawsuits** are settled **out of court** through negotiation between the two parties.

Legal professions

Listen to extracts from interviews with four business lawyers at the international law firm DavisLaing Associates. Complete the table.

Which of the jobs described do you find the most interesting?

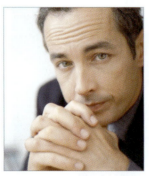   

Name	Marvin Hunt	Louise Grainger	Marsha Maspero	Samuel Chase
Speciality				
Example case				

Speaking

Read some examples of cases where people have sued. If you were judging the case, would you award compensation (if so, how much?) or would you dismiss the case?

- A woman sued a fast food outlet after she spilled a cup of coffee over herself and suffered burns.
- A group of consumers sued a restaurant chain because they claimed the food it served was making them put on weight.
- A father sued the school basketball coach when his son was left out of the school basketball team.
- A young woman sued a local hospital after recognising her mother in a TV commercial (infomercial) for the hospital's emergency service. Her mother had been filmed receiving emergency treatment.
- A computer user sued the manufacturer after his computer was attacked by a virus which destroyed some important files.

Reading

Company liability

1 Read the text on the opposite page quickly. Which paragraphs contain information about the following?

a   a strategic decision which exposed a company to litigation *para 1*

b   the different forms that litigation against companies can take

c   how the attitude of some judges and courts is changing

d   how litigation can affect a company's stock price

e   what happened when a company acquired another business

f   the lack of information available about the real cost of litigation

g   the arguments used to justify litigation

Glossary

Bubble Wrap™ protective plastic film used to protect goods

in restrospect looking back to the past

blunder mistake

teeter be in danger of falling

trigger (n) mechanism that activates a process; (v) to activate

get out of hand become unmanageable

Company liability

The people vs the USA

Along with creditors and shareholders, a third group is developing significant ownership claims on American companies: litigants

1 SEALED Air, the manufacturer of Bubble Wrap™, should have been protected from a financial collision as well as any product wrapped in the firm's famous plastic. The corporation's margins and growth prospects are good, its patent protection strong. Several years ago, however, Sealed Air made what in retrospect can be seen as a classic American blunder: it thought it was merely acquiring another plastic-packaging company; instead, it was buying a legal nightmare.

2 The problem was the seller, W.R. Grace, a conglomerate that now teeters on the edge of bankruptcy from asbestos litigation. Attorneys pursuing Grace reckoned Sealed Air's profits could be theirs if a court could be convinced that along with the acquisition of any Grace subsidiary came Grace's full liabilities – despite the fact that asbestos-related products had never been produced by the firm which was bought by Sealed Air. When word of the litigation spread, Sealed Air's shares and bonds were both hit hard. Regardless of the outcome of the court case, Sealed Air, as the defendant, is already paying a higher cost for lawyers, and a higher cost for capital.

3 Of the many ways in which companies can end up owing vast sums of money in litigation, six currently stand out. Product-liability cases are the single most common area, followed (in no particular order) by suits concerning antitrust, intellectual property, employee conduct, contractual failure and, increasingly, shareholder actions. There is nothing new about the categories themselves; what has changed is that each has become, in essence, a huge industry in itself, which has been fed by ever larger settlements.

4 Because litigation risk is difficult to analyse, when the financial markets do wake up to these concerns, they often panic. As a result, the indirect costs from higher financing charges can become as important as any potential verdict or settlement. Often, litigation is not the trigger for a company's share-price decline, but rather the result. This is because any company whose share price falls sharply is exposed to legal action. Law firms say these suits prompt much needed change. But it is questionable whether they make economic sense, as they typically end up taking money from firms (i.e. shareholders) and returning it to them minus lawyers' fees – which can be one-third of the settlement.

Regulation through litigation

5 On the face of it, why shouldn't a company that does something wrong pay the price? This sense of justice, after all, is why Americans love the novels of John Grisham and movies such as *Erin Brockovich*, with Julia Roberts. The trouble is, there is no incentive for a plaintiff lawyer, or a jury, to weigh up the broader economic consequences of huge awards against companies, especially multi-million-dollar punitive damages.

6 Pushing for reform would no doubt be easier if there were more precise information on the cost of litigation. Remarkably, that information ranges from poor to outright wrong, says Deborah Hensler, a professor at Stanford Law School. State courts often provide no data, while data provided by federal courts can be misleading. Most litigation is threatened and settled, leaving no financial trace. With more effort, these costs could be captured. Federal agencies routinely collect data from companies on employee benefits and pension plans for statistical surveys, notes Ms Hensler. The same methodology could be used to compile information about litigation payouts.

7 Reacting to a sense that verdicts have got out of hand, the Supreme Court has heard a number of appeals and even thrown back a multi-million-dollar verdict which had been triggered by a repair job at a car dealer that was estimated to be worth only $4,000 in compensation. Penalties, the judges ruled, must be tied more closely to harm. It is not yet clear that anyone is listening ∎

2 Choose the best options (a–c) for questions 1–6.

1 What was the principal mistake made by Sealed Air?
  a It didn't protect its patents.
  b Its margins were too low.
  c It didn't foresee potential problems.

2 Why is W. R. Grace nearly bankrupt?
  a It was involved in asbestos litigation.
  b It sold a subsidiary to Sealed Air.
  c It paid too much to its lawyers.

3 Why is litigation costing companies more money than before?
  a Levels of compensation are higher.
  b New industries have emerged.
  c The categories of litigation have changed.

4 Which of the following is often a direct result of litigation against companies?
  a Share prices rise.
  b Financial markets panic.
  c Shareholders receive more money.

5 How could changes be brought about?
  a by requiring companies to agree to settlements
  b by obtaining more information
  c by collecting data about employee benefits

6 What has the Supreme Court decided?
  a to limit the number of appeals
  b to impose stricter penalties
  c to reduce compensation awards

3 Paragraph 3 lists the six most common categories of litigation. In which category would you include the following cases?

1 The Microsoft Corporation is accused of using its dominant position on the personal computer market to put other companies out of business.

2 The Merck corporation has decided to withdraw its drug Vioxx after complaints that it has dangerous side effects.

3 A member of staff has accused his employer of sexual harassment.

4 MetaSoft Ltd has been taken to court after repeatedly failing to meet the deadline for installing new software for one of its clients.

5 InterStat claims that a competitor has illegally copied technology that it developed.

6 Investors in MaxInvest claim that the CEO did not disclose compromising information about the company's results.

Speaking In some countries, more and more people are prepared to litigate either against businesses or professional people. Is this a good thing or not? Do you think this will benefit society in the long term?

What cases do you know of involving litigation in your country?

Writing Your organisation is considering purchasing a company in the USA. Write an email to your legal department giving details of potential problems. (See *Style guide*, page 20.)

1 Match the words with their meanings.

1	settlement	a	money paid to a professional for services
2	damages	b	a qualified legal adviser
3	plaintiff	c	use of the legal system to settle an argument
4	lawyer	d	money paid to the victim of an injustice
5	fee	e	a problem brought to a court of law
6	judge	f	a company providing legal advice
7	jury	g	the official who controls a court
8	verdict	h	a person who litigates
9	defendant	i	an agreement reached between two parties in a lawsuit
10	law firm	j	an official judicial decision
11	(law)suit	k	a person seeking to prove his/her innocence in court
12	legal action	l	a group of people who evaluate evidence presented in court

2 Which of the words above have the following synonyms?

a award (n)   c attorney

b compensation   d litigant

3 Which of the words in 1 and 2 above would you include under the following headings?

1 People (or groups of people) involved in a lawsuit

2 Money paid out during or after a lawsuit

4 Complete the expressions with the verbs.

take	suffer	make	provide	reach	file	award

1 to _____ a lawsuit   5 to _____ legal action

2 to _____ an accusation   6 to _____ evidence

3 to _____ damages   7 to _____ injuries

4 to _____ a settlement

Practice   Complete the article with the appropriate form of words from this Vocabulary section.

In the Hollywood movie of the same name, Julia Roberts plays the role of Erin Brockovich, a Californian single mother who is involved in an unsuccessful ¹ _lawsuit_ where she is seeking ² _____ for injuries that she has sustained in a car accident. The ³ _____ who is defending her loses the case but offers her a job with his ⁴ _____ instead. During her work she discovers that a large corporation has contaminated the water supply of a local school. She tries to convince the local population to take ⁵ _____ and eventually persuades 600 people to become ⁶ _____ and join in a class action suit. At the hearing, the ⁷ _____ rules in their favour and ⁸ _____ ⁹ _____ amounting to $333 million.

The passive

1 Study the sentences taken from the text on page 61.

a ... *Sealed Air's shares and bonds* **were** both **hit** hard. (para 2)

b ... *Sealed Air* **made** ... *a classic American blunder.* (para 1)

Which of the two sentences:

1 mentions the people/things responsible for something happening

2 focuses on the result or outcome of an action

Which sentence is in the passive form and which is in the active form?

2 Look through paragraphs 1–4 of the text on page 61 and find the passive equivalent of the following active forms in **bold**. Which tenses are used?

1 This is because a sharply falling share price **exposes** any company to legal action.

2 ... despite the fact that ... the firm which Sealed Air **bought** ...

3 ... a huge industry in itself, which ever larger settlements **have fed**.

4 ... the firm **had** never **produced** asbestos-related products ...

5 ... if lawyers **could convince** a court ...

6 The manufacturer of Bubble Wrap **should have protected** itself from a financial collision ...

3 Rewrite the sentences in the passive.

1 TV and the media have covered the case in detail.

The case has been covered in detail (by TV and the media).

2 Attorneys are suing the company for negligence.

3 The jury is to announce the verdict later today.

4 The company would pay compensation to all victims.

5 The judge is going to postpone the trial.

 For more information, see page 160.

For more information, see page 160.

Practice Complete the article with the active or passive form of the verbs in brackets. Use the appropriate tense.

When the US pharmaceutical company Merck first announced that its best-selling drug Vioxx was going to (¹pull) _be pulled_ from the market, the reaction on the stock markets was immediate: the firm's share price (²drop) _____ 30 per cent in one day. Internal documents that (³leak) _____ to the press shortly after the announcement suggest that the company (⁴know) _____ for several years that Vioxx could produce harmful side effects. If that information (⁵communicate) _____ to the press, it could have affected both the company's profit performance and its share price. It (⁶estimate) _____ that more than 80 million people around the world have taken Vioxx since the drug (⁷introduce) _____ in 1999. In 2005, Carol Ernst became the first litigant to (⁸award) _____ damages, totalling over $250 million, when a jury in Texas (⁹find) _____ the firm guilty of negligence. This has brought home to pharmaceutical companies the dangers of aggressive marketing: it only succeeds when products (¹⁰guarantee) _____ to be 100 per cent safe.

Negotiating

Interacting with other people in a formal or informal context often involves some degree of negotiating. Before you negotiate, you should have a clear idea of your objectives and strategy. You should also find out what common ground you share with the other side and understand which points will be the hardest to negotiate. Look at the following phrases, which can be used when negotiating.

a *Another option is …*
b *Here's what we have in mind …*
c *That's out of the question!*
d *Of course, you'll have to …*
e *No way!*
f *You've got a deal!*

g *I'm prepared to offer you …*
h *Alternatively, we could …*
i *Done!*
j *I'll have to think that over.*
k *We'll need more time.*
l *Take it or leave it!*

Match phrases a–l with the following stages of the negotiating process.

1 presenting an initial offer
2 refusing an offer
3 imposing conditions
4 making a counter-proposal
5 reaching agreement
6 postponing a decision

Listening ⊙

1 Listen to three dialogues. What is the subject and the outcome of each negotiation?

2 Listen again. Which of phrases a–l above are used? Identify one phrase from each dialogue to add to the list (a–l) above. Indicate which stages the phrases correspond to.

Speaking

Work in pairs. Take the role of one of the people involved in the following situations. Prepare the arguments that you would use and then negotiate with your partner.

1

You have decided to rent out your apartment for two months while you are working abroad. You are meeting a person who is interested in renting it from you. Negotiate the price and conditions.

2

You are a supplier and your contract with your principal customer is about to expire. You know that the customer will propose a new contract but at a reduced price (5 per cent less). You can only accept this under certain conditions (longer contract and larger orders). Meet your customer.

Writing

Write a letter to the person you negotiated with to confirm the outcome of your negotiation. (See *Style guide*, page 16.)

Culture at work

Bargaining

In some cultures, people spend considerable time bargaining over the price of the things they are buying. This is often an accepted part of the interaction when making a purchase. What happens in your culture? Are there certain situations and settings where people are more likely to bargain?

Dilemma & Decision

Dilemma: Beauty and business

Brief

Glow Industries was born when Terri Williamson, an experienced Californian businesswoman, decided to start her own company specialising in beauty products and perfumes. Terri launched a very successful line of products under the 'Glow' name, which she sold from her shop in Hollywood. Two years later, she discovered that hers was no longer the only company selling beauty products with the 'Glow' name. Jennifer Lopez was launching her own line of beauty products: 'Glow by JLo' through Sweetface Fashion. Terri immediately decided to take legal action against Sweetface Fashion to stop it from launching its products on the market.

For both businesses, the consequences of prolonged legal action could be serious: Glow Industries may lose its access to the mass market and Sweetface may have to review its international plans. What should they do?

Task 1

Before further legal action is taken, lawyers representing the two companies have agreed to meet to see if they can reach a negotiated settlement. Work in pairs. Student A, you represent Sweetface. Turn to page 137. Student B, you represent Glow Industries. Turn to page 138. Prepare a list of your objectives for the negotiation.

Task 2

Meet and conduct the negotiation.

Task 3

Join another pair and compare the outcomes of your negotiations.

Write it up

Write a short memo to your staff informing them of the outcome of your negotiation. (See *Style guide*, page 24.)

Decision:

⊙ Listen to what David Schapiro, a business lawyer, has to say about this case.

Unit 8 Brands

www.longman-elt.com   www.economist.com

Keeping it exclusive

Keynotes

Brands are more than just product names. They are a mark of quality, and it is the **brand name** that distinguishes a product from other similar products and gives it a **brand identity**. **Global brands** have the ability to cross both geographical and cultural boundaries, building international **reputations** of quality. Creating brands and **brand awareness** is the job of the **brand manager** or **brand asset manager**. Once the brand name has been established, the makers sometimes engage in **brand extension**, which involves using the brand name on a range of products. In the case of **luxury brands**, companies have to be careful to avoid **overexposure**, which could damage the exclusive aspect of the **brand image**.

L'ORÉAL
PARiS

SONY

Brand awareness

Discuss the following questions about the global brands shown.

   – What emotions and feelings, e.g. desire, satisfaction, importance, do you associate with each brand?

   – What image, e.g. prestige, reliability, exclusivity, is each brand trying to convey to the public?

Listening 1 Listen to a brand management consultant talking about why a brand can lose its image. Which of the reasons below does she mention? Can you think of any other reasons?

1 counterfeit products weakening exclusivity image
2 giving licences to too many retailers
3 choosing the wrong people to endorse the product
4 stamping the brand name on too many and too diverse products
5 poor pricing policy, making brands too cheap

Reading **The luxury business**

1 Read the following sentences taken from the text on the opposite page. Then read the text and complete it with the sentences.

1 A strategy to increase distribution expanded the market to thousands of retailers, detracting from the brand's essence of exclusivity.
2 Fashionable celebrities such as Grace Kelly and Audrey Hepburn were counted among the enthusiastic collectors.
3 Its watches alone number more than a dozen distinct models and are exclusive items, generating millions in revenue.
4 The Gucci group was amongst those reporting far fewer profits during that period.
5 The two men responsible for this revival were the creative director Tom Ford and the president/CEO Domenico De Sole.

2 Read the text again and put these events in the correct order.

a Guccio Gucci's grandsons took over the business.
b The rich and famous started buying the brand.
c Guccio Gucci died.
d The first shop opened in Florence.
e A new image campaign was launched.
f Stores opened in London and Paris.

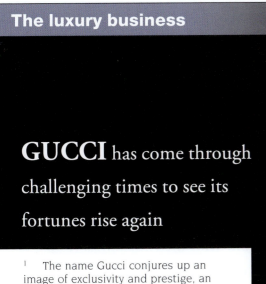

GUCCI has come through challenging times to see its fortunes rise again

1 The name Gucci conjures up an image of exclusivity and prestige, an Italian brand of quality. As one of the world's leading purveyors of personal luxury goods, Gucci stands for more than just fine quality shoes or suits. The Gucci Group is now a multi-brand conglomerate, with a collection of high-fashion brands like Balenciaga, Stella McCartney, Boucheron and Yves Saint Laurent, YSL Beauté, Bottega Veneta, Bédat & Co and Sergio Rossi under its finely crafted umbrella. Gucci sells its brand of leather goods, shoes, clothes, ties, scarves and jewellery in directly operated stores around the world as well as outlets licensed to sell their products. (a) _____

2 The beginnings of the Gucci empire go back to Florence, Italy, in 1921, when Guccio Gucci opened an exclusive leather shop. He understood the importance of building a reputation for his brand and did so by putting an identifier on his special edition creations. He concentrated on producing fabulously high-quality products, making them status symbols synonymous with luxury.

3 After Gucci died, his sons Aldo and Rodolfo took over the management and led the brand to iconic status in the 1950s. They succeeded extremely well in promoting the brand to the rich and famous. (b) _____ The Guccis took note of this popularity and expanded aggressively, opening stores in glamorous locations such as London, Paris and Palm Beach. However, for all the glamour Gucci represented externally, there were increasing disagreements within the family. Aldo and Rodolfo each had two sons who began pulling the brand in different directions in the eighties, and decisions made about product distribution affected the brand's reputation. (c) _____ Eventually, retailers were selected more judiciously and the brand's reputation returned. However, during this period of disagreement over distribution the brand went from headlines to sidelines, perceived as an old standard in the fashion world.

4 Since then, smart leadership has driven the Gucci brand to more visibility and success than ever before. (d) _____ Tom Ford was responsible for the design of all product lines from clothing to perfumes and for the group's corporate image, advertising campaigns and store design from 1994 to 2004. It was his elegant vision that placed this once staid brand back on the backs of the wealthy. Known today as one of the world's leading visionaries in fashion, Ford has accumulated a great number of accolades on his way to the top.

5 Italian-born attorney Domenico De Sole was the other half of this dynamic duo. By integrating elaborate advertising and communication campaigns with a marketing strategy that placed the focus on Gucci's core leather products and ready-to-wear, De Sole brought the much needed attention back to the quality of the brand while streamlining the back-end of the business and expanding the network of directly operated stores. He has received as many prestigious accolades as Ford, and his efforts were recognised by the European Business Press Federation, which selected Gucci as European company of the year from among 4,000 other companies.

6 Strong leadership and an image revamp literally breathed life back into the Gucci brand. Even so, the rocky economic climate of the past few years has made for a really bumpy ride for the luxury goods market. (e) _____ Despite the numbers, however, analysts still cite Gucci as one of the stocks with the greatest upside potential, giving it plenty of room for further development.

Glossary

staid sober and unexciting

accolade prize, award

back-end behind the scenes administrative activities

---

3 **Answer the questions.**

1 How did Gucci's founder establish a reputation for quality?

2 Why did the brand's image need renewing? How was this achieved?

4 **Which of the problems in Listening 1 has Gucci experienced?**

Speaking   **Which current stars would you choose to endorse Gucci today? Why?**

1 Find synonyms in the text for the following words and phrases.

1 _____ (para 1)   providers, suppliers

2 _____ (para 1)   corporation, group of diverse firms

3 _____ (para 1)   stores, points of sale

4 _____ (para 2)   signs of importance or wealth

5 _____ (para 3)   attractiveness, beauty

6 _____ (para 4)   commercial, business

7 _____ (para 4)   plans of action, strategies to succeed

8 _____ (para 6)   renovation, improvement

2 Study the following sentences taken from the text and match the verb–preposition combinations in bold with their meanings (1–3).

*The name Gucci **conjures up** an image of exclusivity ... (para 1)*

*... Gucci **stands for** more than just fine quality shoes or suits. (para 1)*

*He **concentrated on** producing fabulously high-quality products ... (para 2)*

1 represent   2 give attention to   3 make one think of

3 Complete the verbs with the following prepositions. Some verbs can be followed by more than one preposition.

to (x2)	of (x2)	in (x4)	from (x2)	on

1 refer _____   4 benefit _____   7 consist _____ , _____

2 approve _____   5 belong _____   8 depend _____

3 believe _____   6 result _____ , _____   9 succeed _____

Complete the article using your answers from exercise 1, and the appropriate form of verbs and prepositions from exercise 3.

Eric Bernat bought a troubled Spanish confectioner in the 1950s. He [1] *believed in* the importance of creating one brand and knew that success ultimately [2]_____ eliminating the majority of the company's 200 products to concentrate on building one truly global product — a lollipop, or 'candy on a stick'. This innovative product allowed children to eat candy without getting their hands and clothes dirty. Suddenly Eric Bernat was on the way to becoming the world's leading [3]_____ of candy that parents worldwide would [4]_____ their children eating!

His strategy had several phases, and the first one [5]_____ finding a name that would appeal to children everywhere and then promoting it worldwide. He chose Chupa Chups (from the Spanish *chupar*, to suck) and then asked the famous surrealist painter Salvador Dali to design a colourful logo to accompany the marketing and advertising [6]_____ . The product's reputation soon [7]_____ his careful positioning tactics, and within five years his famous lollipops were being sold in 300,000 [8]_____ throughout Spain.

Bernat's company now sells four billion lollipops a year in 170 countries around the world and has [9]_____ creating a truly global brand. They even hope to win the war on sugar and have started a complete [10]_____ of the image of their candy — the latest product under study: lollipops that whiten the teeth and prevent cavities.

Adjectives and adverbs

Study the examples taken from the text on page 69, showing adjectives and adverbs used in different ways.

1 **Adjectives**

– after the verbs *be, become, seem, appear, look, feel, remain*

Tom Ford was **responsible** for the design of all product lines ... (para 4)

– in comparatives and superlatives

He has received **as many prestigious** accolades **as** Ford ... (para 5)

... one of the stocks with **the greatest** upside potential ... (para 6)

2 **Adverbs**

– after verbs

The Guccis took note ... and expanded **aggressively** ... (para 3)

– before adjectives and other adverbs (as intensifiers)

De Sole brought the **much needed** attention back ... (para 5)

– before past participle adjectives to show how something is done

... under its **finely crafted** umbrella. (para 1)

... in **directly operated** stores around the world ... (para 1)

For more information, see page 160.

Practice

1 Find the adjectives in the text on page 69 that describe the following.

1 Gucci's position in the luxury goods market (para 1) *leading*

2 the first Gucci shop (para 2)

3 the type of status Gucci acquired (para 3)

4 Ford's vision (para 4)

5 Gucci's promotional activities (para 5)

Find the adverbs plus the adjective or adverb they intensify in the text on page 69 that describe the following.

6 the products he focused on (para 2)

7 how Gucci's sons marketed the brand (para 3)

8 the ride this market has had recently (para 6)

2 Complete the article with the appropriate form of the words in brackets.

Companies in the (¹high) _*highly*_ competitive electronics industry are discovering something (²surprise) _____ and curious: brands matter almost as much as exciting new technology. This has been (³clear) _____ demonstrated by Samsung Electronics, which made a (⁴dramatic) _____ new entry into the (⁵particular) _____ difficult digital market this year.

Once best known for microwave ovens, it has transformed itself into a (⁶real, cool) _____ brand and is (⁷success) _____ selling (⁸style) _____ flat-screen TVs, digital cameras and mobile phones. Their sales figures have done (⁹increase, good) _____ and they are positioned to beat Motorola as the second biggest manufacturer of mobile phones. Samsung has proved that a combination of clever brand building and (¹⁰good, design) _____ products can work miracles. They have understood that a brand without good products will lose popularity (¹¹incredible, rapid) _____ , but the (¹²amaze) _____ thing is that the opposite is also true. The market is (¹³crowd) _____ with firms with a few great products, but weak brands. To succeed and grow as (¹⁴fast) _____ as Samsung has requires a strong brand, as well as (¹⁵true, innovate) _____ products.

Corporate brands

1 **Listen to an interview with a corporate identity and brand asset manager. Are the following statements *true* or *false*?**

1 Brand management and corporate identity management present two very different 'faces' of the company.

2 Pricing is the most important part of establishing a brand identity.

3 Survival without a clear brand identity is perhaps possible if there is a lack of competitors.

4 Companies need to check corporate brand effectiveness every year.

5 Keeping a low corporate profile always protects brands from corporate scandals.

2 **Listen again and take notes in order to answer the following questions.**

1 What exactly is meant by the 'face' of the company?

2 Why is pricing so important?

3 How is brand effectiveness checked?

Speaking Can you think of any examples of a company or brand suffering from bad publicity? Did they survive, and how?

Would you continue to buy your favourite brands of clothes, sports shoes or perfume if the company that made them was found to be employing children in sweatshop conditions? Why / Why not?

Do you know who owns the following global brands?

Check your answers by looking at the company websites.

Writing Write a formal email to a colleague in marketing, telling him/her about the content of the interview you heard in Listening 2. Explain that you agree with what was said and recommend that your company takes its corporate and brand identity more seriously. (See *Style guide*, page 20.)

Dealing with people at work

In an ideal world, co-workers are always professional, positive and efficient. Unfortunately, there are exceptions and you have to develop strategies for dealing with difficult situations and difficult personalities. This requires intelligence, tact and professionalism. Look at the following useful phrases for dealing with people.

a *Before we start, I think you should know ...*
b *This is good – it just needs a few minor changes.*
c *Let's work on this together.*
d *I wanted to tell you before anyone else does – we're planning to ...*
e *I like this idea, but it's not what we need right now.*
f *We're all ultimately working towards the same thing.*

Which of phrases a–f would you use in situations 1–3?

To develop good interpersonal skills and avoid problems, co-workers should always:

1 try to anticipate potential conflicts
2 find common goals
3 be as positive as possible

Listening 3 **Listen to an extract from a dialogue where people didn't handle a situation in the best way. Answer the questions.**

1 What should the man have done before the meeting?
2 Which of phrases a–f above could he have used?
3 What did the woman fail to see?
4 Which of the above language could she have used to improve communication?

Speaking **1** Work in pairs. Take the role of each person in the dialogue above. Role-play the conversation that they should have had before the meeting. Avoid problems by using the appropriate language and tactics.

2 Work in pairs. Tell your partner about problems you've had dealing with difficult people and the solutions you've found. Discuss what other possible ways you could have dealt with the problems/people.

Can you think of other difficult personality types and ways of dealing with them?

Culture at work ## Interpersonal relationships

In some business cultures it is considered important to have close interpersonal and relatively informal relationships with co-workers. Colleagues are encouraged to socialise together, and all levels of the hierarchy can mix in a social environment outside office hours. In other cultures, formal relationships are preferred and there is never a hierarchical mix at social events. Which corresponds best to your culture? How could different attitudes cause problems in a multicultural situation?

Dilemma & Decision

Dilemma: The two faces of Burberry

Brief

Burberry, 'the original British luxury brand', launched its first logo in 1900 and registered the signature check pattern as a trademark in 1920. It was an established luxury brand for wealthy middle-class conservatives for several decades, but sales declined in the 1980s as the brand began to appear old-fashioned. Then in the 1990s, CEO Rosemary Bravo revamped its image, repositioning the Burberry brand in line with its luxury and exclusive heritage. Ads were designed to depict the essence of the 'new' Burberry, giving a modern feel combined with classic British elitism. This marketing strategy reached the intended target, and even Prince William has been seen at many events wearing Burberry. However, the brand has also become popular with hip-hop artists and football fans. The question now being asked by business analysts and journalists is: 'If Burberry embraces the new audience, will they lose their core customers?'

Task 1

Read below the options open to a brand facing this type of positioning dilemma and discuss which ones you agree/disagree with. Can you think of other arguments?

The case for extension

- Increased sales from the 'unintended' market are doubling turnover.
- Our brand is ranked eighth on American Brandstand for 'most mentioned brand' in popular song lyrics.
- We should recruit hip-hop artists whose fans are already brand enthusiasts, to endorse the brand officially.
- Young customers will stay loyal to the brand throughout their lives, while sales to ageing traditional target customers will fall off.

The case against extension

- We should ignore these new customers and reinforce the 'traditional and classical' image.
- A British newspaper has run a potentially damaging article about 'design hooligans', describing the bad behaviour of British football fans who were wearing designer brands.
- Fashions change quickly in the world of hip-hop and rap. We should concentrate on our loyal customers, who don't change brands as easily.
- If young, less wealthy people buy our brand, it should be for the same reasons and for the same brand image as our core customer base.

Task 2

You are the marketing manager of a company facing a similar dilemma. Decide which action the company should take. Prepare fully-developed arguments from the notes on page 139 and be ready to present your arguments at a meeting.

Task 3

Work in small groups. Hold a meeting and decide which course of action the company should take.

Write it up

You are the marketing director of Clearly Chic. Write a memo to all the staff informing them of the decision that has been made concerning their present dilemma, and explaining why this decision has been taken. (See *Style guide*, page 24.)

Decision:

⊙ Listen to what a brand asset manager thinks about this issue.

The rewards of risk

Keynotes

Most business ventures start as investments by **entrepreneurs,** who hope to make financial gains or **returns on investment (ROI)**. Money for a new business may come from banks, or from **venture capitalists** and **business angels**, who also give **entrepreneurial advice**. As businesses grow, they invest in their own projects in order to increase **profits** and **dividends** for shareholders. Some businesses such as insurance companies and investment banks employ professional **fund managers** to oversee investment **portfolios** of different types of **shares** (US *stock*) and **bonds** on the global stock markets as their main profit-making activity. Although all businesses aim to make a profit, some organisations think it is important only to make **ethical** investments, possibly with lower returns, in projects that, for example, don't harm the environment.

Investor profiles

1 Work in pairs. What should a business person be in order to be a successful investor? Choose the five most important characteristics from the list. Compare and discuss your choices with another pair.

reckless	pessimistic	opinionated	optimistic
calculating	ambitious	determined	analytical
opportunistic	intuitive	focused	
greedy	flexible	prudent	

2 Read the profiles of four famous investors. Choose two adjectives from exercise 1 which best describe each of them.

Jessie Livermore the legendary stock trader, who was known as 'The great bear of Wall Street' He took big investment risks but always analysed the market carefully. He gave his opinion readily but didn't always follow his own advice. He once said, 'A man must believe in himself and his judgement if he is to make a living in this game.' Whenever his judgement failed him, he incurred huge losses.

Nick Leeson the trader who caused the bankruptcy of Barings Bank He specialised in futures (an agreement to buy or sell something in the future at a specific price) and options (a contract which gives you the right but not the obligation to perform a transaction at a specified time). Not only did he lose money from the start but he also systematically increased the risks. He falsified accounts and lost a staggering total of £208m.

Warren Buffett known on Wall Street as the greatest investor ever His performance over five decades has never been bettered. His best deals were in low-risk, blue-chip stock with such giants as Coca-Cola and The Washington Post. He advises investors to buy and hold and never act rashly.

Paul Allen co-founder of Microsoft with Bill Gates; his first investment earned him $17 billion! He then became an angel, investing in movies, 1960s art, rock music and space travel. His companies are so innovative that it is still hard to say whether they are head-in-the-clouds losers or far-sighted pioneers. He once said, 'The advantage of having the resources I have is that you can be a more patient investor.'

If you were making investments, which of the famous investors would you be most like?

Investor beware!

1 Look at the title of the text and the cartoon on the opposite page. What do you think the text is about? Read the text to check your answer.

Which of the following adjectives best describes the average investor?

pessimistic	flexible	irrational	wise

Glossary

folly foolishness, lack of good sense

myopia short-sightedness

boom years years of economic prosperity

Investor beware!
Freud, folly and finance

Human intuition is a bad guide to handling risk

1 PEOPLE make strange decisions about the future. The evidence is all around, from their investments in the stock markets to the way they run their businesses. In fact, people are consistently bad at dealing with uncertainty, underestimating returns from some investments and overestimating others. Surely there must be a better way than using intuition?

2 Daniel Kahneman, a professor at Princeton, was awarded a Nobel prize in economics for his work in the field of behavioural finance, a science which applies psychological insights to economics. Today he is in demand by investors and Wall Street traders. But, he says, there are plenty of others that still show little interest in understanding the roots of their poor decisions.

3 What surveys have shown is that people's forecasts of future stock market movements are far more optimistic than past long-term returns would justify. The same goes for their hopes of ever-rising prices for their homes or doing well in games like the lottery or poker. They seem to ignore evidence and hard facts and prefer to trust their inner instincts.

4 Not only are first encounters decisive in judging the character of a new acquaintance but also in negotiations over how much money to invest in new ventures. The asking price quoted by the seller in a property sale, for example, tends to become accepted by all parties as the price around which negotiations take place, whereas this figure could be at best simply inaccurate or at worst completely dishonest. However, people find it difficult to question their first impressions.

5 Similarly, no one likes to abandon the generally accepted idea that the earlier a decision has been taken, the harder it is to give up. However, companies really should decide earlier rather than later to cancel a failing research project to avoid wasting money. The problem is they often find it difficult to admit they have made a mistake. This human weakness can cost them a lot of money.

6 Another problem is that people put a lot of emphasis on things they have seen and experienced themselves, which simply may not be the best guide. For example, somebody may buy an overvalued share because a relative of theirs has made thousands on it, only to lose money. In finance, too much emphasis on information that is easily available helps to explain the so-called "home bias", a tendency by most investors to invest only within the country they live in, even though they know that this is not responsible behaviour and that diversification is good for their portfolio.

7 Fear of failure is another strong human characteristic, which may be why people are much more concerned about losses than about gains. It is this myopia in the face of losses that explains much of the irrationality people display in the stock market.

8 More information is helpful in making any investment decision but, says Kahneman, people spend proportionally too much time on small decisions and not enough on big ones. They need to adjust the balance. During the boom years, some companies put as much effort into planning their Christmas party as into considering strategic mergers.

9 Regretting past decisions is not just a waste of time; it also often colours people's perceptions of the future. Some stock market investors trade far too frequently because they are running after the returns on shares they wish they had bought earlier. But at least when businesses try to assess their risks, they have to worry only about making money. Governments, on the other hand, face a whole range of conflicting political pressures. This unfortunately makes them even more likely than businesses to take irrational decisions ■

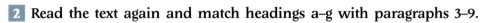

2 **Read the text again and match headings a–g with paragraphs 3–9.**

a   Misplaced priorities

b   Counterproductive regret

c   Initial feelings

d   Being too cautious

e   Being over-optimistic

f   Winning and losing

g   Accepting when you are wrong

3 **Answer the questions.**

1   Where can we find evidence of people's bad decisions about the future?

2   What is *behavioural finance*?

3   Why don't companies abandon projects on which they are losing money?

4   Why is it irrational to invest only in your own country?

5   Why are people more concerned about losses than gains?

6   How does regretting bad decisions affect stock market investors' future decisions?

| Speaking | **What kind of risk taker are you?** |

You have just inherited $100,000 and you want to invest it for five years. Which of the following appeals to you, and why?

–   a bond issued by an organisation or a government, which is guaranteed and will pay you an interest of 2 per cent per year

–   a junk bond (high-risk bond) that could earn you 20 per cent per year, but there is a high risk of not earning any interest at all

–   blue-chip shares which will almost certainly pay a minimum of 4 per cent even in poor economic conditions

–   high-tech company shares with high-risk but high-return potential of 10 per cent per year

–   a new business venture offering a position on the board and a 5 per cent share of potential profits; impossible to forecast possible returns

Which of the above do you think would have appealed to the famous investors on page 76?

| Vocabulary 1 | **Match the words from the text with their meanings.** |

1	returns (para 1)	a	a range of investments
2	traders (para 2)	b	to estimate
3	diversification (para 6)	c	people who buy and sell stocks and shares
4	portfolio (para 6)	d	varying investments
5	losses (para 7)	e	money earned on investments
6	to assess (para 9)	f	money lost on investments

Prefixes

1 Look at the following sentence from the text on page 77. Think about the meaning of the prefix *over*. What does *overvalued* mean?

For example, somebody may buy an **overvalued** *share because a relative of theirs has made thousands on it ... (para 6)*

2 Match the prefixes (1–6) with their meanings (a–f).

1	post	a	between / among a group
2	pre	b	more than one / many
3	multi	c	later than / after
4	bi	d	two / twice / double
5	inter	e	before / in preparation
6	under	f	not enough

3 Add prefixes from exercises 1 and 2 to the following to make new words.

emphasise   estimate   lingual   value   national   arranged   date (v)   spend

4 Make a list of other words you know with the prefixes above.

Practice   Complete the article about art as investment with the appropriate form of words from Vocabulary 1 and 2.

It is difficult to ¹ *overemphasise* the risk involved in buying fine art as an investment, even if investors often claim that they are making greater returns and getting more pleasure from their Van Gogh than from their equity fund. It may be a good opportunity for ² _____ , but it is highly unlikely that they are making more money. Art is frequently ³ _____ and the industry is infamous for ⁴ _____ value inaccurately.

The main attraction of buying on the ⁵ _____ art market, apart from the pleasure of having the works around, is to vary the investment ⁶ _____ . However, most businesspeople are put off by the uncertainty of whether the work will increase in value or not. For example, a Japanese businessman definitely ⁷ _____ when he paid $82.5m for Van Gogh's *Portrait of Dr Gachet*, which has since sold for an eighth of the price. But despite ⁸ _____ like these, some people have made a fortune on works such as Egon Schiele's painting of Krumau (shown right), which sold at Sotheby's for £12.6m in 2003.

Speaking   Discuss the pros and cons of investments such as art, antiques, rare books and wine. Prioritise them in terms of highest/lowest risk.

Emphasis

1 Study these examples taken from the profiles on page 76 and the text on page 77. How would these sentences be written if the writer didn't want to emphasise them?

a   **Not only** did he lose money from the start **but** he also systematically increased the risks. (Nick Leeson)

b   **What** surveys have shown **is that** people's forecasts of future stock market movements are ... (para 3)

c   **It is this** myopia in the face of losses **that explains** much of the irrationality ... (para 7)

2 Study these examples of inverting the auxiliary verb and subject. Rewrite the sentences without emphasis.

1   **On no account should you invest** in such a risky business.

   You should on no account invest in such a risky business.

2   **Rarely has so much money been lost** by one person gambling with his company's assets.

3   **Never has a work of art risen** in value by so much in such a short time.

4   **Only** in exceptional circumstances **can an investor** take high risks and still be successful.

 For more information, see page 161.

Rewrite the following sentences using inversion.

1   Investors have never had to work so hard to make a reasonable return.

2   Forecasts of how the markets will change are rarely 100 per cent accurate.

3   People are not only afraid of losing money but also of appearing stupid.

4   They shouldn't have expanded their portfolio on any account, because their track record was so poor.

5   People should only listen to financial advisers if they really trust them.

 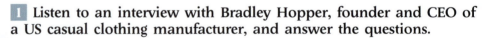

1 Listen to an interview with Bradley Hopper, founder and CEO of a US casual clothing manufacturer, and answer the questions.

1   Why did Hopper go into textiles?

2   What was his main goal?

3   What does he say about the competition?

4   What does he say about environmentally friendly products?

5   What are his future plans?

2 Listen again and change the sentences to what he actually says.

1   I was interested in clothes more than anything else.

2   Profit drives me.

3   Making money has to be your first priority.

4   Knowing where to cut costs and where to invest keeps me one step ahead.

5   The hands-on part really interests me.

3 Practise saying the sentences, paying particular attention to the words which are emphasised.

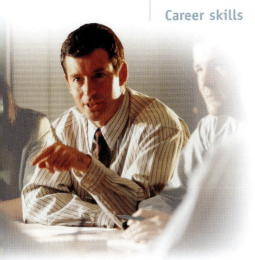

Prioritising

Setting priorities means deciding what it is you most want to achieve and then organising your time and activities in the best possible way to reach those goals and targets. Look at the following phrases, which can be useful when prioritising.

a *This is absolutely imperative.*
b *No need to do this.*
c *Let's get Susan to do that.*
d *This might be useful.*

e *I ought to do this urgently.*
f *Forget about that.*
g *That's a job for Marco.*
h *The next step should be …*

The following questions are helpful to ask when prioritising. Match phrases a–h with the questions.

1 What is absolutely essential for me to do?
2 What is a good idea but has no negative consequences if it isn't done?
3 Which task(s) can I delegate and assign to someone else to do?
4 Which task(s) can I eliminate because they are really not urgent or relevant to my specific goals?

Speaking **Work in groups. Your project team has brainstormed ideas for setting up a new ethical investment fund. Prioritise the following tasks that you have come up with.**

- Establish a list of ethical companies to propose to our clients.
- Meet the CFOs of companies on our 'sustainable company' list.
- Attend a conference on sustainable development in Frankfurt next month.
- Meet journalists to give interviews about our new socially responsible investment product.
- Come up with criteria to evaluate companies according to financial, social and environmental performance.
- Recruit two new specialised fund managers to manage the new portfolios.
- Prepare a brochure to send to existing clients about the new product.

Listening 2 **1** Listen to the team leader summing up decisions taken so far at the prioritising session. Which task on the list does he say is not essential, which is impractical and which is of vital importance?

2 How does this compare with the way you prioritised the tasks?

Writing **Write a memo telling management what the plan of action is for the new service. (See *Style guide*, page 24.)**

Culture at work ## Status and society

Some cultures are money driven and it is perfectly acceptable for businesses and people to measure their success in terms of how rich they are. In other cultures, priorities are different and businesses can be judged on such things as the quality of their products and the conditions they provide for their employees. What is common in your country? How might this difference cause misunderstanding in multicultural teams?

Dilemma: Your money or your reputation?

Brief

Two young Californian entrepreneurs, Steven Evans, a successful businessman, and his younger brother Max, a recent MBA graduate, have just inherited the family fortune and have decided to invest in the manufacturing sector. They plan to supply the European and US screen print market with mass-produced, blank T-shirts. Their rivals include giants like Fruit of the Loom, but they feel confident that there is room for another competitor in this highly lucrative but risky sector. They both agree that their main goal is to establish a successful business as quickly as possible, then sell it and reinvest the profit in other ventures in order to build up a much larger fortune to leave to their own children. However, they have very different ideas on how best to achieve this goal. Read their respective business plans.

Task 1

Work in pairs. Role-play a discussion between the two brothers as they explain their business plans to each other.

Task 2

Join another pair and discuss as a group which business plan has the best chance of succeeding. Prepare to tell the class about both plans, saying which is better, and why. Consider what is: of vital importance to the success of a business; a nice idea but not essential; impractical for the moment.

Task 3

Present your ideas to the class.

Write it up

Steven or Max has sent their business plan to your company, looking for financial backing. Write a letter giving your response and the reasons for it. (See *Style guide*, page 16.)

Decision:

Turn to page 146 to find out what choice the now successful founder of American Apparel made when he was faced with the same dilemma a few years ago.

Steven's business plan

Set up factories in south east Asia
- Minimum wage in US $893 per month + liability insurance + health insurance.
- High staff turnover in US due to monotonous and uncomfortable nature of the job.

Reduce risk of bad reputation
- Pay more than minimum wage requirement ($18.53 in Bangladesh and $63.75 in Guandong province in China).
- Allow trade unions and make conditions relatively better.

Get a competitive edge
- Ensure we stay in business by being able to offer highly competitive prices.
- Avoid risk, copy successful competitors.

Minimise advertising
- Informing potential customers of quality to justify high prices would require a large communication budget.
- No guarantees that this campaign would work.
- It will take a long time to make real returns.

Better safe than sorry!

Max's business plan

Buy manufacturing site based in California
- Build up an 'ethical employer' reputation and establish a name based on integrity and fairness.
- Set up teams to reduce boredom, increase turnaround time and reduce staff turnover.

Maintain control over quality
- Sell to big, well-known brands, whose fear of consumer lobby investigations into their suppliers will convince them to pay more. Many brands have been damaged by negative publicity lately.

Charge higher prices
- People will pay more for quality.
- Higher profits will offset cost of investing in salaries and conditions.

Invest in advertising
- Building a good reputation and brand image is a necessary long-term investment. Consumer attitudes are changing – the future is 'ethical clothing'. Competitors will have to do the same sooner or later.

Nothing ventured, nothing gained!

Review 3

Language check

The passive

Underline the passive forms in *italics* that are incorrect. Correct them.

1 The new legislation *is to introduce* six months from now.

2 Lawyers for the defence say they *are not being giving* a fair chance to defend their client.

3 It now looks as though an agreement *will reach* and there is a good chance that the accusations *will be withdrawing*.

4 Clients *are defended* by their lawyers.

5 All evidence *must produce* in court.

6 Although some litigants *had not informed* of the changes, most were aware of the new procedures.

7 How much will the company *ask* to pay the victims in compensation?

8 The jury is *going to be selected* one month before the trial begins.

9 The plaintiff claims that his reputation *has damaged*.

10 The courts *may force* by the government to reduce the level of damages that litigants *award*.

Adjectives and adverbs

Complete the sentences with one word from each box.

surprisingly	particularly	highly	much
directly	clearly		

difficult	little	sophisticated	cheaper
operated	demonstrated		

1 Perhaps the company doesn't want any publicity – so far _____ information has been given to the press.

2 The latest devices use _____ and innovative laser technology.

3 The marketing manager said that conditions have become _____ as a result of cheap imports.

4 Falling prices of some components mean that the new models will be _____ than initially indicated.

5 Most of the company's outlets are _____ by franchisees in each of the main national markets.

6 The success of the new brand is _____ in this diagram.

Emphasis

Rewrite the sentences starting with the words given.

1 It's the first time I have ever seen a company's shares collapse as fast as this.
Never _____ .

2 Private investors are hardly ever able to match the performance of professional fund managers.
Rarely _____ .

3 Investors shouldn't on any account concentrate all their shareholdings in one business sector.
On no account _____ .

4 Today, I'd like to focus on how to identify stock market opportunities.
What _____ .

5 In the long run, the return on an investment is the most important thing.
It's _____ .

6 The psychology of investors is the thing that has always interested me most.
What _____ .

Consolidation

Choose the correct forms of the words in *italics*.

Johnathan Harper [1] *has sued / has been sued* his previous employer in a [2]*high/highly* unusual lawsuit: he claims that he was a victim of discrimination because he [3]*was forced / forced* to go to work dressed in a shirt and tie while his female colleagues were allowed to dress more [4]*casually/casual*. When the case [5]*brought / was brought* to trial [6]*more early / earlier* this month, Harper [7]*was awarded / awarded* £10,000 in damages by the Labour Tribunal. [8]*No sooner / Sooner* had the decision been announced than lawyers for his ex-employer appealed. However, the effects of the decision are already [9]*to be felt / being felt*: [10]*not only / only not* are thousands of other male employees across the country now saying that they too have been discriminated against, but they are also seeking compensation.

Vocabulary check

1 Put the words in the correct groups.

image target entrepreneur case identity
publicity dividends judge risk damages
promotional sue portfolio verdict bonds

Law	Brands	Investment

2 Complete the article with the appropriate form of words from exercise 1.

Reputation is easy to lose

The biggest [1]_____ any company faces are losing its good name and damaging brand [2]_____ . Nowadays, [3]_____ pay close attention to anything that could have a negative impact on their brand or lead to bad [4]_____ in the media.

Wal-Mart, the giant US retailer, attracted the wrong kind of publicity when it was [5]_____ for employing illegal workers it had hired through a contractor. The [6]_____ decided that the company should be made to pay [7]_____ even if it didn't know the workers were illegal.

Companies try to protect themselves by hiring a Chief Legal Officer to take care of brand and corporate [8]_____ . He or she is employed to reduce the chances of the company being involved in expensive and damaging court [9]_____ , but as Jack Welch, GE's former CEO said, it is imperative to avoid becoming a [10]_____ for or a victim of criticism in the first place.

Career skills

Negotiating

Put the dialogue in the correct order.

- [ ] a That's a good compromise – you've got a deal!
- [ ] a I suppose I could go to £300.
- [ ] a How much are you selling your camera for?
- [ ] a That's much too expensive for me.
- [ ] b Is it? Well, what price are you prepared to pay then?
- [ ] b £300! No way, but I'd consider £400.
- [ ] b I'm asking £500 for it.

Dealing with people at work

Find and correct the mistake in each sentence.

1 Let's to work on this together.

2 This is good – it just needs few minor changes.

3 I wanted to tell you before anyone else more does.

4 I like this idea, but it's not what we need have right now.

5 We're all ultimately working towards a same thing.

Prioritising

Match 1–5 with responses a–e.

1 Shouldn't we get those figures done urgently?

2 I think I'm too busy for an appointment today.

3 What would happen if we changed the order of things?

4 Can we get Frédérique to do that?

5 What should the next step be?

a Well, you should try to make time – you shouldn't delegate this to someone else.

b Yes, it's not essential that you do it personally.

c I think we ought to contact all our salespeople at this point.

d Yes, it's of vital importance.

e I don't think it would make any difference.

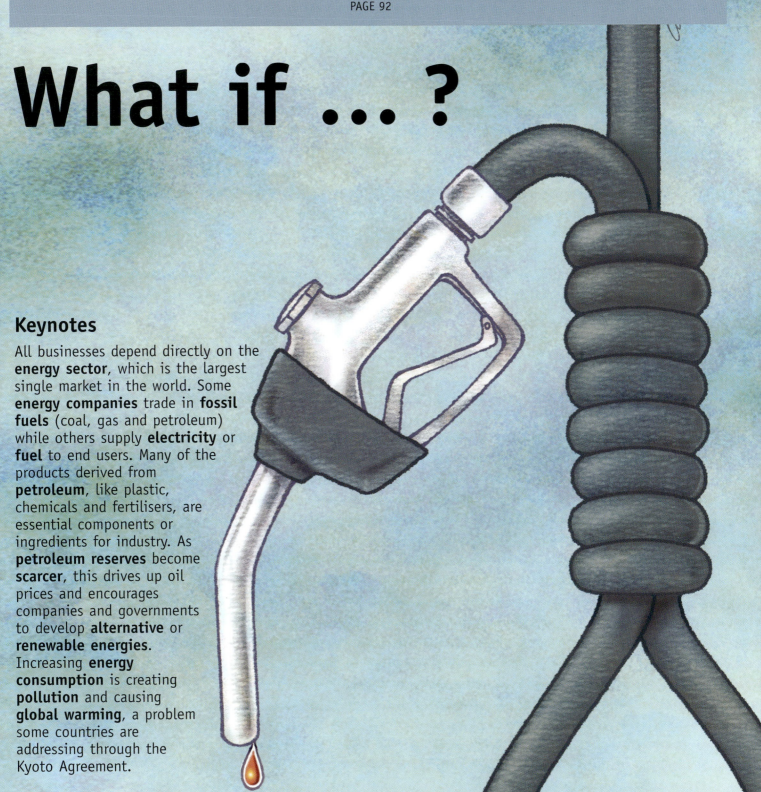

Unit 10
Energy

www.longman-elt.com www.economist.com

Fossil fuel dependency
PAGE 87

Conditionals
PAGE 90

Career skills: Problem-solving
PAGE 91

Dilemma: The power of money
PAGE 92

What if ... ?

Keynotes

All businesses depend directly on the **energy sector**, which is the largest single market in the world. Some **energy companies** trade in **fossil fuels** (coal, gas and petroleum) while others supply **electricity** or **fuel** to end users. Many of the products derived from **petroleum**, like plastic, chemicals and fertilisers, are essential components or ingredients for industry. As **petroleum reserves** become **scarcer**, this drives up oil prices and encourages companies and governments to develop **alternative** or **renewable energies**. Increasing **energy consumption** is creating **pollution** and causing **global warming**, a problem some countries are addressing through the Kyoto Agreement.

The energy quiz

Do the following quiz and find out how much you know about the energy industry. (Answers are at the bottom of the page.)

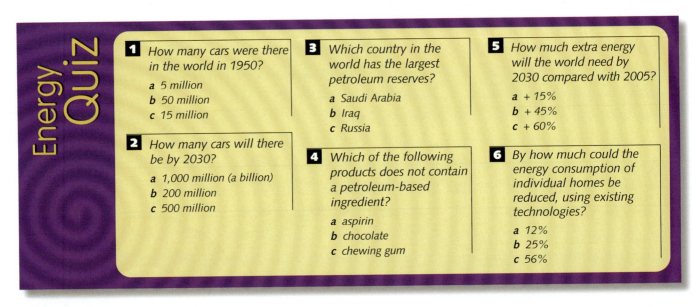

Energy Quiz

1 How many cars were there in the world in 1950?
- **a** 5 million
- **b** 50 million
- **c** 15 million

2 How many cars will there be by 2030?
- **a** 1,000 million (a billion)
- **b** 200 million
- **c** 500 million

3 Which country in the world has the largest petroleum reserves?
- **a** Saudi Arabia
- **b** Iraq
- **c** Russia

4 Which of the following products does not contain a petroleum-based ingredient?
- **a** aspirin
- **b** chocolate
- **c** chewing gum

5 How much extra energy will the world need by 2030 compared with 2005?
- **a** + 15%
- **b** + 45%
- **c** + 60%

6 By how much could the energy consumption of individual homes be reduced, using existing technologies?
- **a** 12%
- **b** 25%
- **c** 56%

Speaking — Work in pairs. Look at the list of some of the things that people could do to reduce the amount of energy that they use. Answer the following questions.

1 Which of these things do you do already?

2 Which ones would you be prepared to do in the future?

3 Are there any other things people could or should do to save energy?

Reduce the temperature at home by one degree or more.

Use public transport instead of using your car. / Use your car less often.

Change to fluorescent lighting at home.

Recycle all containers and packaging.

Watch less television.

Turn appliances off at the mains instead of leaving them on standby.

Use ventilation instead of air-conditioning.

Have a shower instead of taking a bath.

Reading — **Resource depletion**

1 Look at the chart. What do you think the two curves show? Read the text on the opposite page. Is there anything in it to support either of the projections shown in the chart?

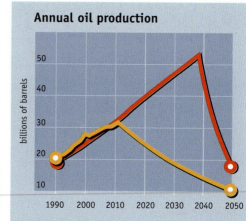

Annual oil production

billions of barrels

50, 40, 30, 20, 10

1990 2000 2010 2020 2030 2040 2050

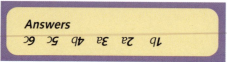

Answers

Fossil fuel dependency

Uncertainty over estimates causes the energy debate to heat up

[1] Gasoline prices have reached their highest mark ever in the United States – just as some oil companies have slashed their petroleum reserve estimates by 20 per cent. While soaring prices at the pump have the public worried about another 1970s-style oil crisis, waiting in line might ultimately be the least of our concerns. An increasing number of prominent petroleum geologists have warned that official estimates of available global oil reserves are dangerously exaggerated.

[2] They may well be right. For energy companies, proven oil and gas reserves are their primary indicator of economic health. They have every incentive to boost reserve estimates: the more oil they can claim, the more competitive and attractive to shareholders they appear. But private companies are not the only ones with an incentive to inflate estimates. In the mid-1980s, global oil reserve estimates jumped overnight, but this wouldn't have been the case if OPEC had not decided to factor in member states' reserves when determining their market share. Today, the more oil a country can claim – the methods each uses to determine this are a closely guarded secret – the more influence it has on the global energy scene.

[3] As a result, say the geologists, there may be considerably less oil in the world than the oil-producing countries and energy companies claim, and it would be logical to expect that global oil production could peak far sooner than predicted. If that happened, then getting at the remaining oil would become increasingly difficult and expensive. For an economy still reliant on fossil fuels, the effects would be catastrophic. As the oil supply shrinks, essential petroleum-dependent products (that is, nearly everything in modern society, from transportation to electricity to basic foodstuffs) are rendered either unavailable or unaffordable. Eventually, as companies employ even more complex and invasive drilling techniques, the energy required to extract a barrel of oil exceeds the amount it can generate, and oil ceases altogether to be an energy source.

[4] Of course, all major players in the oil business – private and public – insist that there will be enough oil to last well through the twenty-first century. But it would be irresponsible not to question their estimates when the official figures are so notoriously unreliable. Compounding the problem, most governments and all major energy companies insist that an oil shortage – and thus the point at which the world needs to find an alternative energy source – will occur only when the final drop is pumped from the ground. It does not take a petroleum geologist to surmise that demand will outpace supply long before the last bit of oil is gone.

[5] The optimistic oil-reserve estimates also fail to take into account one vital question: what will happen if global demand for energy continues to rise, particularly among developing nations? China itself could render the figures obsolete: Chinese oil imports rose by 30 per cent last year and the country's energy demand is expected to grow significantly in the next 25 years. To put the size of China's energy problem in perspective, in the last two years its electricity use has increased by an amount equal to the total power consumption of Brazil.

[6] The consequences of overestimating the global oil supply would be devastating. In the best-case scenario, industry would recover by turning to less efficient and more polluting fuels, accelerating the already noticeable effects of global warming. But if the worst came to the worst, there would be a total economic collapse, with today's rising gas prices in the United States and sporadic blackouts across China merely the mildest previews of what is to come.

[7] Granted, it is quite possible that there will never be an oil shortage, that global reserves are healthy enough to last until well after a replacement energy source is discovered. But given that those responsible for measuring the supply have a vested interest in making it appear high, the accuracy of their estimates cannot be taken for granted. The future of oil may not be as bright as it seems, either to the energy industry at large or to anyone who relies on their computer, their car or their planet.

Glossary

gasoline/gas (US) petrol

OPEC Organisation of Petroleum Exporting Countries

factor in include as a component of an equation

barrel standard unit of measurement for selling oil (159 litres)

sporadic occasional

2 Each of the following statements summarises information presented in one of the paragraphs in the text. Match the statements with the correct paragraphs.

a If no alternative energy source is found to replace petroleum, many everyday products will become prohibitively expensive.

b The potential effects of a shortage of oil could include environmental damage and the interruption of power supplies.

c Some scientists doubt that levels of petroleum reserves are as high as the petroleum companies have said they are.

d New sources of energy will only be seriously developed once petroleum becomes scarce.

e The economies of some countries are growing fast and will require greater quantities of energy.

3 Answer the questions.

1 Who has questioned the validity of the estimates of petroleum reserves? Is there any evidence to suggest that they are right?

2 Which groups have a vested interest in exaggerating oil reserves, and why?

3 How would a shrinking oil supply affect the following groups?

a energy companies   b consumers

4 What would be the least/most serious consequences of a diminishing supply of petroleum?

Speaking How do you think people will be affected by developments in the energy industry over the next ten to twenty years?

Vocabulary 1

Negative prefixes

The negative prefixes *un-, non-, il-, im-, in-, ir-* can be added to certain adjectives to give them the opposite meaning, e.g. *possible – impossible*.

1 The following are definitions either of adjectives in the text or of adjectives that can be made by adding a negative prefix to an adjective in the text. Write the correct forms of the adjectives.

1 (para 2) less efficient or more expensive than something else _____

2 (para 3) not sensible or reasonable _____

3 (para 3) not easily found or bought _____

4 (para 3) too expensive to purchase _____

5 (para 4) not worrying about the potentially negative results of an action _____

6 (para 6) clean, not producing waste or harmful emissions _____

2 Look at the following list of adjectives. Which negative prefix is used with each group?

1	_____	partial	perfect	plausible
2	_____	valid	correct	significant
3	_____	rational	regular	relevant
4	_____	existent	negotiable	renewable
5	_____	sustainable	economic	profitable
6	_____	legal	legitimate	literate

Vocabulary 2 Look at the list of words that can be used to form collocations with the words *oil, energy* and *power*. Which of these words can be placed before *oil / energy / power* and which can be placed after them?

solar (x2)	plant	crude	policy	renewable	grid
field	nuclear (x2)	refinery	cut		

Practice Complete the article with the appropriate form of words from Vocabulary 1 and 2.

Energy sector

A new report by GlobalResources presents three scenarios for the future of the energy sector.

The best-case scenario foresees a world of relative political stability, where international concern about the security of the Middle East region, with its huge [1] _oil fields_ , diminishes. Petroleum supplies are readily [2]_____ to individual consumers and businesses. However, petroleum companies are forced to focus more on [3]_____ development and ensure that they leave a positive economic legacy in countries where natural resources have been depleted.

A second scenario predicts that energy companies from Russia and China will become more [4]_____ in order to secure markets and supplies for their national industries. This will make it more difficult for companies to invest in [5]_____ and other environmentally friendly energy solutions. Governments will be increasingly reluctant to subsidise [6]_____ , and plans to build costly atomic reactors will consequently be shelved.

In the worst-case scenario, the energy supply chain is disrupted by regional and local conflicts. Operations become less [7]_____ as the cost of insuring [8]_____ and other energy installations rises. Access to energy is limited and markets contract. Some countries become import dependent for their energy and are forced to adopt new [9]_____ to control domestic consumption. Supplies of electricity are regularly interrupted by [10]_____ .

Listening 1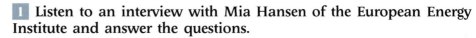

Renewable energy

1 Listen to an interview with Mia Hansen of the European Energy Institute and answer the questions.

1 What is renewable energy?
2 Is Mia Hansen in favour of developing renewable energies?
3 What is the UK government's target for 2025?

2 Listen again and answer the questions.

1 What are the two categories of energy that Mia Hansen talks about?
2 Which five types of renewable energy rely on the sun? Which two don't?
3 What are the two advantages and three disadvantages of renewable energy?
4 What are the four main uses of energy in the UK?

Writing You were a member of the audience at the conference where Mia Hansen was interviewed. Write an email to your company's managers, explaining the main points that Mia Hansen made. (See *Style guide*, page 20.)

Language check | Conditionals

Conditionals are generally used to predict the consequences of likely situations (Type 1) or of unlikely or hypothetical situations (Type 2) or to talk about hypothetical situations in the past (Type 3).

Find an example of each type in the text on page 87.

Mixed conditionals contain two clauses, each of which refers to a different time (future, present or past).

Which time is referred to in each clause in the following example?

If there **hadn't been** *an oil crisis in the 1970s, people* **wouldn't be** *so worried today.*

 For more information, see page 161.

Practice

1 Complete the following mixed conditional sentences using the appropriate form of the verbs in brackets. Does each clause refer to the future, the present or the past?

1 Pollution levels (be) <u>would be</u> lower today if planners **had designed** cities for pedestrians and not for cars.

2 I (buy) _____ an electric car already if they **were** cheaper and more reliable.

3 If I (not/have) _____ so much work to finish by this evening, **I'd have gone** with you to the conference.

4 If the government **is** not planning to build new nuclear power stations, then they (say) _____ so before they were elected.

5 If nuclear waste disposal (not/be) _____ such a problem, then more power stations **would have been built** by now.

6 The local people **would be** much poorer if oil (never / be discovered) _____ .

2 Choose the correct forms of the words in *italics*.

In the late 1970s, NASA decided to abandon its SSP (Space Solar Power) project using satellites to transmit solar energy from space. If the project (¹*had succeeded*)/ *succeeded*, many energy specialists and government planners ²*would/will* be less worried than they are today. But it didn't. Constructing the satellite ³*would have cost / would cost* $78 billion and it ⁴*will take / would have taken* 30 years to install it in space.

NASDA, the Japanese space agency, has now taken up the challenge and is currently doing its own research into a similar system. Their scientists are confident that if everything ⁵*goes / has gone* according to plan, they ⁶*would/will* be able to make their first satellite power transmission to Earth before 2025. But transferring solar energy to the planet by satellite won't be easy. In fact, if cheaper launch systems for space vehicles ⁷*are not / will not be* available in the near future, the cost of transporting and assembling even a simple system ⁸*will/would* remain prohibitive. However, one thing is clear: if there ⁹*wasn't/isn't* a slight chance of making the system work, the Japanese ¹⁰*would not have invested / will not invest* so much money.

Speaking

Make notes about something you planned to do in the past but weren't able to do, and something you dream about doing now but can't. Discuss the situations with a partner, using appropriate conditional forms.

Career skills

Problem-solving

When a problem surfaces at work, it is important to identify its source and to analyse the points of view of the people who are directly affected by it. This makes it easier to find an appropriate solution which everyone involved will understand and accept. Look at the following useful questions and responses.

a *Actually, we're one week ahead.*
b *Where do we go from here?*
c *Is everything going smoothly?*
d *I wish I knew.*
e *If the worst comes to the worst, ...*
f *Any idea what the problem is?*

Complete the table with the questions and responses above.

Keeping track	
How are things going with ... ?	Couldn't be better.
1	Yeah. It's working out just as we thought.
So, how did it go?	Not that well, actually.
Are you still on schedule?	2

Identifying the source of a problem	
So what exactly seems to be holding things up?	There's still no sign of the parts we ordered.
What's gone wrong?	3
4	It looks like it's the ...
What's up?	We're in big trouble.

Proposing a solution	
How can we sort this out?	Get someone onto it fast.
5	We'll just have to ...
How do you suggest we deal with this?	Let's just take it one step at a time.
What's the best way to fix this?	6

Listening 2 ⊙

1 Listen to three dialogues between managers and members of their teams. Identify the problem that is mentioned and the solution that is proposed in each case.

2 Listen again. Which of the questions and responses above are used?

Speaking

Work in pairs. A manager is talking to a team member who has discovered a problem. Decide together on an appropriate course of action in each of the situations on page 142. Take turns to play the roles of manager and team member.

Culture at work

Approaches to problems

How people approach problems depends on the culture in which the problems have arisen. In some (universalist) cultures, people interpret and react to problematic situations in terms of what is generally considered to be right or wrong. In other (particularist) cultures, however, problems are approached in the light of the relationships of those involved, and people try to find a solution that fits the specific circumstances. How do people approach problems and problem-solving in your culture?

Dilemma & Decision

Dilemma: The power of money

Brief

The World Bank is an international institution which provides loans and finance to countries and governments around the world. The decisions that it makes are particularly important as they provide the guarantee that other financial institutions need before they will agree to contribute additional funding to a new development project.

The Bank is currently conducting a review of its policy on energy. World demand for energy is set to rise considerably during the coming years, and the role of the Bank will be critical in determining how that demand is met. Over the last decade, the Bank has financed hundreds of fossil fuel projects which will substantially increase the levels of carbon dioxide in the atmosphere and accelerate the effects of global warming. The dilemma that the Bank now faces is whether to continue to finance such projects or to change to a radical new policy which would promote cleaner or renewable energies.

The Bank has appointed a special commission to prepare a report that will present recommendations for its future policy in the energy sector.

Task 1

You are members of the commission, which has representatives from three groups: the energy industry, developing countries and non-governmental organisations. Work in groups. Group A, you represent non-governmental organisations. Turn to page 137. Group B, you represent the energy industry. Turn to page 138. Group C, you represent developing countries. Turn to page 140. Prepare the arguments that you will present to the commission and choose a spokesperson to present them.

Task 2

A meeting takes place, at which the spokesperson for each group presents his/her group's viewpoint. Take notes about the proposals that the other groups make.

Task 3

All members of the commission should give feedback and express reactions to what has been proposed. At the end of the debate, agree on an outline of the future policy that you will advise the Bank to adopt.

Write it up

Write a short report on future policy that the commission will submit to the World Bank. (See *Style guide*, page 28.)

Decision:

Turn to page 146 and read the extract from a news article about the commission's report.

Unit 11
Going public

www.longman-elt.com   www.economist.com

Searching for shareholders

Keynotes

An **Initial Public Offering (IPO)** takes place when a private company **raises capital** by introducing its shares on the **stock market** and becomes a **public limited company (plc)**. Before a private company can **go public**, it must comply with the requirements of the **regulators** of the **stock exchange** (**Securities Exchange Commission** in the US) and **file an application** giving full details of its **accounts**. Most companies prefer to use the services of an **investment bank** to manage or **underwrite** the offering.

Stock market launches

1 Listen to an expert talking about why companies decide to go public. Match the three companies that she mentions with the reasons that she gives for their IPOs.

1	DreamWorks	a	to pay off debt
2	Virgin Blue	b	to pay back investors
3	Domino's Pizza	c	to pay for future expansion

2 Read the following statements. Which show the advantages of going public and which show the disadvantages?

1 Management will face pressure to produce positive quarterly results.
2 Outsiders may impose their views on management.
3 The value of the business may suddenly fluctuate.
4 More people will be aware of the company's existence.
5 The company will be obliged to disclose financial information.
6 The company can obtain finance without having to repay a debt.
7 Employees can exercise stock options.
8 Capital will be available for expansion.

Speaking

Work in pairs. Discuss the following statement made by Richard Branson before he decided to take Virgin Blue public and answer the questions below.

The delightful thing about not being a public company is that we don't have to worry about foolish analysts who say stupid things.

1 Why do you think Richard Branson changed his mind?
2 When is it better for a company to go public rather than stay private?
3 How would you decide whether or not to buy the shares of a company that was going public?
4 Can you think of an example of a company that has gone public? How successful has it been?

Reading ## Wall Street wonderboys

1 Read the extract from a letter written by Larry Page and Sergey Brin, the founders of Google, the internet search company.

Google is not a conventional company. We do not intend to become one. Throughout Google's evolution as a privately-held company, we have managed Google differently. We have also emphasized an atmosphere of creativity and challenge, which has helped us provide unbiased, accurate and free access to information for those who rely on us around the world.

What do you know about the company?

2 Read the text on the opposite page and answer the questions.

1 What is unusual about the way Google organised its IPO?
2 What are the two principles on which Google is founded?

PAGE AND BRIN'S DARING IPO

The new men on the block fight the Wall Street cartel

1 LARRY Page and Sergey Brin, the founders of Google, are doing something that has never been risked before. Not by Microsoft's Bill Gates. Not even by Apple's Steve Jobs. The Google guys are telling Wall Street to drop dead.

2 Those entrepreneurs from an earlier era played the game of going public the way it had always been played. Before Google came along, when a company was ready to sell shares, it hired big Wall Street investment firms such as Goldman Sachs and Morgan Stanley. The firms offered the stock to their favorite customers at a big discount. The privileged few were guaranteed quick profits, but the company received less money for its IPO. And the newly public company paid a high price for the honor. The investment firms' commission was typically as high as 7 per cent of the money raised. That fee could run into the hundreds of millions of dollars.

3 Page and Brin aren't putting up with this racket. Their plan is to use a public auction to offer Google's shares to anyone willing to pay the market price. Google will receive an estimated $100 million more by handling the sale this way. And while major firms like Morgan Stanley will be managing the auction, their role – and their fees – will be much diminished.

4 Why did such famous risk-takers as Gates and Jobs put up with the Wall Street shakedown? They didn't have much choice. The brokerages were able to act like a cartel because they held a near monopoly on information. CEOs had no idea what was happening to their stock

price unless they called their brokers. And the buyers of equities were mostly big financial institutions – pension funds, insurance companies – that paid commissions to the big brokerage firms for research and advice. The investment houses essentially gave kickbacks by cutting them in on IPOs.

5 Cracks began to appear in that cartel in the late 1990s, when WR Hambrecht & Co. and Wit Capital pioneered the auction approach. But few entrepreneurs chose these Wall Street reformers for their IPOs. Why? For one thing, many founders and CEOs picked traditional investment banks to take them public because they wanted the services of the firms' "analysts" – who notoriously hyped clients' stocks under the guise of providing objective stock research. Page and Brin built Google by applying their hyper-mathematical logic to the internet; now they have focused the same rationality on the IPO industry. In so doing, they might revolutionize Wall Street just as they revolutionized the internet.

6 Of course, the huge popularity of Google's brand makes it possible for the company to bypass Wall Street. The Google guys are relying on the fact that by the time the public come to decide whether to buy, they will have seen that the old way was collusive and corrupt while their way is rational and fair. That's a great leap of faith. Alienating the powers that be in investment banking has risks, too. The first time the newly public company reports disappointing results, Wall Street will be a very lonely and dangerous place, where everyone is gunning for Google and few allies are to be found.

7 Page and Brin are going to take that chance. Google is based on the twin principles that brains will trump brawn and that a democracy will always supplant a hierarchy. This democratic impulse forms the very core of Google's technology; so it goes with the IPO: Google has put its future in the hands of the people, not Wall Street. Larry and Sergey are not your typical courageous leaders. But they are at the forefront of a new breed of technocrat kings who are gambling that they can outthink – and outflank – the status quo.

3 Read the text again and study the following statements. Which refer to the way that companies traditionally issued shares, which refer to the public auction approach adopted by companies like Google and which apply to both?

	Traditional	Auction	Both
1 Stocks are sold directly to the public.		✗	
2 The company pays fees to a brokerage firm.			
3 Stocks are sold mainly to financial institutions.			
4 Shares are sold at a reduced price to favoured customers.			
5 The company receives more money from the sale.			

4 Statements 1–6 paraphrase information given in paragraphs 3 and 4. Which of the following groups of people does each statement refer to?

a   entrepreneurs like Bill Gates

b   institutional investors / investment funds

c   Larry Page and Sergey Brin

1   They did not have the information to allow them to track the performance of their companies on the stock exchange.

2   They were the principal purchasers of newly issued shares.

3   They represent a new generation of business leader.

4   They paid high commissions for information from stock specialists.

5   They needed to keep on good terms with analysts.

6   They paid for information and consulting services.

Speaking   What are the disadvantages of not following the traditional route and bypassing Wall Street when going public?

Do you think that Google will be successful in the long term or will it suffer as a result of having antagonised the Wall Street community?

Listening 1 ⊙   **An analyst's view**

Listen to Jonathan Harper giving his views of the Google IPO. Complete the table below.

Capital expected from the IPO		Capital raised	
Number of shares expected to be sold		Number of shares actually sold	
Projected share price		Share price obtained	
Mistakes made	1		
	2		
	3		

Writing   Your CEO has asked you to give your opinion about whether your company should plan to launch its new IPO by auction or by using an investment bank. Write a short letter saying which method you would recommend, and why. (See *Style guide*, page 16.)

Vocabulary 1

Find words in paragraphs 3 and 4 of the text on page 95 and match them with their meanings.

1 *(public) auction* a method of selling where people bid against each other

2 _____ the price determined by supply and demand

3 _____ companies specialised in selling stocks

4 _____ a group of companies that form an alliance to control a sector

5 _____ a situation where there is only one supplier of goods or a service

6 _____ the price of a company's shares

7 _____ stocks and shares

8 _____ the percentage paid on transactions

Vocabulary 2

Prefixes

The prefix *out* can be added to certain verbs to indicate that something is done better. Study these examples from paragraph 7.

outthink think in a more intelligent way

outflank have a more effective plan of attack

Match the verbs with their meanings below.

outlast	outscore	outmanoeuvre	outnumber
outperform	outbid		

1 use tactics to gain advantage

2 compete more effectively

3 buy something with a higher offer

4 obtain a better result

5 be of longer duration

6 be more numerous

Practice

Complete the article with the appropriate form of words from Vocabulary 1 and 2.

Investors who are looking to add some new [1] __*equities*__ to their portfolios will get the chance to do just that when Fairfax Inc goes public. It announced recently that it will be going ahead with plans for its IPO, and a company spokesman said that they would be offering two million shares. They expected that the initial [2] _____ would be between $25 and $30. The IPO is unlikely to affect the management of Fairfax's business affairs as the votes held by the original shareholders will [3] _____ those of investors acquiring a stake in the company. Fairfax said that although they had originally intended to hold a [4] _____ of the shares on the internet, they have now decided to use the services of the Randsfeld Investment Bank, which will be organising the sale in collaboration with several of the major Wall Street [5] _____ . Fairfax has refused to disclose the details of the agreement, but it is rumoured to be paying the bank a [6] _____ of eight per cent on the IPO. The company has consistently [7] _____ its competitors in its sector, and analysts are saying that they anticipate strong demand for Fairfax shares. This should result in a rapidly rising [8] _____ once investors start trading on the exchange.

Future forms

1 **Match the following with the situations (1–6) in which they are used.**

| future with *going to* | future perfect | present simple |
| modals *may* or *might* | future with *will* | future continuous |

1 to describe actions in progress in the future
2 to talk about things that someone wants to happen or intends to do
3 to talk about uncertain future events and make tentative predictions
4 to describe actions which will be completed by a particular time in the future
5 in clauses introduced by e.g. *when, as soon as, if, before*
6 to make firm predictions

2 **Match the examples taken from the text on page 95 with 1–6 above.**

a *Google **will receive** an estimated $100 million more ...* (para 3) _____
b *... Morgan Stanley **will be managing** the auction, ...* (para 3) _____
c *In so doing, they **might revolutionize** Wall Street ...* (para 5) _____
d *... they **will have seen** that the old way was collusive ...* (para 6) _____
e *The first time the newly public company **reports** ...* (para 6) _____
f *Page and Brin **are going to** take that chance.* (para 7) _____

 For more information, see page 161.

Practice

Choose the best options (a–c) to complete the sentences. There may be more than one correct answer.

1 Analysts will know more about the company's financial position when it _____ its prospectus next month.
   a is going to publish b publishes c will publish

2 The auditors say that they _____ the final version of the income statement by the end of next week as they'd planned.
   a will not have finished b are not going to finish c will not be finishing

3 Personally, I _____ any shares because I don't think the company will ever be able to pay a dividend.
   a will not buy b am not going to buy c might not buy

4 CEOs can make all the predictions they like, but ultimately it's the markets which _____ .
   a will decide b will be deciding c will have decided

5 I _____ buy a few shares, but only if the market looks good.
   a might b will c am going to

6 Our Chief Financial Officer _____ the first presentation to analysts on 21 June.
   a makes b will have made c will be making

Speaking

Make a list of things in the future that you intend to do, you will have done by a certain time or you will be doing at some point. Discuss your list with a partner.

Making a presentation

When you are making a presentation, it is important to include appropriate language to show your audience what you are doing at different moments. This will make it easier for them to follow what you are saying and will signal the transitions between the different sections of your presentation.

Look at the following language, which can be used to signal the different sections in a presentation.

a	*for instance*	h	*to put it in simple terms*
b	*in other words*	i	*i.e.*
c	*in brief*	j	*I'll come back to that later.*
d	*as you can see here*	k	*moving on to*
e	*to go on to (the next point)*	l	*as this chart shows*
f	*to sum up*	m	*that brings me to*
g	*such as*	n	*another way of putting that*

Which of a–n above would you use to do the following?

1   illustrate your presentation with examples (or visuals)
2   simplify or summarise sections of the presentation
3   show that you are changing to a different section of the presentation
4   reformulate or paraphrase what you have said

Listening 2 **Listen to the introduction to a presentation given by Andrea Herra to a group of analysts and answer the questions.**

1   What will the main sections of her presentation be?
2   Which of a–n above does she use?

Practice   **Work in groups. Choose one of the next sections of Andrea's presentation (section 1 below, sections 2–5 on page 141). Read the notes and then prepare and present your section.**

INNOVATex

Section 1	Who we are	
	Registered in 2003	founded by Gary Patton and Francis Fairbank
	Sectors of activity	new materials research (chemical and bio-engineering)
	Products	patented biodegradable plastics
	Number of employees	250
	Head office and research centre	Pasadena, California
	CEO	Andrea Herra

Culture at work

Presentation styles

When you give a presentation to an audience in another country, you may have to adapt the style of your presentation. In some cultures, audiences may react negatively to a presentation that is considered to be too flashy and over-optimistic. What style of presentation do people in your country use? Is it considered acceptable to use humour in a presentation?

Dilemma & Decision

Dilemma: **Which way to Wall Street?**

Brief

Hi Wire Ventures was the parent company of *Hi Wire* magazine – a popular business magazine for Silicon Valley entrepreneurs and executives. When the internet boom was in full swing, Hi Wire Ventures had big plans: launching new multimedia start-ups and new titles that would position the group as one of the leading interactive media companies. Financing that plan meant taking the company to the Stock Exchange. But it wasn't all going to be quite as simple as Chief Executive and founder Mario Rossini might have imagined.

The company had already been forced to cancel their first attempt at an IPO at the last minute when stock prices started to fall. But now, two months later, Rossini is convinced that the market is ready for the launch. He has found a bank to manage the launch and they have just finished doing the 'road show', a series of sales presentations where professional investors are invited to commit themselves to buying shares. Representatives of the bank and of Hi Wire's senior management team are now meeting to discuss the results and decide on the future of the IPO.

Task 1

Work in groups. Group A, you represent the bank. Turn to page 142. Group B, you represent Hi Wire senior management. Turn to page 144. Prepare the arguments that you will present at the meeting.

Task 2

Have the meeting with the representatives of the other group. Discuss your arguments and reach a decision about what action to take for the IPO.

Task 3

Each group should prepare a short presentation of the final decision and give their presentation to all the senior managers of Hi Wire and the bank.

Write it up

Write a short press release explaining the decision. (See *Style guide*, page 30.)

Decision:

⊙ Listen to Larry Elgin talking about what went wrong with the Hi Wire IPO.

Unit 12 Competition

www.longman-elt.com　　www.economist.com

Winner takes all

Keynotes

Businesses **compete** against each other to sell their products and to increase or defend existing **market share.** When a company succeeds in creating a new market, **competitors** enter the industry, offering similar products but at a lower price. To stop their customers from **switching** to alternative products, businesses must maintain a **competitive advantage.** This can be achieved by **differentiating** the product or service, by having a lower **cost of production**, possibly through **economies of scale**, or by controlling the **source of supply** or

Protecting a market

Listen to Robert Njiki, a professor of business studies, talking about how companies can analyse their competitive position in a market. Complete the diagram with the terms that he mentions.

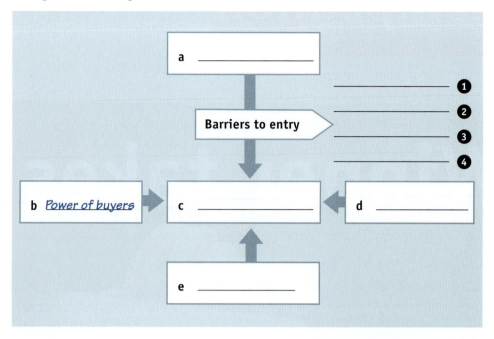

a _____

Barriers to entry

1 _____
2 _____
3 _____
4 _____

b *Power of buyers*   c _____   d _____

e _____

Speaking

All businesses have to adapt as their markets evolve and new opportunities emerge. Can you match the following companies with the products or services they originally sold? Do you know of other companies which have recently entered new markets?

1	American Express	a	forestry and wood
2	Nokia	b	mining and minerals
3	Nintendo	c	glass containers and bottles
4	3M	d	ornaments and decorations
5	Shell	e	mail delivery
6	Danone	f	playing cards

How might established companies be affected by the following new products entering their industries?

digital camera   mobile phone   MP3 player

Writing

Choose a company that you know well. Imagine a new market that this company could enter. Write a press release explaining how it will do this. (See *Style guide*, page 30.)

Reading

Competitive advantage

1 Read the text on the opposite page and answer the questions.

1 Who is Apple's principal competitor and how is the company trying to deal with it?

2 Which of the barriers mentioned in Preview has

  a   so far prevented Apple from gaining market share in the PC sector?

  b   made it difficult for companies to compete with Apple?

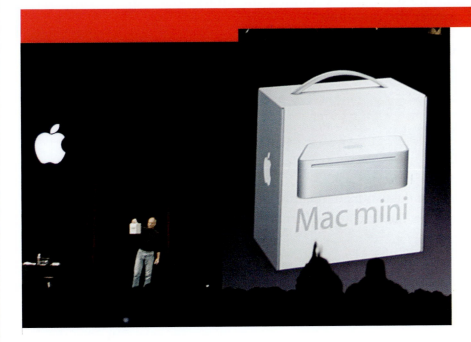

Glossary

hip fashionable, trendy

unveil reveal, disclose

cede give up, abandon

dabble get involved in as an amateur

peripherals printers, scanners and other devices used with a computer

revered respected and admired

Competitive advantage

Crunch time for Apple

Apple's Steve Jobs is having another go at the mass market for computers

1 During the first week of the year, Steve Jobs, the chief executive of Apple Computer, manages to look like the hippest boss in his industry. Every January, he coolly stands aside while other industry bosses go to Las Vegas for the Consumer Electronics Show. Then, in the second week, Mr Jobs mounts a stage in San Francisco at Apple's MacWorld conference. There, to oohs and aahs, he unveils Apple's latest products, all inevitably stunning in their design elegance and user-friendliness.

2 But this week Mr Jobs went one step further. Encouraged by the runaway success of the iPod, and by profits that were up by 368 per cent on the same quarter a year earlier, he announced what is, in effect, a new corporate strategy. Instead of settling for being a niche player selling beautiful but expensive computers, the firm is returning to contest the mass market that it long ago ceded to Microsoft, Dell and others.

3 That this challenge is even conceivable is due entirely to the iPod, which is going from strength to strength. The iPod's market share has grown from about one-third to two-thirds in the past year, at the expense of cheaper "flash" players.

An Apple for everyone

4 But Mr Jobs wants to attack even that remaining third of the market and this week he unveiled an Apple flash player, the iPod Shuffle. For Mr Jobs, who has never previously dabbled at the bottom of – nor explicitly attempted to dominate – any market, all this is unprecedented.

5 Even though the iPod now outsells Apple's computers by volume, most of the firm's revenues still come from the computers. So Mr Jobs still needs to fix Apple's long-standing problem in its core business, which is that its global market share in computers seems stuck at about 3 per cent. Using the iPod's success to convert mainstream (i.e. Microsoft Windows) computer users might be the way to do it.

6 This is why Mr Jobs also announced his most radical product, the Mac mini, a fully-fledged but tiny computer. The twist, in Mr Jobs's words, is that it is BYODKM, or "bring your own display, keyboard and mouse". Buyers are expected to plug in whatever monitors and peripherals they have already. Leaving out these bits makes the Mac mini Apple's first truly low cost computer, "so that people who are thinking of switching will have no excuse," says Mr Jobs.

7 Cutting the price tag by leaving out the peripherals is a shrewd way of minimising two risks: it is unlikely to cannibalise the sales and profit margins of Apple's more expensive models; and it is likely to snap many Windows users out of their inertia and into making the switch.

8 Mr Jobs hopes that as its seamlessly integrated range of products grows further, Apple will become the most revered brand in the digital home and in consumer electronics. This is why Mr Jobs has opened 101 retail stores around the world, their locations hand-picked by a former Gap manager. It also helps that an ecosystem of accessories is blooming. That growth will continue further once Mercedes, Nissan, Volvo and Ferrari have joined BMW and started to offer iPod controls in their steering wheels, as announced by Mr Jobs this week. And it helps that Mr Jobs, also the boss of Pixar, a hugely successful animated-film studio, understands the world of entertainment better than probably any other boss in his industry.

9 Apple leads the market for online music with iTunes, which works only with the iPod, while Microsoft is pushing a rival software format, Windows Media, in an attempt to make it the industry standard. Mr Gates could come from behind once again. On the other hand, Mr Jobs has been more circumspect this time around – designing iTunes to work with Windows, for instance, doing marketing deals for the iPod with Hewlett-Packard and Motorola and, with this week's announcements, fighting off competition from lower cost rivals. It is too early to tell which of these two generals is still fighting the last war ■

2 Read the text again. Complete the tables about Apple Computer and answer the questions.

Apple Computer Inc.
Competitive overview

1 Original market

Products	Competitors	Current market share	New product
personal computers			
Market objective			

a What are the two main qualities of Apple products?

b How does the Mac mini differ from other Apple computers?

2 New markets

Products	Competitors	Current market share
1		
2		
3		
Market objective		

a How is Apple trying to defend itself against its competitors?

b What structural change has it introduced to distribute its products to a wider market?

c What agreements has Apple made with other companies?

Speaking **What are the main reasons why Apple does not have a larger share of the personal computer market?**

Do you think that Apple's new strategy for the personal computer market will be successful? Why / Why not?

Vocabulary 1 **Expressions with *have***

Look at the subheading of the text on page 103. *Having another go at* can be paraphrased as *making another attempt to succeed in*. Use the appropriate form of *have* with the following phrases to paraphrase the underlined words in the sentences below.

trouble with	a look at	a right to	a stake in	no idea	in mind

1 Could you <u>check out</u> the latest sales figures and let me know what our share of the computer market is?

2 What sort of marketing campaign <u>are you considering</u>?

3 We've <u>encountered some problems with</u> the software on the new operating system.

4 Blackthorn Industries <u>owns a percentage of</u> the company.

5 All employees <u>are entitled to</u> know where we stand in relation to our competitors.

6 I <u>don't know</u> what they're planning to do. But the rumour is that they're bringing out a new version.

Compound nouns

Join nouns from the two boxes to form compound nouns from the text on page 103. Complete the definitions below with the compound nouns.

mass	niche	core	market	profit

business	margin	share	player	market

1 _____ (para 2)   a company that is present in a small segment of a market

2 _____ (para 2)   the largest source of customers

3 _____ (para 3)   the proportion of a market that a company occupies

4 _____ (para 5)   the central activity of a company

5 _____ (para 7)   the difference between costs and sales

Practice   **Complete the article with the appropriate form of words and phrases from Vocabulary 1 and 2.**

Pixar, the highly successful computer animation company, was originally a division of George Lucas' company, Lucas Films. In 1986 Steve Jobs, who [1] *had a stake* in the company, bought out George Lucas and took control. Originally, Pixar's [2]_____ was the creation of computer systems for visual processing. However, the company was never more than a [3]_____ in this sector and its [4]_____ was insufficient to justify further investment. Pixar was soon facing a critical situation as they were [5]_____ sales of their machines. To promote sales and improve [6]_____ , John Lasseter, the creative director, prepared a series of commercials, but he [7]_____ that one day film-making would become Pixar's main source of revenue. Today, Pixar is one of the most successful operations in its sector and has produced some of the most popular animated pictures for the [8]_____ , such as *Finding Nemo* and *The Incredibles*.

Listening 1   **Listen to a business analyst talking about the history of Honda. Take notes and complete the table.**

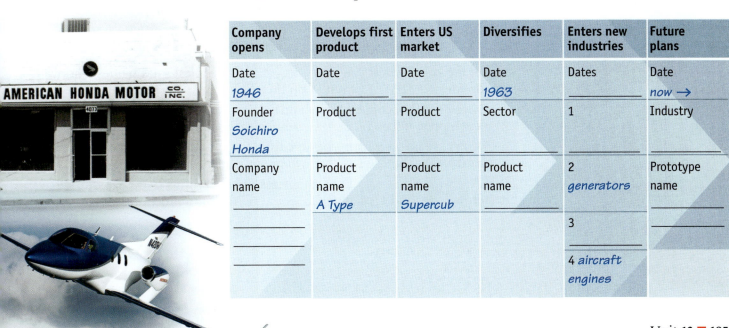

Company opens	Develops first product	Enters US market	Diversifies	Enters new industries	Future plans
Date	Date	Date	Date	Dates	Date
1946	_____	_____	1963	_____	now →
Founder	Product	Product	Sector	1	Industry
Soichiro Honda	_____				
Company name	Product name	Product name	Product name	2	Prototype name
	A Type	Supercub		generators	
_____			_____		_____
_____				3	
_____				_____	
				4 aircraft engines	

AMERICAN HONDA MOTOR CO. INC.

Time clauses

Study the examples taken from the text on page 103.

a *Every January, he coolly* **stands** *aside* **while** *other industry bosses* **go to** *Las Vegas ...* (para 1)

b *Mr Jobs hopes that* **as** *its seamlessly integrated range of products* **grows** *further, Apple* **will become** *the most revered brand ...* (para 8)

c *That growth* **will continue** *further* **once** *Mercedes, Nissan, Volvo and Ferrari* **have joined** *BMW and* **started** *to offer iPod controls in their steering wheels ...* (para 8)

1 Which of the examples above includes the following?

1 a time clause and a main clause both in the present tense

2 a time clause in the present perfect and a main clause in the future

3 a time clause in the present and a main clause in the future

2 Which of the verbs in **bold** above could be replaced by a present simple form?

3 Study the conjunctions that can be used in time clauses. Which could be used to replace the conjunctions in the examples above?

while	as	once	until (till)	before/after
whenever	by the time		as soon as	when

 For more information, see page 162.

Practice

Complete the sentences with the appropriate form of the verbs in brackets. You may need to use negative verb forms in some cases.

1 We (make) <u>will make</u> every effort to get our new medicine onto the market **before** our main competitor (release) _____ theirs.

2 **As soon as** we (find) _____ a supplier who can provide the circuits, we (move ahead) _____ with the production phase.

3 **Whenever** a new competitor successfully (enter) _____ a market, profit margins (tend) _____ to fall.

4 The new vehicle (go) _____ on sale **until** it (complete) _____ its road trials.

5 Let me know **when** you (get) _____ the latest sales figures, and we (decide) _____ what to do then.

6 **Once** the salespeople (understand) _____ the advantages of the new model, it (be) _____ much easier for them to sell it.

7 I don't see how we (can / be able to) _____ confirm the orders **until** we (know) _____ when our dealers will receive the goods.

8 Sandra (make) _____ the necessary alterations to the website **while** Jodie and I (prepare) _____ the sales brochures.

Handling conflict

When conflict occurs at work, it is important to deal with it appropriately before it causes further problems. Look at the following phrases, which can be used when handling conflict.

a *Whether you like it or not ...*
b *Can we set aside our differences?*
c *I don't see what all the fuss is about.*
d *What are your views on this?*
e *I'm sorry, but there's no point discussing this any further.*
f *I'm sure that won't be a problem.*
g *I know we don't see eye to eye on this but ...*
h *Let's keep things in perspective.*

Look at three strategies for handling conflict and match them with phrases a–h.

1 Minimise: ignore a conflict or try to make it seem less important.

2 Accommodate: try to find a compromise solution that is in the interests of all those involved.

3 Dictate: use your authority to impose a solution to the problem.

What do you think the advantages/disadvantages of each approach are?

Listening 2 ⊙ **1** **Listen to three dialogues. What is the source of conflict in each dialogue, and which strategy is used by each of the six colleagues?**

2 **Listen again. Which of phrases a–h above are used?**

Speaking **1** **Work in pairs. Turn to page 143 and read the descriptions of situations involving conflict between a manager and member of staff. Take turns to play the roles of manager and member of staff, using a different strategy each time.**

2 **Think of a situation where you have been involved in conflict. What was the cause of the problem? What attitude did you take? How successful were you at resolving the conflict? Do you think you reacted in the right way?**

Culture at work ## How much confrontation?

Some cultures consider conflict to be a normal part of working life and see it as a factor that can enhance performance and generate creativity. Other cultures, on the contrary, believe that interpersonal conflict should be avoided at all costs and that the interests of the individual should be subservient to those of the group or the community. Which of the two attitudes is closest to your culture?

Dilemma & Decision

Dilemma: The cola comeback

Brief

Parle Ltd is an independent company that produces and distributes soft drinks and sodas, including its best-selling Thums Up cola, on the market in India. Until recently, the company had been protected from outside competition by government regulations which prevented foreign competitors from entering the market. However, the government has now changed to a free-market policy, and foreign companies are now able to set up plants and distribution networks inside the country. Parle is well aware of the power of the US giants, Pepsi and Coca-Cola. But what can they do to protect their market?

Task 1

Work in groups of three. You are directors of Parle and you have arranged a meeting to decide what strategy your company should adopt to prepare Thums Up for the free market. Choose a role on page 143 and prepare the arguments that you would use to convince your fellow directors to follow your advice.

Task 2

Hold a meeting and present your arguments.

Task 3

Decide together on the best course of action for the company to adopt.

Write it up

Write an email confirming the decisions that you have made. (See *Style guide*, page 20.)

Decision:

⊙ Listen to Dinesh Madhur talking about the strategy that was adopted for Thums Up.

Review 4

Language check

Conditionals

Complete the dialogue with the correct form of the verbs in brackets.

A You know, if you (¹use) _____ public transport instead of driving to work every day last year, I'm sure you (²save) _____ a lot of money!

B You're right. And if petrol prices (³keep) _____ going up the way they have done recently, it (⁴start) _____ to cost me even more. But it's not just the money – it's so much more convenient by car. If I (⁵not/own) _____ a car, I (⁶have to) _____ take the bus to the station and then take the train, adding an extra hour a day onto my journey.

A Well, if I (⁷be) _____ you, I (⁸make) _____ an arrangement with a colleague and take it in turns to drive. That way, you (⁹not/waste) _____ any time and you (¹⁰save) _____ money, too.

B You're right. That's exactly what I should do.

Future forms

Choose the correct forms of the words in italics.

1 The company has confirmed that it *might go / will go* ahead with its IPO as long as the market remains stable.

2 Company spokesperson Gregory Hansett said that his firm *will intend / intends* to offer five million shares for sale.

3 The share price has yet to be fixed, but analysts say that it *will / might* probably be in the order of $10–15 per share.

4 By the time its new flagship hotel *is opening / opens* in February, the group *will become / will have become* the market leader in Asia.

5 Some analysts say that the CEO *will be asking / will ask* for trouble if he takes the company public at such a difficult moment.

6 Economists are predicting that overcapacity *erodes / will erode* profit margins for the industry as a whole.

Time clauses

Complete the sentences with the following words.

as soon as	whenever	when	until
after	while		

1 _____ we first introduced the product, it was the only one on the market.

2 _____ looking at all the facts, the management has decided to stop manufacturing in Europe.

3 The contract is coming by express delivery. _____ you get it, sign it and send it back. It's urgent!

4 _____ we run into design problems like this, it always seems to take so long to sort things out.

5 I can give you an answer, but not _____ I've had time to look at the latest sales figures.

6 At least we'll be able to do some work at home _____ the office is closed for renovation.

Consolidation

Choose the correct forms of the words in italics.

Chevron, the US oil company, announced that it has made a bid to acquire Unocal for $18 billion. The planned acquisition comes at a time ¹*when / while* many industry analysts are warning that oil prices ²*rise / will rise* even higher than the recent peak of $58 per barrel. If the specialists at Goldman Sachs ³*are / will be* right, the oil markets ⁴*continue / will continue* to become even more volatile as world reserves ⁵*are starting / start* to diminish. ⁶*Before / After* Chevron decided to make the deal, one thing was already clear: if it ⁷*hadn't bought / didn't buy* a competitor with access to reserves of natural gas, it ⁸*won't be able / wouldn't be able* to supply its clients' growing appetite for this type of fuel. However, there is no doubt that even if petroleum prices eventually ⁹*fall / had fallen*, Chevron ¹⁰*would not waste / will not have wasted* its money as it is paying for the acquisition with shares.

Vocabulary check

1 Correct the adjectives in *italics* by adding or removing prefixes where necessary.

1 One of the arguments that is often used against wind energy is that it is not only *uneconomical* but also extremely *reliable*.

2 It is very hard to increase market share with products that are not *uncompetitive*.

3 Although solar energy will only become *expensive* once cheaper solar panels are *available*, it does provide a source of energy that is *polluting*.

2 Choose the best options (A–C) to complete the sentences.

1 The companies have formed a(n) _____ which fixes prices and production levels.

   A monopoly   B cartel   C agreement

2 The products have been designed for the _____ and will be sold worldwide.

   A mass market B niche market C stock market

3 Companies can protect their markets by creating barriers _____ .

   A to enter   B to entry   C of entrance

4 Another word for *stocks* and *shares* is _____ .

   A capitals   B accounts   C equities

5 The advantage of _____ energies is that the reserves they consume can be replaced.

   A renewable   B fossil fuel   C electrical

6 They've bought another two million shares, giving them a 20% _____ in the company.

   A stock   B stake   C part

Career skills

Problem-solving

Match the questions with the responses.

1 So, how are things going with the modifications?

2 What seems to be holding things up?

3 What's the best way to fix this?

4 So, how did it go?

5 Are you still on schedule?

a There have been some minor delays but nothing too serious.

b Well, if the worst comes to the worst, we may have to rewrite the entire program.

c Not that well, actually. I got stuck in traffic and missed my flight.

d The delay is because we don't have authorisation.

e Couldn't be better. We've just got two more to finish.

Making a presentation

Complete the extracts from a presentation with the following phrases.

moving on	in brief	in other words
sum up	for instance	as you can see

Our company has always had a reputation for inventiveness – [1]_____ , we were the first to develop a viable biodegradable alternative to plastic. And we're an innovative company, [2]_____ , we're the type of organisation that responds to challenges by finding original solutions.

Before [3]_____ to the next point, I'd like to say a few words about our financial performance – [4]_____ from this slide, we've increased our profit margins for the last year by 1.5 per cent.

Before I conclude this talk, I'm going to [5]_____ the main points that I have mentioned here this morning: [6]_____ we're young, we're dynamic and, most important of all, we're profitable.

Handling conflict

Put the dialogue in the correct order.

☐ a But you've known about it for ages.

☐ a But people are still saying the colours are wrong.

☐ a Well, not if it's going to ruin our sales!

☐ a I don't think I can get things ready in time.

☐ b Listen. I know we don't see eye to eye on this, but it is just a minor detail. Right?

☐ b Well, you'll just have to, whether you like it or not.

☐ b Oh, please, let's keep things in perspective! It's a good product, people like it and it will sell. Stop worrying!

☐ b Well, we can't change them now. So there's no point discussing it any further.

Unit 13
Banking

www.longman-elt.com   www.economist.com

Money matters

Keynotes

The **banking sector** has four main types of institution. **Central banks** implement the **monetary policies** of governments / countries and fix **interest rates** for other banks. **Commercial banks** or **clearing banks** take **deposits** and **make loans** to private individuals and businesses. **Investment banks** or **corporate banks** provide advice and specialist services to corporations or large individual customers. **Microcredit banks** or **microfinance institutions** (MFIs) lend sums of money to people in developing countries for small business development.

Banking institutions

Which of the following banks do the things listed below?

Central	Microcredit	Commercial	Investment

1 give loans to people who have very limited resources
2 advise companies who want to go public
3 fix the exchange rate of a national currency
4 issue chequebooks and credit cards

Speaking   What are the main banking institutions in your country? What banking services do you use? How do you carry out your banking transactions (by phone / on the internet / at a branch, etc.)?

Listening 1   Look at the table, which shows the main departments and services of an investment bank. Listen to three employees talking about their jobs. Which department does each one work in?

Advisory/ Research	Portfolio management	Investment	Capital and debt	Private asset management
business risk	market information	start-up companies	IPOs	client management
business sector analysis	stock reports	venture capital	corporate debt	taxation
strategy and management	stock trading			pension planning

Frank _____   Matt _____   Claudia _____

Speaking   Which of the departments do you find the most interesting?
What do you think it would be like to work in an investment bank?

Reading   Investing in development

1 Read the text on the opposite page. What is the main difference between Mr de Lesseps' investment bank and the one described in Listening 1?

2 Read the text again. Are the following statements *true* or *false*?

1 Microcredit institutions generally make loans up to a maximum of $1,000.
2 Microcredit loans are less likely to be repaid than other high-risk loans.
3 Over $3 billion is currently on loan under microfinancing schemes.
4 Microcredit loan interest rates are based on risk assessments.
5 20% of the potential for microfinancing is currently being exploited.

Speaking   Do you agree that investment will help to solve some of the developing world's problems?

Do you think that it's possible to mix business and philanthropy?

What other ways of reducing poverty can you think of?

A path to helping the poor

Microfinance institutions see the sense of investing in the developing world

1   "IN New York, people are always asking me the same question," Alexandre de Lesseps says: 'Why do you want to lend money to poor people in developing countries?' Mr de Lesseps, 54, an international investment banker, has a ready answer. "The only way to solve the problems of poverty and terrorism in the world today," he says, "is through investment." As a co-owner of BlueOrchard Finance, a corporate bank in Geneva, he is one of the leading figures in the world of microfinance. His firm manages a fund that currently makes about $50 million in short-term loans to microcredit lending institutions in more than 20 developing countries around the world, and BlueOrchard and its investors make a profit in the form of interest payments on the loans that they make to such institutions.

2   Microfinance institutions typically make loans in amounts of $1,000 or less to poor people in developing countries who are ignored by commercial banks. As a rule, microcredit loans are not backed by collateral, leaving no means of financial recovery for the lender if they are not repaid. But leading microcredit institutions claim that only five per cent of the loans they make are never repaid. This compares with five to ten per cent in the consumer finance industry for borrowers with bad credit histories. Just less than $500 million is committed to microcredit loans worldwide, according to BlueOrchard's estimates. But Mr de Lesseps says he believes that today the total market for such loans may be nearly $3 billion.

3   He acknowledges that the aims of his microfinancing ventures are not purely philanthropic. "The reason we lend money to poor people in developing countries is not only so that they can make money," he said, "but also so that our investors can make money." The latter, of course, have to be his primary concern. His involvement in microfinancing began a little over two years ago, when a Swiss banker and friend approached him about investing in BlueOrchard, which was founded by microfinance specialists Cédric Lombard and Jean-Philippe de Shrevel, one-time employees of the United Nations.

4   When de Lesseps and his team arrive in a country, they visit the central bank or leading aid institutions, the ones generally doing microfinancing. Later, on-site research often takes them to interior villages, where families may live on less than $10 a month. "I visited a village in Cambodia where the people used microcredit loans to buy irrigation equipment and seed, which they use to grow vegetables," Mr de Lesseps said. "They are now selling the vegetables to exporters and to a local hotel. Such villages are being transformed from dust to being productive. You don't ask for collateral on the loans because they don't have it. But they will die to pay you back because you are giving them a first-time chance. It's a matter of pride."

5   BlueOrchard typically charges two to seven percentage points more than Libor, the international benchmark for interest rates, for loans to local microcredit institutions, which then charge rates to their borrowers based on assessments of risk factors. "I know that sounds pretty high," Mr de Lesseps said. "But you have to remember that other forms of locally available credit are five times higher than that."

6   Mr de Lesseps said he believed that 80 per cent of the potential for microfinancing worldwide remained untapped, and that the industry would easily be able to absorb more than $10 billion. "For me, the only way to make a difference," he said, "is to make sure that the money going to developing countries is properly managed and not just thrown away."

Glossary

collateral assets that can be used as a guarantee for a loan

philanthropic benevolent, interested in people's well-being

Libor **L**ondon **I**nterbank **O**ffered **R**ate (the rate of interest at which London banks offer loans to each other)

Expressions with *make*

1 **Look at the following example from the text.**

Microfinance institutions typically **make** *loans* (= lend money) ... (para 2)

Complete the following expressions with *make* from the text. (Each can be followed by the preposition(s) in brackets.)

1 get/produce a return on an investment (para 1)
   make _____ (on/from)

2 get/produce a return on an investment (para 3)
   make _____ (on/from)

3 have a positive influence on something (para 6)
   make _____ (to)

2 **Look at more expressions with *make* below. Complete them with the prepositions *of, for, on* or *with*.**

1 make allowances _____   4 make an impression _____
2 make a habit _____   5 make a mistake _____
3 make a deal _____

Look at the collocations from the text.

Why do you want to **lend money** *...?* (para 1)

... only five per cent of the **loans** *they* **make** *are never repaid.* (para 2)

Which of the following verbs can be used to form collocations with *money* and *a loan*?

pay off	borrow	lend	secure	invest	deposit	negotiate
raise	lose	apply for	save			

Complete the article with phrases from Vocabulary 1 and 2.

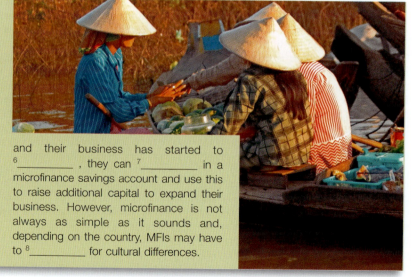

Today, 90 per cent of people living in poverty are unable to ¹ _borrow money_ from commercial banks, which refuse to ² _____ without financial guarantees. That means that their only available sources of credit are either family, or moneylenders who charge interest at rates as high as 100 per cent per month. Microcredit banks, where investors can obtain funds despite being unable to ³ _____ their _____ , can really ⁴ _____ to the lives of future small business owners. In order to protect investments, these banks often lend to groups; if one member of the group is unable to ⁵ _____ , the other members of the group can do so for them. Once a microentrepreneur has become successful, and their business has started to ⁶ _____ , they can ⁷ _____ in a microfinance savings account and use this to raise additional capital to expand their business. However, microfinance is not always as simple as it sounds and, depending on the country, MFIs may have to ⁸ _____ for cultural differences.

Write a short letter to the communications director of the company you work for explaining why you think the company should contribute money to support microfinance. (See *Style guide*, page 16.)

Investment bank for sale

Read the extract from a newspaper article about Cazenove, a British investment bank, and answer the questions.

1 What services does Cazenove provide for its clients?
2 Why do you think major investment banks wanted to buy Cazenove?

Cazenove, a small British investment bank, is the object of desire of many of the world's biggest financial institutions. It is the banker for 43 of the UK's top 100 companies and also manages the finances of many of the members of the British Royal Family.

Cazenove provides corporate finance advice and manages funds on behalf of its clients worldwide. The bank acts as financial adviser in merger and acquisitions transactions, both public and private, and offers an extensive shareholder analysis service.

Even though they are not specialists in all areas and charge relatively little for each of their services, when they announced they wanted to sell, all the major investment banks were interested in buying them.

Listening 2 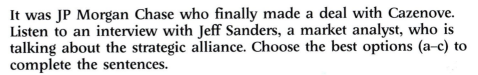 **It was JP Morgan Chase who finally made a deal with Cazenove. Listen to an interview with Jeff Sanders, a market analyst, who is talking about the strategic alliance. Choose the best options (a–c) to complete the sentences.**

1 The alliance is a
   a takeover.
   b merger.
   c joint venture.

2 The price JP Morgan Chase paid for the deal is
   a much less than other recent alliances they made.
   b much more than other recent alliances they made.
   c 50 per cent less than other recent deals.

3 Cazenove is attractive because it
   a is a very powerful bank.
   b has very important clients.
   c is Britain's biggest investment bank.

4 Cazenove's shareholders are
   a mostly made up of employees.
   b unhappy about the deal.
   c concerned about losing control.

5 The speaker says that in five years' time JP Morgan will probably
   a pull out of the deal because of the penalties they have to pay.
   b sell Cazenove to another US giant.
   c pay penalties in order to gain complete control of Cazenove.

Reference words

We use the reference words *this*, *that*, *these*, *those*, *such*, *the former*, *the latter*, *one* and *ones* to refer to something mentioned before.

Study the examples taken from the text on page 113 and decide what the words in bold refer to.

a   *But leading microcredit institutions claim that only five per cent of the loans they make are never repaid.* **This** *compares with five to ten per cent in the consumer finance industry ...* (para 2)

b   *"... we lend money to poor people ... not only so that they can make money ... but also so that our investors can make money."* **The latter***, of course, have to be his primary concern.* (para 3)

c   *... they visit the central bank or leading aid institutions,* **the ones** *generally doing microfinancing.* (para 4)

d   *"I visited a village in Cambodia where the people used microcredit loans to buy ...* **Such** *villages are being transformed from dust to being productive."* (para 4)

e   *BlueOrchard typically charges two to seven percentage points more than Libor ... "But you have to remember that other forms of locally available credit are five times higher than* **that***."* (para 5)

For more information, see page 162.

1   Read the extract from an article about a banker and decide what the words in *italics* refer to.

Jonas Okembo is a microfinance manager. [1]*This* involves calculating the interest rates the bank should charge customers on their loans. It also means deciding how long it will take disadvantaged customers to repay both the principal and the interest on the loans. [2]*The former* is the actual sum lent and [3]*the latter* refers to the percentage charged by the bank for the lending period. Rating the credit-worthiness of [4]*such investors* can be the most difficult part of the job, but as it often involves travelling to interesting places, it is [5]*the one* he enjoys most.

2   Read another extract from the same article. Replace the words in *italics* below with *the latter*, *that*, *such*, *the ones*, *these* or *the former*.

He was first attracted to the microfinancing sector by a desire to help people in developing countries. They are *the people* [1]_____ whose projects he found the most challenging, and their motivation and enthusiasm were contagious. '*Their motivation and enthusiasm* [2]_____ are the things that make them interesting and worthwhile to work with,' Jonas says. 'It's a great position to be in, and I'm sure that if I didn't work in *this type of* [3]_____ an environment, I would probably have set up my own business. Originally, I wanted to go into the technology sector and then I thought about a career in international relations, but *the technology sector* [4]_____ suffered a slump in my final year in business school, and I wasn't really qualified for *international relations* [5]_____ . However, being a microfinance account manager is what I want now and *being a microfinance account manager* [6]_____ is all that matters for the moment.'

Persuading

Persuading colleagues to agree with your point of view or follow the course of action you recommend can sometimes be a difficult task. You may need to use different approaches depending on the personalities and relationships involved. Look at the following useful phrases.

a *Unless you're prepared to ...*
b *Bearing all things in mind ...*
c *We're all in this together.*
d *All things considered, I think ...*
e *It's in all of our interests to ...*
f *If you don't do it this way, then ...*
g *After looking at all sides of the argument ...*

Match phrases a–g with the following approaches.

1 **Coercion** introducing a threat in order to get what you want

2 **Reasoned argument** showing that your point of view / solution is the most logical or reasonable

3 **Shared interest** creating a sense of common purpose

Which of the approaches do you think is the most effective?

Listening 3

1 Listen to three dialogues. Which of phrases a–g above are used?

2 We tend to use a mix of approaches when persuading. Discuss the tactics or strategies the speakers use in the three dialogues and say which you think are most effective, and why.

Speaking

1 Work in pairs. Which of the following would you have to be persuaded to do? Take turns to try to persuade each other to do them.

– lend your new car to a friend for the weekend
– invest your savings in a friend's new business scheme
– participate in a team training session where you will have to do a bungee jump
– live without your TV, mobile phone or computer for one month
– write a report criticising a colleague who is a friend of yours

2 Tell your partner one other thing you would never do. Your partner must try to persuade you to do it.

Culture at work

Exerting influence

If an attempt is being made to persuade them to do something, people in different cultures react in different ways, whatever approach is used. Junior colleagues may feel they have to accept whatever a superior suggests, or they may feel they should present an alternative argument or put forward an opposing view if that is what seems right to them. What is the situation in your culture?

Dilemma & Decision

Dilemma: Reliable research?

Brief

LVMH, the company famous for Dior cosmetics and Vuitton handbags, is suing the US investment bank Morgan Stanley for 100m, accusing its research analysts of giving false reports about its financial health. LVMH claims that the bank compared them unfavourably with their biggest rival, Gucci, who is a client of Morgan Stanley, causing the LVMH share price to drop. The bank counterattacked by seeking damages of 10m and the publication of the judgement, if it was in their favour, in 20 magazines and newspapers.

Task 1

Work in groups. Read the claims below put forward by the two sides. Discuss whether you think these claims are valid. Why / Why not?

Task 2

Work in groups. Based on the claims, prepare a list of persuasive arguments which could be used by the spokespeople from each party. Assign the roles of spokespeople to two members of the group and listen as they argue the points. Did you feel more convinced by some arguments than others?

Task 3

Discuss what you would do if you were the judge in this case. Would you award the requested damages to either side? Compare your decision with those made by other groups.

Write it up

Write the minutes of the meeting your group had in Task 3. (See *Style guide*, page 26.)

Decision:

Now turn to page 140 to find out what happened.

LVMH – The Case

- The company claims that the bank was deliberately and systematically unfair to them in its stock research because of the direct conflict of interest concerning the bank's client, Gucci.
- Clare Kent, the bank's analyst, is supposed to have stated that LVMH stock had peaked and wouldn't increase in value any more, thus causing a dramatic drop in their share price.
- Morgan Stanley sent an email to their clients to inform them that LVMH's credit rating was about to be downgraded. This had a very bad effect on their market credibility.
- Morgan Stanley made negative predictions about the impact of the weak yen on LVMH profits, and also suggested they would have problems integrating clothes retailers they had bought.

Morgan Stanley – The Case

- The bank admits that they did seek to promote their own client by giving favourable information about them, but they also insist that they never tried to make LVMH's situation look worse than it was.
- They argue that Clare Kent is one of their best analysts, and was voted European Luxury goods analyst of the year by *Institutional Investor* magazine.
- They say that investors know that analysts make mistakes. For example, they were uniformly positive about technology stocks in the late 1990s, and nobody is suing them now.
- They argue that the credit downgrade was based on a report by the rating agency Standard and Poor's, and that they are not responsible for the accuracy of information given by them.
- They claim that they were right about the impact of the yen and the integration of clothes retailer Donna Karan.

www.longman-elt.com   www.economist.com

Practice makes perfect

Keynotes

Professional development opportunities or **in-company training courses** are offered to working people who need to develop new **skills** to become more competent at their jobs.

The courses usually take place **in-house** or in specialised training **centres**, as well as **online**. Organisations pay for them out of the **training budget**, and the courses generally take place **in company time**. As well as improving business performance, offering staff opportunities for training has a positive impact on **motivation** and **staff loyalty**. It has been proved that staff generally feel greater **job satisfaction** and a personal **sense of achievement** as a result of any training they do.

Training solutions

1 Do you think it is important for a company to have a training budget for its staff?

If you had to select a training course in one of the following areas, which would you choose to do? How would you make your choice?

– foreign languages (Japanese, Italian, Russian, Arabic or other)
– computer skills training (Web design, Microsoft Office, Database or other)
– management skills training (Teamworking, Cross-cultural awareness, Presentations or other)

2 Read the four extracts from brochures advertising training courses. Which ones would appeal to you, and why?

a

ITD THE INSTITUTE FOR TRAINING AND DEVELOPMENT
Our account directors will help you to define your organisation's exact training needs and will work in partnership with you to develop and manage specific training programmes to suit your business requirements. Whether you need to invest in technical training or general management skills, we can offer experienced trainers and a combination of different courses to suit all levels of the hierarchy. Our customised training leads to ITD qualifications, and our flexible solutions packages include face-to-face and online classes to suit all budgets.

b

Java Tutor

The selection of instructor-led courses are designed for all computer users: non-programmers, novice programmers and Java professionals alike. We provide a complete range of Java computing solutions, from introductory to expert level. Through hands-on experience – labs, exercises and tutorials – trainees learn to issue programming commands effectively. Special corporate discounts are also available for private classes scheduled for your employees only.

c

Tanya Becker Group
Our seminars will help your employees to learn about Stress Management and to apply those lessons to their working lives. Directly inspired by Tanya Becker's award-winning book Stress Remedies, *we run courses in companies and organisations of all types and sizes and help hundreds of delegates each year to recognise stress in themselves and others. Participants will focus on Tanya's ten strategies for coping with stress, which will empower them to manage pressure effectively and take control of their lives. The course format ranges from a one-day intensive workshop to regular weekly sessions.*

d

StageCoach
We provide a unique programme of interactive executive training events, using theatre and drama techniques. Reliving the dramas faced by characters from a range of well-known plays forms the basis of our acclaimed training method, which has been specially designed for executives and senior managers. Working with selected extracts from the works of such famous playwrights as Bertold Brecht and Anton Chekov, participants are invited to take part in debate and discussion, and to perform role-plays on stage. Our seminars and workshops cover a wide range of management issues: ethics and motivation, crisis management, succession planning, and more. Act now and enrol for this unforgettable training event!

3 Read the statements below and decide which of the institutes or courses they refer to.

1 This company gives advice on appropriate training for your staff.
2 A well-known specialist designed this course.
3 Part of these courses can be completed by computer.
4 The course is designed to help managers and high level executives only.
5 This course is cheaper if participants are from the same organisation.
6 This course uses examples from literature to illustrate business problems.

Write an email to your HR manager, asking for permission to attend a training course of your choice. (See *Style guide*, page 20.)

Motivational training

1 Read the text on the opposite page about a training organisation called 'Movers and Shakespeares' and answer the questions.

1 Which Shakespeare plays does it refer to?
2 Why is Shakespeare good for business trainers?

A leadership lesson in Shakespeare

Dramatic training courses bring dramatic results in the world of business training

1 ONE of the executives gathered at the Aspen Institute for a day-long leadership seminar using the works of Shakespeare was discussing the role of Brutus in the death of Julius Caesar. "Brutus was not an honourable man,"

he said. "He was a traitor. And he murdered someone in cold blood." The consensus was that Brutus had acted with brutality when other options were open to him. He made a bad decision, they said – at least as it was portrayed by Shakespeare – to sanction and lead the conspiracy to murder Julius Caesar. And though one of the executives acknowledged that Brutus had the good of the republic in mind, Caesar was nonetheless his superior. "You have to understand," the executive said, "our policy is to obey the chain of command."

2 During the last few years, Shakespeare has assumed a prominent place in the management guru field, as business executives and book writers looking for an innovative way to advise corporate America have begun exploiting his wisdom for profitable ends. None more so than husband and wife team Kenneth and Carol Adelman, well-known as advisers to Ronald Reagan, who started up a training company called "Movers and Shakespeares". They are amateur Shakespeare scholars and Shakespeare lovers, and they have combined their passion and their high level contacts into a management training business. They conduct between 30 and 40 seminars annually, focusing on half a dozen different plays, mostly for corporate clients, but also for government agencies.

3 The seminars all take the same format, focusing on a single play as a kind of case study, and using individual scenes as specific lessons. In *Julius Caesar*, for example, Cassius's sly provocation of Brutus to take up arms against Caesar was the basis for a discussion of methods of team building and grass roots organising. The funeral orations provided a basis for a debate about the relative merits of logic and passion in persuasive speech making.

4 The programmes do conform to certain familiar contours of management training: the day's final exercise always involves each participant reciting "what I learned" and "what I'll do". But the sessions also include clips from film versions of the play at hand; the Caesar seminar, for example, showed Marlon Brando beseeching "Friends, Romans and countrymen" to lend him their ears. In addition, the Adelmans travel with certain props, and throughout the day executives were prompted to deliver text readings wearing Roman helmets and togas.

5 Although neither of the Adelmans is academically trained in literature, the programmes contain plenty of Shakespeare tradition and background. Their *Henry V* seminar, for example, includes a helpful explanation of Henry's winning strategy at the Battle of Agincourt. But they do come to the text with a few biases: their reading of *Henry V* minimises his cynicism and more or less excuses his abuse of power. Instead, they emphasise the story of the youth who seizes opportunity and becomes a masterful leader. And at the Caesar seminar, Mr Adelman had little good to say about Brutus, saying "the noblest Roman of them all" couldn't make his mind up about things.

6 Many of the participants pointed to very specific elements in the play that they felt to be pertinent. Caesar's arrogance, which led to his murder, and Brutus's mistakes in leading the conspirators after the assassination, they said, raise crucial questions for anyone serving in a hierarchy: when and how do you resist the boss?

7 And it did not escape the notice of those in the room that the conspirators' hurried act of revolt failed to consider its aftermath, the lesson being that thorough planning, for any leader, is paramount. Those who would depose Caesar had, in effect, no exit strategy. In the end, a more philosophical discussion evolved about leadership itself, something the men and women in the room agreed was worth considering more often than they do.

Glossary

sanction	officially agree to
sly	cunning
grass roots	fundamental or basic level
beseech	invite
props	theatrical costumes and scenery (property)
toga	long robe, item of clothing
aftermath	period of time after a terrible event

2 Read the text again and answer the questions.

1 What kind of man did the group of managers think Brutus was?

2 In what way was Brutus's planning insufficient?

3 What assets do the Adelmans have which have contributed to the success of their training firm?

4 Which executive skills do they explore using *Julius Caesar*?

5 Which aspects of the training are similar to more conventional management courses?

6 What are the virtues of Henry V, according to the Adelmans?

7 What did the participants think they should do more often?

3 According to the text, which of Shakespeare's leaders are guilty of the following faults?

1 dishonour   3 cynicism   5 arrogance

2 manipulation   4 indecision   6 short-sightedness

Speaking

1 Discuss the following questions.

1 Would you enjoy a training course where you had to act out scenes from Shakespeare's plays?

2 How would you feel about wearing a Roman toga and helmet during a training session?

3 Can you think of other leaders like Henry V who could be used as leadership models on business training courses?

4 What other plays or films might be useful to business trainers?

2 Read the extract below from Shakespeare's *Henry* V and the notes about it. What lessons could this speech teach managers about motivating their staff? Discuss the following questions.

1 What does Henry V say to make the listeners feel part of a team?

2 What rewards does he offer them?

3 What does he say to make them feel that their project is worthwhile?

What else could managers learn from this speech?

Henry V speaks to his soldiers before they go into battle, and tells them how they will always be remembered if they fight bravely alongside him. He then continues with:

We few, we happy few, we band of brothers;
For ¹he to-day that sheds his blood with me
Shall be my brother;
This day ²shall gentle his condition
And gentlemen in England now ³a-bed
⁴Shall think themselves accursed they were not here

Language notes

1 Shakespeare changes from the plural *we* to the singular *he* to speak about individuals.

2 *He will become a gentleman*

3 *in bed*

4 *will be sorry they were not here*

Listening 1 Listen to a trainer who is using this speech to illustrate his course on motivation. Compare what he says with your answers above.

Vocabulary

1 Put the following words, taken from Preview and the text on page 121, into four groups: Teachers, Sessions, Students, Methods.

seminar   instructor   trainee   case study   delegate   programme
course   role-play   participant   trainer   tutor

2 Read the text on page 121. Find verb–preposition combinations which have the following meanings.

1 (para 3) concentrate on _____
2 (para 4) comply with _____
3 (para 6) mention (as important) _____
4 (para 6) be the cause of _____

3 Which prepositions are used with the following verbs?

1 result _____ , _____   3 react _____
2 relate _____   4 report _____ , _____

Practice

Complete the dialogue with the appropriate form of words and phrases from this Vocabulary section.

Sue: Hi, Mike. I've just signed up for that [1] _course_ , 'New issues in management'.

Mike: Yeah, me too. I hope they're going to [2]_____ ethical issues in management. That's something I've been trying to get people around here interested in for some time.

Sue: They probably will. I heard the [3]_____ are pretty radical people and don't exactly stick to traditional methods. The last time they did sessions here, it [4]_____ some pretty dramatic changes. Some people didn't [5]_____ them very well and a few of our more conservative colleagues resigned!

Mike: I remember that. I'm not sure we need to change things all that much, but it would certainly be nice for [6]_____ like us to have the chance to talk about our own particular problems here.

Sue: Yes, that's true, but things can get a bit unpleasant if we have to discuss how we [7]_____ management – and each other.

Mike: I'm not worried about that as long as we don't have to do too many [8]_____ like last time – they're sure to ask me to take the part of the CEO again!

Language check

Clauses and sentence construction

Many sentences contain several different parts, or clauses, each with its own verb. When the main focus of a sentence is contained in one of the clauses, it is referred to as the main clause. The other clauses are subordinate clauses.

Study this example taken from the text on page 121.

Many of the participants pointed to very specific elements in the play
                    main clause
that they felt to be pertinent. (para 6)
        subordinate clause

The main types of subordinate clause are explained in the table on the following page and an example is given for each. The third column shows some of the words that are used to connect the subordinate clause to the other clause(s) in the sentence.

Type	Used to ...	Used with ...
relative (see unit 5)	give additional information about something that is referred to a **which** was conducted over a period of two years	who, which, that ...
conditional (see unit 10)	refer to situations that are possible or hypothetical b **as long as** they can find an English-speaking representative to do the basic work for them	if, unless, as long as ...
time (see unit 12)	give information about the timing or duration of something c **After** interviewing several hundred UK export managers	after, before, while, as ...
purpose	indicate the objectives or intentions behind an action d **in order to** attract the foreign custom they need	to, in order to/that, so that ...
concession	show contrast between two clauses e **despite** the fact that UK managers have very different opinions about the importance of foreign languages	although, though, despite, in spite of ...
manner	describe the way in which something is done f just **like** managers in other groups	as if, like ...
result	explain the consequences of actions or developments g and **as a result**, this group tends to avoid business opportunities	so/such ... (that), so, as a result ...
reason	explain the causes of actions or developments h **Since** they do a lot of their business in non-English-speaking countries	since, because, as, in case ...

 For more information, see page 162.

Practice Complete the extract from a report about language training with the example clauses from the table above.

The objective of the BCC's language survey was to analyse the relationship between foreign language use and export performance. [1] _After interviewing several hundred UK export managers_ , the BCC analysed their responses to a standard questionnaire and used this information as the basis for the report. The findings of the survey, [2]_____ , show that [3]_____ , they do agree on one thing: English has now established itself as the international language of business.

The study divides UK exporters into four distinct groups:

Anglocentrics choose to do business exclusively with countries that have had close historical ties to the UK and a tradition of using English. But this is not a dynamic strategy [4]_____ that present themselves in other parts of the world.

Opportunists do not like to have any direct business dealings in a foreign language. But they are prepared to consider doing business with non-English-speaking countries [5]_____ .

Adaptors go further [6]_____ , and that involves making an effort to present product information and sales literature in the local language.

Enablers are the most sensitive to linguistic and cultural identity and integrate these two factors in their strategic overview. [7]_____ , they ensure that information about all aspects of their business operations is available in the national languages of the markets where they are present. However, [8]_____ , they too are reluctant to actually conduct business in a foreign language.

Career skills

Motivating

When people feel motivated by their jobs, it gives them a sense of personal satisfaction, which results in better quality work. Keeping staff motivated is therefore a priority for managers and supervisors. Look at the following phrases, which can be used to motivate people.

a *We're all in this together.*
b *This is the last chance I'm giving you.*
c *I'm offering an additional commission to whoever ...*
d *It's in everybody's interests to ...*
e *I'm going to let you handle this.*
f *You get the business, you get the bonus!*
g *Come on. You've got to do better than that!*
h *Would you like to take full responsibility for this?*

Look at the following approaches to motivating people. Match phrases a–h with the different approaches.

1 using authority/threats
2 establishing a common purpose
3 giving people a financial incentive
4 empowering people to work autonomously

Listening 2 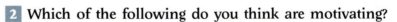 Listen to four dialogues. Identify one sentence from each dialogue to add to the list (a–h) above. Indicate which approaches the sentences correspond to.

Speaking

1 Which of the approaches in the dialogues above would work for you? Which would you adopt if you were a manager and had to motivate a member of your staff?

2 Which of the following do you think are motivating?

- knowing that you are part of a team effort
- knowing that the company is concerned about working conditions
- fear of losing your job
- being recognised for what you have achieved
- working for someone who inspires you
- being offered training courses to improve key skills

3 Work in pairs. Take turns to play the roles of the manager and employee in each of the situations on page 144. As manager, decide which approach you would adopt in order to motivate the employee.

Culture at work

Providing incentives

How people react to incentives to motivate them depends on their cultural background. In some cultures, people are mainly motivated by the desire to achieve power and status, while in others there is less focus on individual achievement and more on the interests of the group as a whole. What would motivate people from your culture? What problems could result from proposing the wrong type of incentive?

Dilemma & Decision

Dilemma: Allocating the training budget

Brief

Ashdown and Kennedy, a manufacturing plant, had to take their absenteeism problem seriously when they discovered that on any given day 10 per cent of the factory staff were off sick. In addition to this, high staff turnover was increasing recruitment costs and reducing productivity. They asked People First, a human resources consultancy, to conduct a full study to ascertain the reasons for these problems and to come up with solutions.

The study revealed that the majority of staff complained of poor relations with line managers, who were said to be authoritative and inflexible, and suffered acute stress due to co-worker disagreements and the generally bad atmosphere in the workplace. Some of the staff obviously had genuine ill-health problems, bad backs being the most common, while more had problems caused by poor diet, being overweight and lack of exercise.

Task 1

In groups, read the extract from the report that People First produced and discuss the benefits and drawbacks of each of the proposals.

Task 2

Decide which option or combination of options you would choose for the short term and for the long term, and give reasons.

Task 3

Present your arguments to the class.

Write it up

Write a short report on the Ashdown and Kennedy problem and how you would solve it. (See *Style guide*, page 28.)

Decision:

⊙ Listen to what Joyce Moorhead, an HR training consultant, thinks about the options available to Ashdown and Kennedy.

One of the best ways to retain staff and keep motivational levels high is to provide incentives through training schemes. We therefore propose that you consider the option of implementing an annual training budget of approximately 5% of the payroll for all kinds of different training. Options to consider in your particular circumstances are as follows:

a) *Health and Fitness Awareness Training* for all staff members

Top Health

- offer courses on occupational health and general fitness awareness (keeping people healthy and showing corporate social responsibility).

Cost: 30% of budget

- could provide gym and fitness facilities on the premises, complete with a fitness trainer, for best long-term results.

Cost: 100% of budget

b) *Stress Management Courses* for all staff members

Key Associates

- claim that stress-related issues are always the main reason for absenteeism.

- help people to think more positively, manage time, enjoy challenges and enhance relationships with co-workers and managers.

- provide

– intensive one-day stress awareness courses.

Cost: 20% of budget

– extensive courses run over several weeks, with a stress consultant available for one-to-one discussions with staff members.

Cost: 70% of budget

c) *Management Style Training* for all line managers

The Future Manager Consultancy

- offer tailor-made training courses for line managers.

- propose a course based on developing good listening skills, setting reachable goals, becoming better communicators and working towards flexibility.

- claim that if you provide dictatorial managers with the appropriate training, you will be taking a positive step towards solving staff absenteeism, turnover and health problems.

Cost: 60% of budget.

The advice business

Keynotes

Professional-service firms provide services to other companies, which often rely on **expert advice** from **consultants** who **advise** on strategy and policy making. **Investment banks** and **finance companies** offer advice on financial transactions, while bookkeeping and **auditing** are often **outsourced** to independent **accountants** or **auditors**. Legal matters are placed in the hands of **law firms**, and **information technology** systems are regularly looked after by external professionals. Some professional-service firms provide '**complete solutions**' by offering legal, accounting and strategic **expertise**. However, in the USA recent legislation limits the extent to which, for example, audit firms can give policy advice on other aspects of business due to the **conflict of interests** this practice gives rise to.

Consulting services

Match the services (1–6) that the Chicago Consultancy Group offers with the following areas of expertise.

branding	corporate development	pricing	strategy
retail	globalisation		

1　We help firms to have a highly co-ordinated approach to the image they want to project.

2　Managers today often assume that they should focus on reducing costs to stay competitive. This is not the only course of action to consider. Sometimes choosing to have expensive products is the best option.

3　Creating above average shareholder value has moved to the centre of the senior-management agenda. We help managers to take the best expansion options.

4　Companies have to deal with many more markets than in the past, and at different levels of economic development.

5　Focusing on the changing needs and behaviour of consumers helps our clients emerge as leaders in this sector.

6　This is the core aspect of all our advice. We help clients plan for the future and put forward the best options to choose from in all areas of their business.

Read about consultants below. What arguments can you think of for and against employing them?

Some people are very sceptical about the value of consultants' advice. There are many jokes about them, such as 'A consultant is someone who borrows your watch to tell you the time.' Top consultancy firms charge clients up to $10 million a year for advice, whether it improves performance or not.

Cross-border consultants

1 Read the text on the opposite page. How did the strategies adopted by the accounting firms differ from those of professional-service firms in general?

2 Read the following sentences taken from the text. Complete the text with the sentences.

1　A small group of firms is showing how this should be done.

2　Russian subsidiaries now tend to be run by Russians, who prefer to buy services from fellow nationals with detailed knowledge of local conditions and rules.

3　Wherever western multinationals went to set up or buy a new business, there too went their accountants, bankers, consultants and lawyers.

4　And what they are looking for is not the biggest global brand name in their neighbourhood directory, nor the firm with the broadest range of services on offer.

5　Things get done among such groups of individuals more by face-to-face persuasion than by impersonal commands used by their clients.

6　For the likes of Arthur Andersen, these problems and conflicts have already ended in disaster.

Cross-border consultants

Global professional-service firms

At last there is an international strategy that seems to be working

1 LIKE the various groups of helpers that accompanied ancient armies on the march, professional-service firms followed their industrial clients as they expanded around the world in the 1980s and 1990s. (a) _____ From Moscow to Buenos Aires, the efficient professional-service firms were ready to advise on what deals to do, how to finance them, how to compute their consequences and how to solve any problems involved.

2 It was heady stuff, and it led some professional-service firms to decide that they should follow their clients' example and go global as well. They dispatched their ambassadors around the world and waited for them to attract the new business that would justify their cost. The accounting firms, which were among the more aggressive globalisers, thought they could be likened to all the groups of helpers as well as to the armies themselves. They took over consultancy businesses, finance companies and law firms, setting themselves up as global chains of one-stop shops with a "we do everything" attitude: "While you're in for an audit why not buy a bit of litigation, too? And by the

way, today we have a special offer on restructuring your company."

3 This was a strategy which created enormous managerial problems, in addition to introducing a cascade of potential conflicts of interest among firms' increasing regulatory and professional duties. (b) _____ For others, such conflicts are still being discovered, a process which is being speeded up by legislation. America's Sarbanes-Oxley Act bans accounting firms from carrying out certain consulting and legal services for their audit clients, and there are growing restrictions on the provision of tax services as well.

4 The "do everything everywhere" strategy looks like a problem for professional-service firms, too, because no matter how multinational their clients, those clients buy very few of their professional services centrally. Purchases are, by and large, the responsibility of local managers. (c) _____ They want the best service for each individual task, and the nature of professional services is such that "the best" invariably involves a combination of superior local knowledge and close customer-client relationships.

5 Besides, the managers of multinationals' foreign operations are less and less likely to be expatriates these days. (d) _____ When those ancient armies had fought their battles and finally won, they left behind locals to run their hard-earned territories. The various groups of helpers returned home with the troops.

6 Yet there is a need for professional-service firms to be international, to a limited extent. Firms in the European Union increasingly need to take a transnational view of things. And someone has to co-ordinate the multinationals' local service-providers, be they auditors or lawyers. (e) _____ The so-called "Charmed Circle" of blue-chip New York law firms has an enviable record of profitability, combined with modest international expansion. Most of these firms have also chosen to join an informal network of top-ranked firms around the world. The network's firms exchange lawyers and run joint training programmes. (f) _____ Until someone proves there is a better approach, this seems the way forward for most other professional-service firms as well ■

3 **Read the text again and answer the questions.**

1 What kind of problems did the accounting firms' strategy create?

2 How has the US tried to solve some of these problems?

3 Why do some global companies not use the services of global consultancies?

4 Why is it necessary to have some international professional-service firms?

5 What have the top New York law firms managed to do successfully?

4 **The text refers to many different groups of people or institutions. Complete the statements below with the following.**

Accounting firms New York law firms Arthur Andersen Managers of foreign subsidiaries The Sarbanes-Oxley Act Industrial clients of professional-service firms

1 _____ decided to go global first.

2 _____ developed a takeover strategy to form conglomerates.

3 _____ prevents audit specialists from giving advice on certain strategic, tax and legal matters.

4 _____ closed after serious financial scandals.

5 _____ are rarely expatriates.

6 _____ have the best approach so far.

Speaking

1 Do you think consultants can be objective when evaluating the strategies they have implemented?

2 What advantages do you think 'face-to-face' persuasion has over impersonal commands from an unknown person in the hierarchy? How would you prefer to receive instructions?

Vocabulary 1

Uses of *like*

1 Study the examples taken from the text on page 129. They all contain expressions with *like*. Complete sentences 1–4 with the correct expressions with *like*.

a *Like the various groups of helpers that accompanied ancient armies ...* (para 1)

b *The accounting firms ... thought they could be* **likened to** *all the groups of helpers as well as to the armies themselves.* (para 2)

c *For* **the likes of** *Arthur Andersen, these problems and conflicts have already ended in disaster.* (para 3 – missing sentence 6)

d *The "do everything everywhere" strategy* **looks like** *a problem for professional-service firms ...* (para 4)

1 _____ is a synonym of to *appear to be*.

2 _____ is used to give an example.

3 _____ refers to a type of person or group of people.

4 _____ is used to compare one thing with another.

2 Complete the article with the appropriate form of expressions with *like*.

Outsourcing to ¹_____ the Chicago Consultancy Group and other big consulting firms can sometimes have a negative impact on the morale of staff. They feel threatened and often ²_____ consultants to messengers of bad news, expecting the 'downsizing' process to start soon after their arrival in the firm. It isn't always ³_____ that, of course, but whatever the effect on individuals or on the company paying the high fees, consultancy ⁴_____ being with us for some time to come.

Vocabulary 2   ## Word building

Complete the table with the other forms of the words taken from the text on page 129.

Verb	Noun (concept)	Noun (person)	Adjective
manage	*management*	manager	managerial/*managing*
finance	_____	_____	_____
_____	_____ / _____ / _____	consultant	_____ / _____
_____	audit	_____	-
-	strategy	_____	_____
_____	_____	_____	regulatory
_____	knowledge	-	_____ / _____

Practice   **Complete the article with the appropriate form of words and phrases from Vocabulary 1 and 2.**

Controlling the controllers

Accounting firms who were originally hired to carry out independent ¹ *audits* on the ²_____ situations of companies saw that they could offer advice at the same time and increase their income through the provision of ³_____ services. However, the Securities and Exchange Commission saw a potential conflict of interests as the big auditors couldn't be expected to give objective feedback on ⁴_____ policies they themselves had suggested implementing. The SEC therefore decided to introduce restrictive measures to ban accounting firms from giving advice on matters other than accounting.

The accounting industry opposed the first attempt at ⁵_____ by getting influential people ⁶_____ congressmen and lawyers to write to the SEC opposing the ban. The SEC withdrew the proposal. Just when it ⁷_____ victory for the accounting industry, a series of corporate scandals involving, among others, Enron and Arthur Andersen occurred. This led to the Sarbanes-Oxley Act, which ensured tighter control on financial statements, by making the senior ⁸_____ staff of companies ultimately responsible for the accuracy of information concerning the value of shares and company performance.

Reported speech

When using reporting verbs like *say* and *tell* in the past, we generally make verb and time changes to the direct speech we are reporting.

'He was here yesterday.' ⟶ She said (that) he **had been there the day before**.

We don't always make these changes, especially when reporting a fact that is still true or when reporting very soon after the direct speech.

'Consultants **can** be helpful because they**'re** objective.'

⟶ They told us (that) consultants **can** be helpful because they**'re** objective.

⟶ ... consultants **could** be helpful because they **were** objective.

We often summarise and use different wording instead of reporting word for word.

'It is important to do some research and check as many of the facts as we can and only then discuss everything so that we can come to a decision about what course of action we should take.'

⟶ He said we should look into it all first and then decide what to do next.

We can use other reporting verbs, which can be followed by:

– an infinitive (*agree, ask, decide, demand, offer, promise, refuse, want*):
'I'll reduce the fees if you like.' ⟶ He agreed **to reduce** the fees.

– a gerund (*admit, deny, mention, recommend, suggest*):
'I made a mistake with the figures.' ⟶ He admitted **making** a mistake with the figures.

– an object + infinitive (*advise, ask, instruct, invite, remind, tell, warn*):
'You should lower your prices.' ⟶ They advised **us to lower** our prices.

 For more information, see page 163.

Listening 1

1 Listen to the managing director of a department store talking to a consultant and take notes under the following headings.

1 market share
2 pricing policy
3 customer survey results
4 options
5 consultant's advice

2 Summarise what the speakers said. Answer the questions below using reported speech and the reporting verbs in brackets.

1 What did the managing director say to the consultant concerning market share? (tell)
2 What did she say about their pricing policy? (admit)
3 Which results of the customer survey did she highlight? (point out)
4 How did the consultant react? (ask)
5 How did she answer him? (explain)
6 What did the consultant tell her to do? (advise)

Speaking

If you were the managing director, would you take the consultant's advice? Why / Why not?

Writing

You are the managing director in the conversation above. Write a formal email to your staff, summarising the conversation you had with the consultant. (See *Style guide*, page 20.)

Reporting

A large part of office life is spent reporting back orally to one's colleagues and bosses about conversations at formal and informal meetings. Reporting back requires accurate observation and memory skills as well as summarising and communication skills. Sometimes the person reporting back is also expected to make a recommendation about a course of action or decision to be taken.

Look at the following useful phrases for reporting back on conversations and meetings.

a *We finally all agreed to ...*
b *He suggested telling them ...*
c *What he was trying to say was ...*
d *In short, she is refusing to ...*

e *What he wants us to do is ...*
f *The bottom line is ...*
g *I recommend / I suggest ...*

Listening 2 **1** **Listen to a line manager reporting back to one of her team members and answer the questions.**

1 What is the first speaker reporting on?
2 How does the second speaker react?

2 **Listen again. Which of phrases a–g above are used by the first speaker?**

Speaking Work in pairs. Student A turn to page 139. Student B turn to page 144. Read the dialogue of the meeting. Imagine you were at the meeting too and report back on it.

Listening 3 Listen to both dialogues and decide if your partner reported all the necessary information.

Culture at work

Reacting to change

Some cultures adapt quickly to change and see it as a matter of course or even progress, development and growth. Some cultures are more conservative: they resist change where possible and perceive it as always being problematic and negative; and they don't like to take advice from an outsider. What is common in your culture? How might this difference cause misunderstanding in multicultural teams?

Dilemma & Decision

Dilemma: **Consultant with a conscience**

Brief

CIC Consultants is proud of the performance of one of its main clients, Power US, a global energy trading company. They have reported high earnings and a 10 per cent growth rate since the consultants started advising them five years ago. CIC not only gives advice on strategy, but its auditing department produces the official figures for Power US as well. Sue Kelly, a senior accountant at the consultancy firm, was first alerted to problems when the CFO of Power US asked her to lie to one of the company's partners about an investment. She refused on moral grounds and soon after that her boss transferred her to another company.

Recently, she discovered that Power US is involved in massive fraud and she is now facing an ethical dilemma: should she report what she knows to an outside financial regulator? Both companies are very powerful and even though she can provide proof, her word may not be taken seriously and in that case, she will never find another job in consulting.

Task 1

Work in small groups. Read the consequences of the two options open to Sue Kelly. Can you think of any other possible outcomes in each case?

Option one If Sue reports the problem to a regulator, and they open an investigation ...
- She will lose her job immediately.
- Power US and CIC Consultants may go bankrupt.
- She will have to testify in court against former colleagues.
- The bosses of both companies will have to pay huge fines and possibly go to prison.

Option two If Sue decides to say nothing and leave CIC Consultants ...
- It is possible that the fraud will never be discovered.
- It is also possible that things will get even worse as time goes on.
- She will feel responsible for not stopping a criminal activity.
- She could probably find work in another consultancy firm but would have to lie about her reasons for leaving CIC.

Task 2

Hold a meeting to decide which option she should take.

Task 3

Choose a spokesperson to report back to the other groups what was said and decided at your meeting.

Write it up

Write the minutes of your meeting. (See *Style guide*, page 26.)

Decision:

⊙ Listen to what someone with a similar dilemma decided to do and what the consequences were.

Review 5

Language check

Reference words

Read the article and decide what the words in *italics* (1–6) refer to. Then complete the rest of the article (7–10) using some of the words from 1–6.

Goldman Sachs, the famous investment bank, can trace its origins back to 1887. [1]*That* was when Marcus Goldman set up his first company in New York. The bank was the first [2]*one* to set up a Mergers and Acquisitions department and a Real Estate Management department. [3]*The former* specialised in advising companies who wished to form partnerships with or acquire other businesses, and [4]*the latter* provided advice for the management and acquisition of business properties. [5]*These* were two of the foundations of the company's success.

The company has always had a unique reputation on Wall Street. [6]*This* is partly due to the fact that the company was one of very few private investment banks. However, all [7]_____ was about to change, and in 1999 it launched its own IPO. [8]_____ was a hugely successful operation, raising a record $3.6 billion. Since then, the company has continued to perform well and increase its range of services. Today, [9]_____ include debt restructuring for governments and asset management for wealthy individuals. Goldman Sachs' client list includes such companies as Samsung and Daimler-Benz. Only recently, it advised [10]_____ during its merger with fellow automobile manufacturer, Chrysler.

Clauses and sentence construction

Complete the sentences with the following words or phrases.

since	unless	in order to	although
despite	until	which	whose

1 Mark Simpson, _____ company specialises in security training, will be leading the first session.

2 _____ some companies do provide systematic language training for all staff, most do not.

3 There is no point in giving employees expensive training _____ it contributes to improving their performance at work.

4 The stress management workshops were introduced _____ reduce the number of workdays lost to stress-related illnesses.

5 We can't fix a date for the training course _____ we know exactly who needs to attend.

6 _____ a 10 per cent decrease in our training budget, we have been able to offer a wider variety of courses than ever before.

7 _____ we do not have the facilities here at head office, we will be running the course at an external training centre.

8 Improving the communication skills of our sales staff is one of the areas _____ we need to focus on.

Reported speech

Find and correct the mistakes in the phrases in *italics*. Some of the phrases are correct.

1 The auditors have *asked we give* them full access to our financial records.

2 Our advisers *have suggested introducing* a standard invoicing procedure for all divisions.

3 They have *refused accepting* responsibility for the programming errors and they have *told that* it is our own fault for installing the system incorrectly.

4 The consultants have *advised that we not* employ any extra staff during the coming year.

5 The firm has *promised to complete* the survey of our accounting procedures by the end of the month.

Consolidation

Choose the correct forms of the words in *italics*.

In the forthcoming fight to eliminate global poverty, [1]*which/that* remains one of the UN's top priorities for the coming decade, microfinance will be playing one of the key roles in the attack. Microfinance is not charity, say [2]*its/their* supporters, [3]*that/who* argue that [4]*it/this* is only another form of investment, [5]*since/although* it provides credit to low-income households. Kofi Annan, [6]*whose/who's* efforts to alleviate poverty around the world are well-known, understands how difficult [7]*it/this* will be to make the UN's Year of Microfinance a success [8]*unless/despite* microfinance institutions and Wall Street investment banks can find a way to work together to reduce poverty [9]*while/when* enabling the rich to stay rich. Speaking at a recent conference, he [10]*advised/suggested* his audience that [11]*for / in order to* achieve this, [12]*the former / the latter* would have to make some fundamental changes to the way they see their role in the twenty-first century.

Vocabulary check

1 Complete the text with the appropriate form of the following verbs.

pay off   loan   borrow   invest   deposit   save

Anwar Khan runs a small bicycle repair shop. He started his business when a microcredit bank agreed to give him a ¹_____ of $100. With the money, he was able to ²_____ in basic equipment and tools for his workshop. After two years in business, Anwar has ³_____ half of his debt to the MFI and he has also ⁴_____ a small sum of money which he has ⁵_____ in a savings account. He now intends to use that money as security in order to ⁶_____ the $500 that he needs to expand his business further.

2 Choose the correct forms of the words in italics.

1   We illustrate our strategic planning course with specific *case studies / tutorials*, which focus on what companies have done in the past.

2   All *trainees/trainers* will be given the choice of attending either an intensive seminar or regular weekly classes.

3   The HR department has announced that there will be a 15 per cent reduction in the training *course/budget* this year.

4   As levels of stress increase, this eventually leads *for/to* lower productivity.

5   In today's seminar, we are going to focus *at/on* some simple exercise techniques.

3 Complete the sentences with the following words, adding an appropriate suffix where necessary.

manage   finance   regulate   knowledge

1   The best way to _____ further development would be to sell a stake to a venture capitalist.

2   It's a pity that Jeff has decided to leave. He is one of the most _____ consultants we have.

3   New graduates always have the technical qualifications but not always the _____ skills needed to supervise staff at work.

4   The SEC acts as the official _____ for the stock exchange, and all listed companies have to comply with its rules.

5   The _____ year is divided into four three-month periods, or quarters.

6   Jane Farley has been promoted to CFO, and she will be joining our senior _____ team.

Career skills

Persuading

Match 1–5 with responses a–e.

1   Unless you're prepared to make an effort I'll have to consider terminating your contract.

2   All things considered, it would be best to postpone the launch for six months.

3   After looking at all sides of the argument, I'm recommending that we cancel the project immediately.

4   I think we should forget our differences and just focus all our efforts on finding a solution as quickly as possible.

5   What will happen if we lose the contract?

a   I agree there's no point in wasting any more money than we already have.

b   But then our competitors will get their products out first, won't they?

c   I don't see how you can say that. I've always done my best, and you know it.

d   I think we know that it's in all of our interests to make sure that doesn't happen.

e   You're right. After all, we're all in this together.

Motivating

Find and correct the mistakes in each sentence.

1   I'm going to let you to handle this.

2   It's in all everybody's interests to sell now.

3   Would you like taking responsibility for this?

4   Come on. You've got to do the better than that.

5   We're each in this together.

Reporting

Put the dialogue in the correct order.

☐ a   And what did they say exactly?

☐ a   What! They're not suggesting we get rid of it completely, are they?

☐ a   So, what did the European director have to say about that?

☐ a   I wonder what the outcome will be.

☐ a   So, what happened at the meeting?

☐ b   They said they wanted us to sell our European subsidiary.

☐ b   Well, the consultants gave us a full summary of their findings.

☐ b   In short, she is refusing to consider that.

☐ b   I'm afraid they are, yes. The bottom line is that we may have to close the whole business if we don't.

Pairwork

Unit 2 — page 22 Dilemma: Student A

One option is to purchase and install additional testing machinery at the factory in France to handle the additional production. You have estimated that you would need between five and six new machines. You are sure that they could be delivered within three months and installed in one to two weeks.

Unit 4 — page 40 Dilemma: Group A (Director of Information)

You represent the US parent company. For you the situation is clear: DigitalVisions has to comply with the new legislation and therefore all employees within the group must accept the new procedures. All employees of the group will be entitled to use the hotline to communicate information about misconduct or alleged misconduct. As far as you are concerned, this will be an advantage for the company as a whole as it will allow senior managers to detect problems that could eventually lead to litigation and prove very costly. It is in everyone's interests to accept the proposal for the hotline, which, in your view, will soon become the standard procedure in all major business organisations.

Unit 7 — page 66 Dilemma: Student A (Sweetface)

Guidelines for the negotiation:
- Annual turnover $100 million
- The legal conflict could delay long-term plans to expand the brand.
- Would 'Glow Industries' be prepared to sell the business and the rights to the name? At what price? How much compensation would they ask for?
- If Glow refuse to sell, you can threaten to take further legal action against them as you have recently acquired a company that also uses the 'Glow' name but which registered it before either Sweetface or Glow Industries were set up. You could sue Glow Industries for using the name.

Unit 10 — page 92 Dilemma: Group A (Non-governmental organisations)

The arguments that you would like to present are the following:
- The natural resources of developing countries should be exploited in a sustainable and environmentally friendly manner.
- Safeguards on pollution levels for fossil fuel projects (coal-fired power plants, etc.) are not respected and there are inadequate international controls.
- Unrestrained development of fossil fuels will create more problems than it will solve (greater use of vehicles for transport, industrial pollution, urban development).
- Statistics show that it is principally developed countries that use fossil fuel energy resources.
- Alternative energy sources must receive World Bank financing as this will help to bring the price down and to make them more cost-effective.

Unit 2   page 22 **Dilemma: Student B**

You think that a good long-term option would be to use an outside company and to conduct all testing externally. You know that there are several organisations that could do the work for you. Infineon would have to pay a fixed rate for each item to be tested. In addition to that there would be a set fee for reserving test capacity – in other words, Infineon would have to pay even when they had no need for the extra testing capacity.

Unit 4   page 40 **Dilemma: Group B** (European Director)

You were not informed of the exact text included in the directive that has been sent to the European subsidiary and neither you nor any member of your management team was consulted. The decision has been imposed on you from above. Your feeling is that it will prove to be a source of conflict among employees, managers and colleagues and may in fact create more problems than it solves. You are in favour of launching an extended discussion phase during which negotiations can be conducted between the different stakeholders to reach consensual agreement.

Unit 7   page 66 **Dilemma: Student B** (Glow Industries)

Guidelines for the negotiation:
* Annual turnover $2–3 million
* Further legal action could be extremely expensive and your budget is limited.
* Your plans to sell through major supermarkets may be compromised.
* It might be possible to sell the company and the rights to the name to Sweetface Fashion. Would they be interested? At what price?
* How would Sweetface compensate you for the effort in establishing the name 'Glow' and for the loss of business?
* If you win your case, you would receive a significant share of the profits made by Sweetface.

Unit 10   page 92 **Dilemma: Group B** (Energy industry representative)

The arguments that you would like to present are the following:
* The world economy needs to meet increasing demand for energy, and fossil fuels are the only available and reliable resource.
* Exploiting these reserves will provide employment and job opportunities around the world.
* The arguments used by environmental groups about the effects of fossil fuels on global warming may be exaggerated.
* Renewable energies are not a viable alternative (too costly and unreliable).
* Providing finance for fossil fuel projects will help to eradicate poverty.

Unit 8 page 74 Dilemma

Clearly Chic are a luxury handbag maker facing a similar dilemma to Burberry's, but with the added problem of cheap fakes of their most expensive models now flooding the market. Some people think the way to deal with the problems is to produce cheaper, more accessible models to a) encourage the new, trendier customer base and b) compete with counterfeit goods.

Prepare fully-developed arguments from the following notes.

The case for extension

Sales up
New target
People will only buy fakes if no extension
New price strategy needed to compete with fakes
New marketing strategies to exploit new target could be ...
Present target getting old

The case against extension

Sales increase only temporary
Young target influenced by trends
Risk losing loyal customers if ...
Risk losing brand image if ...
Cheaper versions give credibility to fakes
Need to reinforce notion of quality to beat fakes, not the contrary

Unit 15 page 133 Reporting: Student A

Production manager: I'm glad to get a chance to speak to you before you prepare your final report. I promised to keep team members informed.

Consultant: No problem.

PM: So, what have you come up with so far?

Consultant: Well, the results of the customer satisfaction survey are pretty bad, I'm afraid. There were a lot of negative comments about delays, high prices and poor quality. This seemed to suggest that the production department just isn't profitable anymore.

PM: So, what are you saying?

Consultant: Well, to be honest, we were thinking of suggesting outsourcing production, but a little further research revealed that your main problem can be solved by changing suppliers. So, we're going to recommend changing to more competitive, efficient and cost-effective suppliers. Do you think there will be any resistance to a change like this?

PM: I'll explain the alternative, which is job losses, and there shouldn't be a problem!

Unit 2 page 22 **Dilemma: Student C**

You are in favour of setting up a new, centralised testing plant that would handle all the testing for all the Infineon plants. The advantage would be that all testing could be planned centrally and co-ordinated with the other plants in the group. You do not yet have a precise figure for the investment that would have to be made to build, equip and staff the new facility. This will require further research.

Unit 4 page 40 **Dilemma: Group C** (Trade Union representative)

You and your members are very unhappy with the proposed code of conduct. You consider that the text of the document constitutes an invitation to employees to communicate confidential/private information about their colleagues. This is not only morally unacceptable, it is also in direct contradiction to the employment laws of several European countries where DigitalVisions operates. In your view, any accusation made against a fellow worker must be backed up by evidence to support the accusation and the person accused must be informed of the accusation and given an opportunity to defend themselves.

Unit 10 page 92 **Dilemma: Group C** (Developing countries)

The arguments that you would like to present are the following:

- Energy resources are vital for economic development.
- Fossil fuel resources can be exploited in a responsible manner, but only if the World Bank is prepared to provide the capital necessary to build plants with low pollution impact.
- Placing restrictions on fossil fuel development will prevent developing countries from exploiting their reserves and will increase poverty.
- Alternative energy can be introduced but fossil fuels can continue to be used at the same time.
- The World Bank has no right to dictate standards of behaviour to developing countries.

Unit 13 page 118 **Decision**

The Commercial French court instructed Morgan Stanley to pay €30m in damages to LVMH and appointed an expert to examine the case, which could lead to Morgan Stanley paying even bigger fines.

The president of the bank's French operation said the decision was bad news for investors both big and small. One fear is that the judgement will lead to analysts giving only positive reports of company performance in order to avoid legal action.

Section 2 Review

	two years ago	last year	this year
Turnover	$2m	$5.9m	$10.6m
Net income	-$3.0m	-$1.8m	$2.0m
Market share	5%	9.7%	11.5%
Number of registered patents	-	39	108
Number of licence agreements	-	5	15

Section 3 Analysis

Potential risks	competitors' development of rival products / economic downturn / availability of specialist staff / dependence on a limited number of major clients / research and production costs
Challenges	continuing development of commercially viable products

Section 4 Structure

Capital

Existing shareholders		
	Gary Patton	30%
	Francis Fairbank	30%
	Venture Associates	35%
	Employees	05%

Management board

Directors	Gary Patton, Francis Fairbank, Daniel Rivers, Bo Larrsen; two new directors will be appointed
Voting rights	Existing shareholders will retain majority
Employee stock options	All employees will be offered 2,000 shares

Section 5 Share offering details

Underwriter	Norman Gradwell Bank
Number of shares proposed	3 million ordinary shares
Price estimate	$10–$16 per share
Launch date	15 October
Auditors	Acclaim Inc.
Stock market	New Jersey Stock Exchange

Unit 2 page 22 Dilemma: Student D

Since all of the existing factories have their own test equipment you think that it should be possible to introduce a new process whereby products to be tested could be 'offloaded', or sent, to another factory which has available excess testing capacity. This would require standardisation of test procedures across the group, the development of an information system to transmit data to the relevant production plants and the setting up of transport and logistics.

Unit 10 page 91 Problem-solving

1 Statistics for accident rates at one of your factories show that there has been an unexplained rise during the last month. Journalists from a local television station have called to ask you for permission to visit the factory and interview workers.

2 Your department has finished developing a prototype personal music system, which you are now planning to bring to the production stage. You have contacted the only company that can supply the battery charger, which is a key component of the system. They have informed you they have just signed an exclusive agreement with a competitor and will not be able to supply you with the chargers.

3 Your company is seeking to qualify for a government subsidy as an environmentally friendly business. You have just been informed by the Department of the Environment that you will need to install an expensive new waste management system in order to qualify.

Unit 11 page 100 Dilemma: Group A (Bank representative)

The bank has only been able to secure firm commitments from their customers for 50 per cent of the 15 million shares that they are hoping to sell.

It is clear that the IPO will not be a success if it is launched at the current price of $30 per share.

The bank cannot afford to disappoint its professional investors by launching an unsuccessful IPO. There are now three options:

- further reduce both the price of the shares and the number of shares that will be offered for sale

- continue with the IPO under existing conditions

- cancel the IPO for the second time

1 Your manager agreed to allow you to take your summer holiday on specific dates during the month of August. He/She has just told you that you will have to take it at a different time as one of your colleagues has been given priority for the same dates.

2 Your sales manager is trying to impose minimum sales of 150 units per month for each sales representative. The reps have already reported that customers are unhappy with the quality of the products and that some are switching to a new competitor's products. You are a rep who feels that it is impossible to meet the target.

DIRECTOR A

You believe that Thums Up has a future as an independent company on the Indian market. In your view, it has various advantages over other western colas: the company is Indian and enjoys a reputation that differentiates it from its future competitors' brands. In addition to this, Thums Up has a stronger taste and appeals to a masculine audience who consider it to be revitalising. You would advise the company to enlarge its distribution network and invest in promoting its brand.

DIRECTOR B

You think that the arrival of the US cola companies will seriously reduce the market share of Thums Up. In your view, Indian consumers will quickly switch to the western brands, which will be backed up by massive publicity campaigns and sophisticated marketing techniques. You would advise the company to change its orientation and diversify into other sectors such as bottled water.

DIRECTOR C

You fear that Thums Up will not be able to resist the invasion of the market and that it will be unable to survive in the long term. You think that the company should negotiate with either Pepsi or Coca-Cola to see whether it would be possible to sell the brand to either competitor. You consider that it might be possible for Thums Up to negotiate a contract with one of the companies to become the official bottler of their products for the Indian market. You would use the proceeds to build up the other soft drink brands that Thums Up owns.

Hi Wire is already committed to a number of new ventures which it intends to finance with money from the IPO.

At the moment, the IPO is proposing 15 million shares at $30 per share.

Without this injection of capital, the long-term plans of Hi Wire would have to be modified.

If the bank has not been able to sell the IPO to its investors, you will have to consider the following options:

- further reduce both the price of the shares and the number of shares that will be offered for sale
- continue with the IPO under existing conditions
- organise the IPO as an internet launch without the support of the bank
- cancel the IPO for the second time

1 A **manager** is conducting an appraisal of an **employee**. On several occasions, the employee has had serious disagreements with his/her supervisor, who has complained about his/her lack of productivity at work.

2 A **computer engineer** has informed the **Director of Information Systems** that there is a potentially dangerous flaw in a software system. His/Her immediate superior has refused to give him/her time to work on finding a solution. The Director of Information Systems needs to ensure that the engineer somehow finds the solution.

3 A **machine operator** has informed the **production manager** that the machines in the workshop are now getting too old and require frequent maintenance, which is causing delays. He/She is suggesting that they are replaced with new machines, but these have not been budgeted for and the old machines will have to stay in service.

Team manager:	Hi, Terry, how are you?
Supplier:	Fine, thanks.
TM:	We have a big order to put in this month and it is pretty urgent.
Supplier:	What kind of deadline are we looking at?
TM:	Two to three weeks maximum.
Supplier:	I don't think we could meet that deadline. I could make you a priority but it would mean a bit of a price increase. You'll have problems finding anyone else in the market with the same quality – it might be worth your while doing a deal with us on this one.
TM:	Look, I'll be honest with you, I'll have to try to find someone else – a price increase won't be accepted in the present climate. I get the feeling our consultants are going to recommend outsourcing production if we don't become more cost efficient.

The following are quotes and extracts from press releases about the alliance between the two companies.

'I got straight onto a plane with a rucksack full of all the good things we do on the environment and safety and in the community and I went to Vermont to see them. I said: "Your choice is you can do your little thing in Vermont or you can be part of us and we can do it everywhere".'
Niall FitzGerald

'Neither of us could have anticipated twenty years ago that a major multinational would some day sign on, enthusiastically, to pursue and expand the social mission that continues to be an essential part of Ben & Jerry's and a driving force behind our many successes. But today, Unilever has done just that. We hope that, as part of Unilever, Ben & Jerry's will continue to expand its role in society.'
Ben and Jerry

Not only will Unilever continue to donate 7.5 per cent of Ben & Jerry's operating profits to charity, but it will use Ben Cohen and Jerry Greenfield to help design its social policy.

Under the terms of the agreement, Ben & Jerry's will operate with an independent board of directors, which will focus on providing leadership for the social mission and brand integrity of Ben & Jerry's.

NESTA decided to give all these companies grants to commercialise their products.

NESTA invested £70,000 in UTDR Research. A spokesperson from NESTA said, 'We are committed to supporting innovative ideas that can help to build a greener, more sustainable future. The UTDR team have found a novel way of dealing with a growing environmental problem and we are delighted to be providing the seed investment to help them to develop their tyre disposal system at this crucial stage of the project.'

Hypertag Ltd received their first financial aid package of £80,000 in 2002 to develop the technology. The Brooklyn Museum launched the 'pocket museum' in October 2004. NESTA said, 'These are exciting times for Hypertag, who have developed a technology that is so attractive to so many markets. It is great that a major US museum has seen the potential for using it for educational purposes.'

Nanosight received £100,000 investment from NESTA. Mark White, director of NESTA, said, 'We are delighted to be investing in this early stage of an idea which applies technology to areas which could have huge social benefits such as defence against the ever-growing threat of bioterrorism.'

Camfed received an investment of £150,000 from NESTA to help them to develop the prototype of their technology to engage major corporate customers. The market for consumer displays is huge. Sales are projected to exceed £10 billion by 2009.

Unit 6   page 56 **Decision**

Following the release of its new adventure game Danger Zone, the video manufacturer Wonder Image Inc has been asked by the ASC to withdraw its first TV commercial in support of the launch. The advertisement, which was first shown last week on national television, sparked a storm of protests from viewers and parents' associations. Bill Bradley, the director of the ASC, explained that the decision to ask the company to withdraw the commercial was taken because of its 'offensive nature': 'The ASC guidelines specify that all advertisements should be in good taste and should on no account promote violent behaviour – which unfortunately was not the case with the Danger Zone commercial.' A spokesperson for Wonder Image Inc said that the decision by the ASC to ban the commercial was 'an exaggerated response to an original and creative television campaign'. The launch of Danger Zone will proceed as planned but without the support of the television campaign, the spokesperson added.

Unit 9   page 82 **Decision**

When Dov Charney, the founder of American Apparel, went into the highly risky T-shirt manufacturing business, he famously said, 'We aim to seek profits through innovation not exploitation.' He refused to outsource and instead pays his employees $12 per hour as well as providing benefits such as healthcare, massages, English lessons and free use of the telephone. He has built up a loyal staff of 1,200 employees and after just six years in business, his turnover reached the $160m mark – higher than many of his direct competitors who outsource. His success proves that people are willing to pay for quality and do care about corporate image and reputation. He says, 'I make more money than my competition who pays 50 cents an hour, because of the efficiencies of dealing with someone face-to-face and paying them a fair wage. My vision is to build new economic models and new kinds of businesses that redesign the entire production, supply and distribution process in a way that makes more people happier.'

Unit 10   page 92 **Decision**

The Extractive Industries Review (EIR) has published its recommendations for the energy policy of the World Bank. Far from comforting the vested interests of the major players in the energy industry, the report has openly criticised the Bank for the way it has handled fossil fuel development projects over the last decade. For energy industry executives, the report reads like a nightmare: funding for coal-related projects should cease immediately and financial support for oil production should be phased out entirely within the next ten years. But the report goes further than that and highlights a number of negative effects that have resulted partly from the World Bank's energy policy. The list is a long one and includes environmental and human rights abuses which reveal an almost systematic failure to respect the rights of indigenous peoples and to protect sensitive ecosystems. As part of its recommendations, the commission has advised the Bank to devote 20 per cent of its future loans in the energy sector to the development of alternative energy projects. How much of the report will eventually become established World Bank policy, however, remains to be seen.

Glossary

acquisition n [C,U] when one company buys another one or part of another one: *Sales from a recent acquisition increased revenues to $85m.*

alliance n [C] an agreement between two or more organisations to work together: *The two companies agreed to form an alliance.*

bid n [C] an offer to buy something at a stated price: *They made a successful bid for an established company.* – bid v [I,T] – bidder n [C] – bidding n [U] Synonym offer n [C] Collocations *make a bid, accept a bid, reject a bid, takeover bid*

conglomerate n [C] a large business organisation consisting of different companies that have joined together: *TWE is a cable TV and film subsidiary of the world's largest media conglomerate.*

corporate culture n [C,U] the attitudes or beliefs that are shared by a particular organisation: *Working late hours seems to be part of the corporate culture.*

merger n [C] the creation of a new company by joining two separate companies: *The merger between the two biggest supermarket chains will have to be approved by the authorities.* – merge v [I,T]

multinational adj a multinational organisation has offices, factories, activities, etc. in many different countries: *Big multinational companies can earn huge profits.*

share n [C] a unit of the capital of the company. Shares in listed companies can be bought and sold on the stock exchange: *Investors are having to pay a higher price for the company's shares.* – shareholder n [C] – stockholder n [C] AmE – shareholding n [C] Synonym stock n [C] AmE Collocations *share capital, share certificate, share dealing, share issue, share price*

strategic alliance n [C] an alliance formed as part of a plan with important aims: *Singapore airlines and Lufthansa have announced a strategic alliance with broad implications for competition.*

synergy n [C,U] additional advantages, profits, etc. that are produced by two people or organisations combining their ideas and resources: *The companies could benefit from cost savings, as well as synergies from combining their manufacturing activities.* – synergistic adj

allocate v [T] to decide officially that a particular amount of money, time, etc. should be used for a particular purpose: *Du Pont has allocated funds for the design of four plants.* – allocation n [C,U]

budget n [C] the amount of money that an organisation has to spend on a particular activity in a given period of time: *The service operates on a very tight budget.* – budget v [I,T] – budgetary adj

contractor n [C] a person or company that makes an agreement to do work or provide goods for another company: *The company has no plans to expand its use of contractors.* – contract n [C]

control v [T] to limit something or prevent it from increasing too much; check that something is as it should be: *To help control costs, the company cut salaries by 12 per cent last month.* – control n [C] – controller n [C]

delay n [C] the situation in which something does not happen or start when it should do: *The government has been blamed for the delay in executing the project.* – delay v [I,T]

estimate v [I,T] to calculate what you think the value, size, amount, etc. of something will probably be: *The value of the deal is estimated at £12m.* – estimate n [C] – estimation n [C]

project n [C] an important and carefully planned piece of work that will create something new or improve a situation: *British Aerospace expected the project to be completed by 2005.* Collocations *project finance, project management, project manager, pilot project*

schedule n [C] a plan of what someone is going to do and by when they are going to do it: *We are running several weeks behind schedule.* – schedule v [T] Collocation *time schedule*

specifications n [usually plural] a detailed description of how something should be designed or made: *They delivered parts that did not conform to contract specifications.* Collocation *job specifications*

stakeholder n [C] a person or group of people who are considered to be an important part of an organisation because they have responsibility within it or receive advantages from it: *When a company is new and small it can stay close to its stakeholders – staff, customers and suppliers.*

subcontractor n [C] a person or company who is paid to do part of the work of another person or company: *Always check whether a contractor is using subcontractors, and who is liable if things go wrong.*

Unit 3   Teamworking

accomplish *v* [T] to succeed in doing something: *We accomplished all our goals on the last project.* – accomplishment *n* [C] – accomplished *adj*

assign *v* [T] to give someone a particular job or task: *The team leader will assign tasks to all the members of the team.* – assignment *n* [C]

collaborate *v* [I] to work with someone on a project: *The two teams collaborated well.* – collaboration *n* [U]

commit *v* [I,T] to agree to do something or say that someone else will do something: *Sorry, I've already committed myself to working on the other team.* – commitment *n* [U] – committed *adj*

co-ordinate *v* [T] to organise all the different parts of something to ensure an effective operation: *Your job is to co-ordinate the different aspects of the project.* – co-ordination *n* [U] – co-ordinator *n* [C]

deadline *n* [C] a date or time by which you have to do or complete something: *The team will never meet these deadlines; they're too tight!*

facilitator *n* [C] someone who helps a team to work together effectively: *A facilitator should remain neutral and ensure everyone follows the agreed ground rules.* – facilitate *v* [T]

feedback *n* [U] advice or criticism about how someone is doing their job: *I'm sure he'll improve if he gets positive feedback after each task.*

goal *n* [C] something that you hope to achieve in the future: *Our goal is to meet all the team's requirements.* Synonyms aim *n* [C] – objective *n* [C]

task *n* [C] **1** a piece of work that has to be done, especially one that has to be done regularly: *Scheduling is a key task for team leaders.* **2** a piece of work that is very difficult but important: *The team is facing the difficult task of installing a new accounting procedure.*

team *n* [C] a group of people who work together to do a particular job: *We have recruited an excellent management team.* Collocations team leader, team player, team spirit, teamwork

Unit 4   Information

data *n* [plural] information or facts about a particular subject that someone has collected: *We cannot tell you the results until we have looked at all the data.* Collocations data bank, data management, data mining, data processing, data warehouse

database *n* [C] an organised set of information stored in a computer: *A database of more than 14,000 training courses is being marketed by an information services company.*

gather *v* [T] to collect information, ideas, etc.: *Successful market research depends on the quality of the information that is gathered.*

hardware *n* [U] computer machinery and equipment: *The continued evolution of computer hardware imposes new challenges.*

information *n* [U] facts or details that tell you about something or someone: *Corporations are making more financial information available to investors.* Collocations inside information, information system, information technology

intelligence *n* [U] information that is collected about the activities of an organisation or individual: *We provide confidential reports and intelligence for companies operating in the biotechnology sector.* Collocations business intelligence, competitive intelligence

measurement *n* [C] the result of an evaluation of the size or dimension of something: *Precise measurements of business performance enable managers to make better decisions.*

network *n* [C] a set of computers which are connected to each other and operate as part of the same system, able to exchange information and messages: *Incoming orders are processed automatically by the computer network.*

procedure *n* [C] the accepted method and order of doing something in a formal situation: *We are currently reviewing our procedures for invoicing our customers.*

process *v* [T] to put information into a computer to be examined and to produce a particular result: *The accounts are processed by the central system.* – process *n* [C] – processor *n* [C] Collocations (electronic) data processing, word processing

software *n* [U] sets of programs put into a computer to perform particular tasks: *There's plenty of good software on the market to help us improve security.*

spreadsheet *n* [C] a computer program that can show rows of figures and perform calculations with them. Spreadsheets are often used to work out sales, taxes, profits and other financial information: *Most spreadsheets can transform data and figures into graphs and charts.*

surveillance *n* [U] the act of monitoring a person or group of people: *Employees must be notified if they are under surveillance at their workplace.*

Unit 5 Technology

chief technology officer abbreviation **CTO** n [C] the manager with the most authority concerning technology: *The Chief Technology Officer announced the company's intention to launch a new consumer electronics product next month.*

component n [C] **1** one part of something: *The microchip department is the main component of our technology division.* **2** one part used in making a piece of equipment: *TTPcom is a firm that designs and manufactures software components for satellite navigation systems.*

download v [T] to move computer software or information from one computing device to another: *You can now download music and video clips from the internet onto your mobile phone.* – download n [C]

invention n [C] **1** a new product that was not available before: *The paperclip was one of the most useful inventions of the twentieth century!* **2** [U] when something is made or designed for the first time: *Mobile phones have changed considerably since their invention.* – inventor n [C] – inventive adj

nanotechnology n [U] a science that combines computer technology and chemistry to build things from atoms: *Nanotechnology could allow us to invent devices that manufacture at almost no cost, by replicating atoms in the way that computers produce information.*

revolution n [C] a complete change in ways of thinking, methods of working, etc.: *Computer technology has caused a revolution in working practices.* – revolutionise v [T] – revolutionary adj

telecommunications n [plural] the process or business of sending and receiving information by telephone, television, the internet, etc.: *Telecommunications is one of the fastest growing industries today.*

upload v [T] to move computer software or information from one computing device to another especially from a local computer to a central server or network: *If you are uploading big files, you'll need a high-speed internet connection.* – upload n [C]

Unit 6 Advertising

audience n [C] the number or kind of people who receive a written or spoken message: *The ad was broadcast on all major channels, giving it an audience of millions.* Collocation *target audience*

billboard n [C] a large sign, usually outdoors, used for advertising: *The agency estimates that one million drivers pass their billboards every day.* Synonym hoarding n [C] AmE

campaign n [C] a series of actions intended to achieve a particular result: *We are launching a campaign to promote the new product.* – campaign v [I] Collocation *advertising campaign*

commercial n [C] an advertisement on television, radio, or at the cinema: *The campaigns were designed to run as television or cinema commercials.*

display n [C] an attractive arrangement of objects for people to look at or buy, for example in a shop: *There was a wide range of goods on display.* – display v [T]

exhibition n [C] a public event where businesses and other organisations show their products or services: *Exhibitions and trade shows are expensive but effective ways to promote products.*

media n [plural] the (mass) media are all the different ways of entertaining and giving information to the public and advertising goods, for example, television, radio, newspapers and the internet: *The company is keen to get its views across in the media.*

product demonstration n [C] an act of explaining and showing how a product works or how something is done: *We organise weekly, live product demonstrations.*

product placement n [C,U] when the maker of a product arranges for it to appear or be used in a film or television programme, as a form of advertising: *Product placement in video games is part of a new strategy by advertisers eager to reach the young consumer.*

promotion n [C] an activity such as special advertisements or free gifts intended to sell a product or service: *ABC has announced a joint promotion with Mullen.* – promote v [T] – promotional adj Collocations *seasonal promotion, promotional campaign, promotional price*

public relations abbreviation **PR** n [plural] the activity of telling the public about an organisation, person, product, etc. so that people think of them in a good way: *Good public relations is always good for a business.* Collocations *public relations officer (PRO), public relations agency*

publicise v [T] to give information about something to the public, so that they know about it: *Car makers are publicising a new generation of fuel-efficient vehicles.* – publicity n [U] – publicist n [C]

sponsor v [T] to give money to pay for a television programme, a sports or arts event, training, etc., in exchange for advertising or to get public attention: *Eagle Star Insurance sponsored the charity's first TV campaign.* – sponsor n [C] – sponsorship n [U]

telemarketing n [U] the practice of telephoning people in order to sell things: *Telemarketing can be used to update your client database.* – telemarketer n [C]

Unit 7   Law

attorney n [C] *AmE* a lawyer, especially one who represents clients and speaks in court: *A company spokesperson said that they would be seeking the advice of their attorneys.* Synonym lawyer n [C] *BrE*

damages n [plural] money that a court orders someone to pay someone else for harming them or their property, or causing them financial loss: *The group is facing claims for damages due to faulty components.* Synonym compensation n [U]

defendant n [C] the person or organisation in a court of law accused of doing something illegal or of causing harm to another person: *The defendant was accused of fraud and tax evasion.*

fee n [C] an amount of money paid to a professional person or organisation for their services: *Legal fees for registering a company range from $500 to $1,000.*

lawsuit n [C] a charge, claim or complaint against a person or an organisation that is made in a court of law by a private person or company, not by the police or state: *Local residents have filed a lawsuit over water pollution.* Synonym court case n [C]

legal action n [C,U] the process of taking a case or a claim against a person or organisation to a court of law: *The European Commission is threatening to take legal action in order to protect the environment.* Synonym litigation n [U]

legal department n [C] the service in a company or organisation that looks after all matters relating to questions of law: *Our legal department is preparing the new licensing agreement.*

litigate v [I,T] to take a claim or complaint against a person or organisation to a court of law: *Angry consumers have announced that they will litigate.* – litigant n [C] – litigation n [U] – litigious adj

settlement n an agreement to resolve a dispute before it is taken to court: *The two companies refused to disclose the financial details of their out-of-court settlement.*

sue v [I,T] to make a legal claim against someone, especially for an amount of money, because you have been harmed in some way. *The company was sued for non payment by their supplier.*

Unit 8   Brands

corporate identity n [C,U] the way in which a company uses similar designs and colours on all its products, advertisements, letters, etc. so that people will become familiar with the company: *People throughout the world recognise our company thanks to our strong corporate identity.*

creative director n [C] someone who is in charge of the work relating to producing advertisements and image campaigns for a company: *The new creative director wants the communications department to start working on a whole new image of corporate social responsibility for the company.*

distribution n [U] the actions involved in making goods available to customers after they have been produced, for example, moving, storing and selling the goods: *The company plans to establish a network of central warehouses to make product distribution more efficient.* Collocations distribution chain / channel / network

exclusivity n [U] the fact that a product is so expensive that not many people can afford to buy it: *Porsche highlighted its exclusivity by aiming at the high end of the luxury-car segment.* – exclusive adj

launch v [I,T] to show or make a new product available for sale for the first time: *The company is launching a new range of perfumes.* – launch n [C]

model n [C] a particular type or design of a machine or device: *This is the most expensive model in our range of luxury watches.*

positioning n [U] the way people think about a product in relation to the company's other products and to competing products, or the way that the company would like them to think about it: *A price reduction may have the effect of damaging the brand's image and positioning.*

pricing n [U] the prices of a company's products or services in relation to each other and in relation to those of competitors, and the activity of setting them: *Aggressive pricing helped increase our sales.* Collocations pricing agreement, pricing policy / strategy, pricing structure, discount pricing

target n [C] a limited group of people or area that a plan, idea, etc. is aimed at: *The main target for Gucci's watches is successful businessmen and women.* – target v [T] Collocations target audience / customers / group, sales target

Unit 9 Investment

angel n [C] a business angel is a private investor who puts money into new business activities: *In the UK, business angels are a more important source of investment for start-ups than venture capital funds.*

blue-chip shares n [plural] shares in a well-managed company with a record of paying profits to shareholders during good and bad economic conditions: *It's far less risky to buy blue-chip shares than to buy shares in a start-up.* Synonym blue-chip stock n [C,U] AmE Collocation *blue-chip company*

business plan n [C] a document produced by a company, especially a new company, giving details of expected sales and costs and how the business can be financed, and showing why the plan will make money: *The bank requires a three-year business plan from anyone applying for a loan for their company.*

dividend n [C] a part of the profits of a company for a particular period of time paid to the shareholders for each share that they own: *The company has announced a dividend of 25 cents per ordinary share.* Collocations *annual dividend, interim dividend, share dividend, dividend yield, dividend payment*

entrepreneur n [C] someone who starts a company, arranges business deals and takes risks in order to make a profit: *State governments had sought to promote economic growth by working closely with local entrepreneurs.* – entrepreneurship n [U] – entrepreneurial adj

forecast n [C] a description of what is likely to happen in the future, based on information that is available now: *The figures for 2015 are forecasts, the others are actuals.* – forecast v [I,T] Synonyms prediction n [C] – projection n [C] Collocations *economic forecast, profit forecast, sales forecast, to make a forecast, forecast growth*

fortune n [C] a very large amount of money: *He made a fortune by investing on the stock exchange.*

lucrative adj an activity, project, job, etc. that is lucrative makes a lot of money: *Investing in the Euro tunnel wasn't as lucrative as investors thought it would be.* Synonym profitable adj

portfolio 1 n [C] a collection of shares owned by a person or a company: *Over 50 per cent of his portfolio is in European shares and the rest is in American and Asian investments.* **2** all the products or services offered by a business: *The company has struck a deal with a biotechnology company of similar size and product portfolio.* Collocations *portfolio management, portfolio manager, portfolio mix*

trader n [C] someone who deals in shares, bonds, currencies, commodities (= oil, metal and farm products), etc. on a market, either for themselves or for a financial institution: *Traders are predicting that the dollar will rise in European markets.* – trade v [I,T]

venture n [C] a new business activity or project that involves risk: *Investors are always looking for business ventures that they think will show a healthy profit.* Collocation *venture capital*

Unit 10 Energy

alternative energy n [C] energy that is not derived from fossil fuels like petroleum and coal: *There is a growing number of firms engaged in alternative energy and power technologies.* Synonym renewable energy n [C]

crude oil n [U] oil in a natural condition, before it has been transformed in an industrial process in order to separate it into different products: *300 million tons of crude oil are exported every year.* Synonym crude n [U] (when used in the context of the oil industry)

end user n [C] the person who actually uses a particular product, rather than someone involved in its production or sale: *End users can often choose who they buy their electricity from.*

fossil fuel n [C] a fuel such as coal, gas or oil that is produced by the gradual decay of animals or plants over millions of years: *Fossil fuels currently account for about 90 per cent of world energy consumption.*

fuel n [C,U] a substance such as coal, gas or oil that can be burned to produce heat or energy: *The rising cost of fuel has prompted protests across Europe.* – fuel v [T]

gasoline abbreviation **gas** n [U] AmE a liquid obtained from petroleum, used mainly for producing power for the engines of motor vehicles: *The US alone consumes well over a hundred billion gallons of gasoline per year.* Synonym petrol n [U] BrE

ingredient n [C] a component or element that is added to form a compound or mixture: *Mineral oil and petroleum are the basic ingredients in many cosmetic products.*

nuclear power n [U] the energy, usually in the form of electricity, that is produced by a nuclear reactor: *The expansion of nuclear power depends substantially on politics.*

power plant n [C] a factory or building that generates electricity, usually by the burning of fossil fuels: *The new power plant will generate enough power to meet the annual residential needs of nine million people.*

reserve *n* [C] an amount of something valuable such as oil, gas, etc., kept for future use: *Most countries have a strategic reserve of petroleum which they can use if supply is interrupted.*

scarce *adj* if something is scarce, there is not enough of it available: *Demand is up, supply is dwindling and new finds are scarce.* – scarcity *n* [U]

shortage *n* [C,U] a situation in which there is not enough of something that people need or want: *Illegal exports and high world oil prices are the main causes of the current fuel shortage.*

sustainable *adj* an action or process that is sustainable can continue or last for a long time: *The benefits from sustainable fuels would be enormous.* – sustainability *n* [U] Synonym renewable *adj* Collocation *sustainable development*

Unit 11 Going public

analyst *n* [C] a specialist in a particular market or industry who gives advice and provides forecasts for that sector: *The company's senior oil analyst said that OPEC may need to cut production to balance the market.* – analysis *n* [C] – analyse *v* [T]

auction *n* [C] a public or online meeting where things are sold to the person who offers the most money: *70 per cent of ebay's sales are from auctions, and the remaining 30 per cent are from fixed price sales.* – auction *v* [T] – auctioneer *n* [C]

brokerage 1 *n* [C] a company or organisation that buys or sells securities, currencies, property, insurance, etc. for others: *The credibility of a brokerage or bank can disappear overnight.* **2** [U] the work done by a brokerage: *The electricity company saved $520,000 in brokerage fees by selling the bonds directly to investors.* – broker *n* [C] – broker *v* [T] Collocation *broker-dealer*

capital 1 *n* [U] money or property used to produce wealth: *Countries around the world are hungry for capital and economic development.* **2** money from shareholders and lenders that can be invested in assets in order to produce profits: *Because Mr Blech is injecting new capital, Ecogen said it is no longer seeking a buyer.* – capitalism *n* [U] – capitalist *n* [C] – capitalise *v* [T] Collocations *equity capital, fixed capital, issued capital, venture capital, working capital, capital equipment, capital gains, capital goods*

cartel *n* [C] a group of companies who agree to set the price of something they produce at a fixed level in order to limit competition and increase their own profits: *The oil cartel, OPEC, has just had its first major success in forcing up oil prices.*

commission 1 *n* [C] an amount of money paid to someone according to the value of goods, shares, bonds, etc. they have sold: *He didn't charge a commission on trades, as other brokers do.* **2** an official organisation that ensures that the law is obeyed in a particular activity: *The Equal Opportunities Commission works to eliminate sex discrimination.*

equity 1 *n* [U] the capital that a company has from shares rather than from loans: *The strong market will encourage companies to use equity to finance acquisitions.* Collocation *shareholder equity* **2** [plural] the shares of a company listed on the Stock Exchange: *Investors are placing funds in equities as they look for higher returns on their investments.*

initial public offering abbreviation **IPO** *n* [C] an occasion when a company offers shares on a stock market for the first time: *The government will sell 40 per cent of the company through an initial public offering.*

issue *v* [T] to make securities such as bonds and shares available for people to buy: *In January, AMR issued five million new shares.* – issue *n* [C] Collocation *share issue*

monopoly *n* [C,U] a situation where a business activity is controlled by only one company or by the government and other companies do not compete with it: *Many national airlines used to be monopolies, but this is no longer the case.* – monopolist *n* [C] – monopolise *v* [T]

Securities Exchange Commission abbreviation **SEC** *n* [U] the US agency responsible for stock market regulation: *The SEC is looking into a large US corporation's investment arrangements, as it thinks they may be illegal.*

stock exchange *n* [C] a market where company shares are traded: *Companies listed on the Madrid stock exchange dropped about 3 per cent this year.*

Wall Street 1 *n* [U] The New York Stock Exchange, situated in Wall Street in Manhattan. **2** American financial institutions and investors in general: *Wall Street analysts predicted that the issue would sell at 96 cents a share.*

Unit 12 Competition

barrier to entry *n* [C] any factor which prevents new competition from entering an industry, for example the need for a lot of capital or strict government regulations: *The aircraft engine industry has high barriers to entry and requires a lot of technological capital.*

competitive advantage *n* [C] an advantage that makes a company more able to succeed in competing with others: *Advanced Micro's chip carries the competitive advantage of using less power than Intel's.* Collocation *comparative advantage*

core business *n* [C] the business that makes the most money for a company and that is considered to be its most important and central one: *US car maker Chrysler is to sell off its $1 billion technology arm to concentrate on its core business.*

differentiate *v* [T] when a company differentiates its products, it shows how they are different from each other and from competing products: *The only viable strategy was to differentiate Citibank credit cards from all the low-cost alternatives.* – differentiation *n* [U]

economies of scale *n* [plural] the advantages that a big factory, shop, etc. has over a smaller one because it can spread its fixed costs over a larger number of units and therefore produce or sell things more cheaply: *Toys 'R' Us buys massive quantities directly from manufacturers and has gigantic stores with huge economies of scale.*

market share *n* [C,U] the proportion of the total market that is supplied by a particular company: *If the two companies' market shares are combined, they'll have 28 per cent of the US market.*

mass consumption *n* [U] buying and using products and services on a large scale: *Mass consumption has transformed not only industry but society as a whole.*

mass market *n* [U] the market for standardised consumer products: *We access the mass market by selling our clothing range in department stores.*

production 1 *n* [U] The process of making or growing things to be sold as products, usually in large quantities: *Toshiba is increasing production of its popular line of laptop computers.* **2** an amount of something that is produced: *In August, production of passenger cars climbed 12 per cent from a year earlier.* – produce *v* [T] – productive *adj* Collocations *just-in-time production, mass production, production costs, production line, production manager, production plant, production process*

profit margin *n* [C] the difference between the price of a product or service and the cost of producing it, or between the cost of producing all of a company's products or services and the total sum they are sold for: *Slow sales have cut profit margins in the industry.*

switch *v* [I,T] to change from one thing to another, usually suddenly: *Consumers are switching to more affordable brands.*

central bank *n* [C] the official bank of a country, which is responsible for setting interest rates, controlling the money supply, producing bank notes and keeping the country's supply of foreign currency and gold, etc.: *China's central bank said that a decline in interest rates is unlikely.*

clearing bank *n* [C] one of the high street banks that issues and accepts cheques and passes them through the banking system: *All cheques have to be authorised by the clearing bank before being accepted.* Synonym *commercial bank* *n* [C]

collateral *n* [U] assets promised by a borrower to a lender if the borrower cannot repay a loan: *When the firm went bankrupt, he lost his home because he had used it as collateral for the business.* Synonym *security* *n* [U]

exchange rate *n* [C] the price at which one currency can be bought with another: *If the euro-dollar exchange rate remains at its current level, US exporters could lose $5 billion in business annually.* Collocations *fixed exchange rates, floating exchange rate*

interest 1 *n* [U] an amount paid by a borrower to a lender, for example by a bank to someone who saves money with them: *Any spare cash is best put in a savings account where it can earn interest.* **2** the rate of interest at which a particular sum of money is borrowed or lent: *Small businesses have to pay interest at 12 per cent and upwards if they go through microfinance institutions.* Collocations *interest rate / rate of interest*

investment bank *n* [C] a bank that buys stocks and shares and then sells them to members of the public, and offers financial advice to businesses: *JPMorgan is a leading US investment bank specialising in asset management.* Synonyms *corporate bank* *n* [C] – *merchant bank* *n* [C]

monetary policy *n* [C] the way a central bank controls the amount of money in the economy at a particular time, for example by changing interest rates: *Unless the Bank of Japan relaxes monetary policy and makes borrowing easier, the stock market is unlikely to improve.*

speculate *v* [I] to buy goods, shares, property, etc. in the hope that their value will increase so that they can be sold for a profit: *Many individuals are now speculating on the stock exchange through special savings schemes provided by their banks.* – speculation *n* [U] – speculative *adj*

absenteeism n [U] the problem of employees not being at work when they should be: *We have a high rate of absenteeism, which is mainly due to stress.* – absent adj

customise v [T] to make, build or adapt especially for a customer: *Our training courses are customised to suit all our customers' specific needs.*

delegate n [C] someone who has been chosen by their company to attend a conference, meeting or training course: *We sent several delegates on a new management training course.* – delegate v [T]

incentive n [C] something which is used to encourage people, especially to make them work harder and produce more: *Training opportunities for staff can be more of an incentive than financial bonuses.*

motivation n [U] willingness, eagerness or desire to do something without being forced to do it: *Some of the staff seem to lack motivation.* – motivate v [T] – motivated adj – motivational adj Collocations *highly motivated, motivational skills, motivational techniques*

seminar n [C] a fairly informal meeting of a group of people, who share information and ideas and often discuss matters relating to work: *The people attending the management training seminar were all from accountancy firms.*

staff loyalty n [U] if staff are loyal to their company, they enjoy working for it, they keep company secrets and tend to stay for a long time: *The Human Resources department has built up staff loyalty by ensuring good working conditions, awarding regular bonuses and providing in-company training.*

stress n [U] continuous feeling of worry about your work or personal life that prevents you from relaxing: *He has been under a lot of stress at work recently, due to tight deadlines and staff shortages.* – stressful adj Collocations *stress-related (illness), stress management*

training n [U] the process of teaching someone or being taught the skills and knowledge for a particular job: *When the new software system was installed, we had to provide training for all the staff in how to use it.* – trainer n [C] – trainee n [C] Collocations *assertiveness training, computer-based training, management training*

audit 1 n [C] an official examination of a person's or organisation's accounts by an expert, to check that they are true and honest: *An audit of the company showed accumulated losses of $1.5 billion.* **2** an official examination of how an organisation behaves, how well it treats its employees, the environment, etc.: *The social audit of Ben & Jerry's commends the company, which gives 7.5 per cent of pre-tax profits to charity.* – auditor n [C] – audit v [T] Collocations *audit report, audit committee, ethical audit, external audit, social audit*

fraud n [U] a method of illegally getting money from a person or an organisation, often using clever and complicated methods: *The external auditor discovered the firm was involved in massive fraud.* – fraudulent adj

network n [C] a group of people or organisations that are connected or that work together: *It is important to build up a network of professional contacts.* – networking n [U] – network v [I]

outsource v [T] to transfer work to an outside supplier: *The company outsourced all their financial operations to an accounting consultant.* – outsourcing n [U] Synonym subcontract v [T]

Sarbanes-Oxley Act n US government legislation introduced to ensure honest accountancy and corporate governance practices in US companies: *The USA's response to Enron and other scandals was to introduce strict financial controls through the Sarbanes-Oxley Act.*

Glossary test

1. As profits are falling shareholders will have to accept a reduction in _____.
   - A salary
   - B bonuses
   - C dividends
   - D stock

2. My job involves carrying out various _____ simultaneously.
   - A tasks
   - B objectives
   - C goals
   - D practices

3. The computers in the R&D lab are getting too old. We really need to replace them with some new _____.
   - A inventions
   - B hardware
   - C telecommunications
   - D software

4. We acquired some sensitive and confidential _____ concerning our competitor.
   - A experience
   - B experiments
   - C intelligence
   - D secrecy

5. The bank will lend us money but they are going to charge 7.5 per cent _____ on it.
   - A repayments
   - B rates
   - C security
   - D interest

6. In some countries, there is already a _____ of fuel, and petrol stations only have limited supplies.
   - A shortage
   - B control
   - C speculation
   - D target

7. There are lots of free _____ available on their website.
   - A media
   - B incentives
   - C uploads
   - D downloads

8. We are working under extremely _____ conditions at the moment in order to finish on time.
   - A eventful
   - B stressful
   - C close
   - D short

9. We have been having difficulty reaching our sales _____, which was too high.
   - A audience
   - B market
   - C forecast
   - D pricing

10. The advertisements will be placed on _____ along the major highways leading into the city.
    - A exhibitions
    - B billboards
    - C placements
    - D commercials

11. The two sides agreed to a _____ six weeks before the court case was due to start.
    - A settlement
    - B lawsuit
    - C legal action
    - D compensation

12. _____ energies like wind power could provide more than 10 per cent of electricity needs within five years.
    - A Crude
    - B Fossil fuel
    - C Alternative
    - D Nuclear

13. The studio has negotiated product _____ with several sportswear and beverage producers, whose brand names will be featured in the new version of the film.
    - A demonstrations
    - B placements
    - C exhibitions
    - D displays

14. We employ specialist _____ to make all our transactions on the US stock exchange.
    - A capitalists
    - B entrepreneurs
    - C end users
    - D traders

15. The department has decided to _____ an extra £50k to cover the costs of hiring an outside consultant.
    - A budget
    - B control
    - C allocate
    - D estimate

16. The survey is going to _____ information about the Asian market.
    - A forecast
    - B gather
    - C upload
    - D publicise

17. Changing the colours and the design of our logo should help us to project a younger and more dynamic _____.
    - A corporate identity
    - B business plan
    - C competitive advantage
    - D corporate culture

18. The _____ is too tight. We need an extension if we are to accomplish our mission.
    - A time
    - B delay
    - C deadline
    - D shortage

19. We've arranged for an extra two million shares to be sold through our _____.
    - A brokers
    - B entrepreneurs
    - C auditors
    - D capitalists

20. We expect our team members to be _____ to their duties.
    - A concentrated
    - B involved
    - C committed
    - D immersed

21 We sent 100 _____ from our company to last year's seminar.

A suppliers B processors
C delegates D characters

22 The textile market is very risky but also very _____ if your business succeeds.

A costly B lucrative
C pricey D expensive

23 The organisers of the extreme sports festival are looking for companies to _____ the event.

A target B issue
C outsource D sponsor

24 If the court decides in their favour, the company will have to pay substantial _____ to the plaintiffs.

A allocations B fees
C damages D reserves

25 Over 20 per cent of our investment _____ is in US bonds.

A file B collection
C blue chips D portfolio

26 Performance bonuses will provide employees with an additional _____ to work more effectively.

A dividend B promotion
C incentive D ingredient

27 We will gain important _____ by combining our resources and working together.

A profits B additions
C extras D synergies

28 If our _____ are reduced any further, we may have to consider selling off the whole business.

A stock markets B profit margins
C business processes D target audiences

29 All our current products are _____ to suit our clients' specific needs.

A customised B transferred
C applied D invented

30 We don't have enough _____ to guarantee our bank loan.

A gains B collateral
C interest D accounts

31 When you say you'll buy something at a particular price, you're making a _____.

A bargain B fee
C quota D bid

32 _____ development is the only way to preserve natural resources for future generations.

A Scarce B Lucrative
C Sustainable D Speculative

33 Our public _____ agency will be sending out press releases and organising a series of press conferences.

A broadcasts B relations
C promotions D media

34 Our _____ managed to convince the judge that the accusations were totally unfounded.

A defendants B plaintiffs
C litigants D attorneys

35 Great. We're almost halfway through the project and everything is exactly on _____.

A specification B schedule
C goal D process

36 The national airline still has a _____ as no one else is allowed to offer flights within the country.

A cartel B synergy
C multinational D monopoly

37 The high rate of _____ is due more to lack of motivation than illness.

A mismanagement B absenteeism
C lateness D unemployment

38 The company is expanding by _____ with one of its competitors.

A purchasing B associating
C sharing D merging

39 The investment bank is asking for a 7 per cent _____ for organising the IPO.

A equity B capital
C commission D brokerage

40 According to the _____ that we have received, the components will have to resist temperatures of 500°.

A specifications B schedules
C goals D processes

Grammar reference

Review of tenses

The present simple has the following uses.

- regular events and repeated actions
  The company's annual report **is published** every June.
- permanent situations
- They **manufacture** electrical goods.
- timetables and scheduled events
  The CEO **arrives** on Friday.
- newspaper headlines
  Miramax **signs** deal with Disney.

The present continuous has the following uses.

- things happening now and changing situations
  We're **negotiating** an alliance with them.
- temporary situations
  We're **not looking** for partners this year.
- future arrangements
  We're **signing** the contract next week.

The present perfect has the following uses.

- changes that affect the present
  Have the shareholders **been informed** yet?
- situations relating to an unspecified past time
  We **have agreed** to share technologies.
- situations that started in the past and continue
  Costs **have been rising** for several years.
- show duration
  He's **been** the CEO for ten years.

The past simple has the following uses.

- finished actions and events
  We **worked** with them for two years.
- definite or finished time periods
  We **merged** with them last year.

The past perfect has the following uses.

- give explanations about past events
  We were celebrating last night because we **had signed** the agreement.
- give background information
  By the time of the acquisition, negotiations **had taken** nearly a year.

will + infinitive has the following use.

- predictions
  The merger **won't be** finalised until next month.

See also Future forms on page 161.

Articles

The indefinite article has the following uses.

- non-specific singular countable nouns
  It will be supervised by **an** internal management team.
- singular things and people in general terms (definitions, jobs, nationalities)
  A deadline is the time limit for completing **a** task.
  Tina is **an** architect. She's **a** Brazilian who lives in New York.
- in certain expressions
  a few, **a** little, **a** great many

The definite article has the following uses.

- nouns already mentioned or specified
  BAA is building a new terminal.
  The terminal will have ...
- things and people that are unique or one of a kind
  The CEO wants it to be finished by May.
- categories or groups of things and people
  The mobile phone has changed communications completely.
- the superlative form of adjectives
  The biggest challenge will be co-ordinating the work of four international teams.

The is pronounced in two different ways.

- Before a word that begins with a consonant sound, it is pronounced / ðə /.
  The deadline is only two months away.
- Before a word beginning with a vowel sound, it is pronounced / ði /.
  The engineers have modified the design to make it lighter.

No article is needed with the following.

- proper nouns and names
  Heathrow will have to be expanded again before very long.

- plural things and people in general terms and uncountable nouns
  Projects of this type are generally managed by specialists.
  Time and money are key considerations.
- abstract nouns
  Hope alone won't get us through this.

Modal forms

Uses of modal forms include the following.
- possibility
  We may / might / could get more people working on the project.
- obligation
  There must be good working relationships between team members.
- advice
  The team should / ought to be experienced enough by now.
- deductions
  positive: *They're not back home yet; they must be working late.*
  negative: *They're very late. They can't know the time of the meeting.*

Past modals have the following uses.

- possibility about a past situation
  The misunderstanding may / might / could have been caused by a lack of communication.
- advice about a past situation
  You should have / ought to have organised that meeting better.
- deductions about a past situation
  positive: *The team must have been very tired after working all weekend.*
  negative: *They can't have done their research properly.*

Question forms

There are four main types of question.

- open questions
- closed questions
- tag questions
- embedded questions

Open, or *wh-*, questions ask for information. They use interrogative words such as *what, when, where, why, who(m), which, how, how long.* (How is often quantified with *much, many, often, long, big, expensive …)*

Open questions generally use an auxiliary.

Who does this computer belong to?

When *who*, *what* or *which* is the subject of the question, no auxiliary is used.

Who uses this computer?
(not Who ~~does use~~ this computer?)

Closed questions expect the answer *yes* or *no*.

Have you finished installing the software?
No, not yet.

Tag questions are used in the following two ways.

- to check information or seek agreement for an opinion
  You'll be arriving at midday, won't you?
  This is really complicated, isn't it?
- to ask a genuine question
  You're dealing with this, aren't you?

Intonation

In spoken English, the intonation the speaker uses tells us what type of tag question it is. If someone uses falling intonation at the end, they are checking information or seeking agreement; if they use rising intonation at the end, they are asking a genuine question.

Tag questions consist of a statement followed by a tag in the same tense; if the statement is in the affirmative, the tag will be in the negative, and vice-versa. Negative tags always use a contraction.

You will be able to get the information, won't you?

In some tag questions, both the statement and the question can be in the affirmative. This indicates surprise or interest. The intonation for this type of question is always rising at the end.

So you are coming to the presentation, are you?

Embedded questions are used to ask questions in a polite way. They have an interrogative question form which introduces a statement.

The answer to an embedded question is always a response to the statement and not to the question that introduces it.

*Could you tell me **how long** it will take to repair the system?*
***It will take** at least two hours, maybe more.*
(not ~~Yes, I could ...~~)

For open questions, an interrogative word is used.

*Do you know **how much** the software costs?*

For closed questions, ***if*** or ***whether*** is used.

*Do you know **if/whether** this software is very expensive (or not)?*

Embedded questions can be introduced by questions such as:

Can/Could you tell me ... ?
Would you mind letting me know ... ?
Do you happen to know ... ?

Embedded questions can also be introduced by tentative statements.

*I wonder **if/whether** you could explain ...*

Relative clauses

Defining relative clauses define or differentiate the person or thing they refer to.

*I'm talking about the phone **that takes photos**.*

The following relative pronouns are used to introduce a defining relative clause.

who, *that* (for people); *which*, *that* (for things); *whose* (possessive)

The relative pronoun can be omitted when it is the object of the clause.

*The scientists **(who/that)** we were working with were highly qualified.*
*The task **(which/that)** they set themselves was almost impossible.*

Non-defining relative clauses add non-essential information to a sentence.

*The phone, **which has been on the market for a month**, is our latest model.*

The relative pronoun can never be omitted and *that* cannot be used.

We usually use commas to separate the non-defining clause from the rest of the sentence.

Non-defining relative clauses are not generally used in spoken English.

In formal English, *whom* can be used as the object in both types of clause.

Shortened relative clauses can be used when the subject of each clause is the same. Either the present participle or past participle (when the verb is in the passive) is used instead of the relative pronoun + main verb.

The designers who develop the best model will win a prize.
➡ *The designers **developing** the best model will win a prize.*

New technology, which is introduced into this industry all the time, is essential if we want to progress.
➡ *New technology, **introduced** into this industry all the time, is essential if we want to progress.*

Gerunds and infinitives

Gerunds have the following uses.

- after prepositions
  *Before **launching** the campaign, the agency did extensive market research.*
- as a noun
  ***Finding** the right person to endorse a product is never easy.*
- after certain expressions
  *It's no good **trying** to sell it now.*

Key words

be/get used to, have difficulty, it's no good, it's no use, it's not worth, look forward to, object to, there's no point

- after certain verbs
  *He proposed **using** TV commercials.*

Key words

admit, avoid, consider, delay, deny, discuss, dislike, enjoy, finish, go, go on, hate, imagine, involve, keep, like, mention, miss, postpone, practise, prefer, propose, recommend, report, risk, suggest

- instead of a relative pronoun + main verb
  *There is a new series of commercials **advertising** their products.*

Infinitives have the following uses.

- after adjectives
  *They are unlikely **to ban** the advert.*

- show purpose
  *The company is sponsoring an extreme sports event **to raise** their profile.*
- after certain verbs
  *They have decided not **to run** the commercial before 10pm.*

- after certain verbs + object
  *I urge you **to think** carefully about the content.*

- after certain nouns
  *Competitors make every attempt **to find** new angles.*

Some verbs can be followed by either a gerund or an infinitive with no difference in meaning.

*The agency continued **promoting** the product despite poor sales.*

*The agency continued **to promote** the product despite poor sales.*

Some verbs can be followed by either a gerund or an infinitive but with a difference in meaning.

*He stopped **sending** emails. (He didn't continue the activity.)*
*He stopped **to send** an email. (He interrupted what he was doing in order to do something else.)*
*They remember **placing** the ad. (refers to past)*
*Remember **to place** the ad. (refers to future)*

The passive

Passives have the following uses.

- when the agent is unknown, unimportant or implied
  *Exactly how the accounts **had been falsified** is still not clear.*
- when the agent has already been referred to
  *The judge ruled in favour of the plaintiff, who **was awarded** substantial damages.*
- processes, systems or experiments
  *First, the jury **is selected** and then a date **is fixed** for the case **to be heard**.*
- report unconfirmed information
  *Several people **are alleged to have been involved** in the scandal.*

Adjectives and adverbs

Adjectives have the following uses.

- before nouns
  *An **interesting** and **exciting** campaign is essential if the launch is to be successful.*
- after stative verbs such as be, appear, look, feel, remain, etc.
  *I'm **interested** in and **excited** about the brand.*

Adjectives ending in -ing describe what things are like and the effect they have on people.

Adjectives ending in -ed describe how we feel.

Adverbs have the following uses.

- after verbs
  *Their image deteriorated **rapidly** after the scandal.*
- before an adjective or another adverb, as an intensifier
  *They experienced an **extremely** fast decline.*
  *The new branding worked **really** well.*

- before past participle adjectives to show how something is done
  Well-*made accessories are part of the range.*

Some adverbs have irregular forms: **well, hard, fast, early, late.**

Adverbs cannot be formed from adjectives ending in -ly, for example *friendly, lively, silly, lovely.* A phrase such as *in a ... way* is used instead.

*Clients are always greeted **in a friendly way** and made to feel at home.*

Emphasis

Emphasis is placed on a particular part of a sentence in the following ways.

- *what ... is/are that ...*
  What *research has shown **is that** long-term investment produces positive results.*
- *it is ... that ...*
  It is *the art market **that** interests us now.*
- inversion after negative sentence openers
  Never *have we seen such terrible share prices.*
  No sooner *had we announced the CEO's resignation than the share value collapsed.*
  On no account *should you invest in art at the moment.*
  Under no circumstances *will we sell our current assets.*
  Not only *is this a good time to invest **but also** to speculate on the stock market.*
- inversion after *only, rarely, little*
  Only *in the property market can prices fluctuate so much.*
  Rarely *does investing in blue-chip companies fail to make money.*
  Little *did I know that the market was going to take off like this.*

Conditionals

Conditional sentences have the following uses.

Zero conditonal

- cause and effect
  *If Opec **increases** production, prices **fall**.*
- request action in the event of a likely situation
  Let *me know if you **get** any more information.*

Type 1

- predict consequences of likely situations
  *The company **will have** to stop production if the political situation **does not improve**.*
  *The company **will have** to stop production **unless** the political situation **improves**.*

Type 2

- predict consequences of unlikely or hypothetical situations
  *If we **had** a better distribution network, **we'd (would) be** able to sell more.*

Type 3

- hypothetical situations in the past
  *If we **had used** a better shipping company, the accident **would never have happened**.*

Mixed conditionals (Types 2 and 3)

*I **would be** in a better position today if I **had accepted** the job.*

*If I **thought** the project wasn't going to be successful, I **would never have invested** all this money.*

Future forms

Different tenses are used to refer to the future depending on the situation and the likelihood of something happening.

will + infinitive has the following uses.

- things that are part of a future plan
  *Our CEO **will make** a statement later today.*
- tentative predictions
  *I think the company's shares **will continue** to increase in value.*
- spontaneous decisions or offers
  *I know – **I'll invest** in that new start-up!*

going to + verb has the following uses.

- personal intentions or predictions
  *She **is going to sell** all her shares and buy bonds instead.*

Modals have the following use.

- predictions about things that are possible
  *They **may / might / could raise** the capital on the markets.*

The present simple has the following uses.

- timetabled events
  The conference **begins** at 9:00am.
- conditions necessary for a future event to happen
  If the price **falls** any further, I'll sell.

The present continuous has the following use.

- events arranged for a certain time
  I'm meeting our advisers next week to discuss our strategy.

The future continuous has the following use.

- actions in progress at a time in the future
  We **will be organising** a presentation for our investors on the 21st.

The future perfect has the following use.

- things that will take place before something else happens
  The London stock exchange **will have been closed** for several hours by the time the Asian exchanges **open** for business.

Time clauses

Time clauses give information about the duration or timing of an event or events which are referred to in the main clause.

- present
  The markets **send** in information about sales as soon as they **receive / have received** it.
- past
  The firm **had** its first major success when it **introduced** disposable pens.

When a time clause refers to an event that will happen in the future, the verb in the time clause is in the present or present perfect and the verb in the main clause is in the future. (Using the present perfect emphasises the completeness of the action.)

We'll **call** you as soon as we **get / have got** the results of the survey.

Reference words

The following are used to refer to previously mentioned words, phrases or ideas.

- the one, the ones
  We are currently developing a new range of customer investment portfolios. However, we can only offer **the** old **ones** for the moment.
- such
  We've had a substantial increase in complaints from our corporate clients recently. We cannot allow **such** a trend to continue.
- the former, the latter
  We advised our client to set up businesses in Latin America and East Asia. **The former** has proved to be a great success, whereas **the latter** has resulted in very little profit.
- this, that, these, those
  Microfinance institutions (MFIs) lend sums of money to people in developing countries with no collateral. **That** may seem very risky, but loans are nearly always repaid.
  The banking sector has four main types of institution: **these** include central and commercial banks.

The ones can have the same meaning as *those*, but is generally used in spoken English and in less formal written English.

Where are the figures? You know, **the ones** we need to show to our client.

Clauses and sentence construction

Complex sentences contain a main clause and one or more subordinate clauses which give additional information. The following are the principal types of subordinate clause.

- Relative clauses (see page 159)
- Conditional clauses (see page 161)
- Time clauses (see above)

Clauses of purpose

- show the intention or purpose of an action
  We've decided to offer more standard features **in order to** match what the competition is doing.

Other conjunctions that are used in this type of clause: *to, so that, in order that, so as to*

Clauses of concession

- show contrast between two statements
  We're still planning to enter the Asian market **despite** the fact that we don't have distributors in some countries.

Other conjunctions that are used in this type of clause: *in spite of, although, though, even though, even if, while, whereas, except that*

Clauses of manner

- give information about how something happens or is done
  Why does the sales manager act **as if** he is the only person who understands what marketing is all about?

Other conjunctions used in this type of clause: *as, just as, like, as though, as much as*

Clauses of result

- show the consequences of an action
  We've received a lot of complaints **so** we're allowing customers to exchange their products for new ones.

Other conjunctions used in this type of clause: *so that, as a result of which*

This type of clause is often preceded by so + adjective or such + noun.

The new version has been **so successful that** some stores are already out of stock.

The new version has been **such a success that** some stores are already out of stock.

Clauses of reason

- give information about why something is done
  The product is outselling all the others **because** it's better and less expensive.

Other conjunctions used in this type of clause: *as, in case, since*

Reported speech

We often make tense, time and pronoun changes in reported speech.

'He **was here yesterday**.' ➡ She said (that) he **had been there the day before**.

We don't always make these changes, especially if a fact is still true or we're reporting soon after the direct speech.

'Jan **is leaving** in a minute.' ➡ She said (that) Jan **is leaving** in a minute.

Verbs apart from *say* and *tell* used to report speech can be followed by:

- a clause
  'The advice wasn't very helpful.'

  She **pointed out** (that) the advice wasn't very helpful.

Key words

complain, explain, feel, imply, point out, report, suggest

- an infinitive
  'I'll reduce the fees if you like.'
  He **agreed to reduce** the fees.

Key words

agree, ask, decide, demand, offer, promise, refuse, want

- an object + infinitive
  'You should lower your prices.'
  They **advised us to lower** our prices.

Key words

advise, ask, instruct, invite, remind, warn

- a gerund
  'Let's go over the figures again.'
  He **suggested going** over the figures again.

Key words

admit, deny, mention, report, suggest

When there is a change of subject, a clause has to be used instead of the gerund.

'Why don't you go over the figures again?'

He **suggested** (that) **I go / went over** the figures again.

Audioscripts

It's nice to see 'a perfect match' alliance – it is so rare! But when Starbucks and Pepsico got together to create the popular coffee-flavoured drink 'frappuccino', it was a great success for both companies. You see, Starbucks wanted to get into the bottled drinks market and this was a perfect way to do it, and Pepsico was interested in creating an innovative product, which they did. Each company met their strategic goals!

Well, you know, I have to say the Daimler-Chrysler merger got off to a bad start. That was mainly because they had very different corporate cultures. But they worked hard to sort out their differences and problems, and everything came right in the end. They had to make sure it did, really, because even though they were powerful players in the automotive industry, they both felt that they couldn't face the competition alone.

As for Disney and Miramax, well, when you think about it, it didn't have a chance from the start. They are so different it couldn't succeed. But Miramax needed the cash and Disney is a very rich company. Disney liked the serious image which Miramax brought and wanted to be linked with that image. But how could the controversial and serious movies of Miramax ever find anything in common with the Disney family movies? Personally, I wasn't that surprised it failed.

Part 1

Well, it hasn't been easy, but we've started to make an excellent recovery and today we've been rewarded for our determination. I have to say the last few years have probably been the most exciting years of my career so far. As you all know, we had lost so much money by 2002 that when Wireless Ltd approached us with the acquisition deal, it looked like the solution to all our problems. We therefore saw the opportunity of an alliance with Wireless as a way to save the company. However, six months into the alliance, we didn't feel like that any more. We had really serious problems trying to integrate our systems and cultures. Our corporate culture was so different from theirs that we worked in a completely different way from them. It was a very difficult time but even so, when they decided that they didn't want an alliance with us any more, it was still quite a shock. We didn't know what to do. By the end of 2003, we needed another strategic partner. The only other alternative was to find a sympathetic bank that would lend us enough money to make a new start independently. We are delighted that the second option was possible and we managed to borrow money to keep operating on our own. So you can imagine how extremely proud I am to be here today to accept this technology company award. Now, I'd like to take this opportunity to thank all the people who ...

Part 2

Well, there were so many points of contention you wouldn't believe it! But, well, I suppose that's not unusual with alliances of all kinds. Different companies often have conflicting approaches to different aspects of doing business. Our first problem was that we managed sales and marketing in a completely different way. I mean, sales and marketing are the basics of running a business, so that created serious problems. The second difficulty was that their products were different from ours. To make an acquisition work, you have to understand how products will work together. We never managed to deal with the differences in products. Then there's communication, which also tends to be quite different from one organisation to another. We have always encouraged our teams to work together, but the bosses at Wireless preferred to interact separately with each team. So, the ways of teamworking differed greatly, too! Yeah, and lastly, and perhaps most importantly, we didn't manage to build relationships with the people at Wireless. It seems so obvious now, but at the time we didn't think of trying to overcome our relationship problems by having some human contact and develop, er, well, *relationships* with their people. We simply never sat down together and discussed all these problems.

A   We're based in Liverpool.
B   So are we. What line of business are you in?
A   We're in video games – and you?
B   We make metal pipes.
A   Oh, really! Where are your main markets?
B   Actually, we've just had a huge order from China.
A   I'm very interested. We are sending a sales delegation to Beijing next month. In fact, we are thinking of sending the team on a cultural awareness programme organised by Culture Plus. Have you heard of them?
B   Yes, we were also thinking of working with them. Maybe we could put our teams together and get a group rate? What do you think?
A   Sounds like a good idea. Look, here's my card. Why don't you give me a call ... ?

It's never easy to give golden rules for project management, and that's because the nature of all projects is that they're fluid – things change, problems appear and you just can't predict exactly what will happen. But, of course, there are guidelines that project managers have to follow and there are a number of tools to help them. I always say that all the phases of a project are critical but that some are more critical than others. And for me, the two most critical ones are initiating and planning. Initiating is critical because if the project doesn't have solid foundations, then it just shouldn't happen. So you have to look at the project as a whole and ask yourself: Is the project feasible? Will it add value? One way to get the answers is by preparing a project overview, or project charter, which lays out the purpose and the strategy behind the project. Once you've done that, then the next phase, planning, becomes much easier. When you plan, you have to do a lot of things – allocate resources, forecast costs, prepare a budget and time schedule and, above all, evaluate the risk factor. Perhaps equally important is selecting the project team because if you've got the right people working together, you're more likely to succeed. If the first two phases have been well prepared, then executing should be relatively easy, especially if you've thought through the potential problems and developed contingency plans if things go wrong. Delivery – well, again, if you've done the planning, you should be able to deliver the project on time and within the specifications. But if you haven't, then there's not much chance of that happening.

Unit 2   Listening 2 page 21

1

Project manager: So, Sylvia, are you ready to take on the market research side of the project?

Sylvia: Well, I really need some more detailed information. What exactly would be involved?

PM: Well, I don't have the specifics yet but I can give you a general idea. We're planning to create a new range of beauty products for women in the Asian and Arab World markets. We're convinced there's a market out there but we need to do some basic research to find out more about the products that are already being used.

Sylvia: OK. So you want us to conduct some interviews and prepare a full market report, is that it?

PM: Yeah. That's exactly it. Your report will tell us what sorts of products we need to design.

Sylvia: So, how many interviews will I have to arrange?

PM: I don't know exactly, but we can discuss that later on. And don't worry, I'm sure the Asian office will be able to help us with all that. That way, you can just focus on the data.

Sylvia: OK. But what about dates? When do I have to get this in by?

PM: Let's say six weeks from now. Does that sound reasonable?

Sylvia: There's no way we can do it by then! I'd say it'll take at least two months, if not more.

2

PM: Thanks for agreeing to do the product development work, Alex. It's great to have someone with your experience working with us.

Alex: No problem. I've read the project summary and this is exactly the sort of thing that we're good at. I'm very happy to be involved. So, what's the schedule for this?

PM: First, we have to get the basic information from the markets before we draw up the final specifications for a full range of beauty products. Once we have those, then I think we should aim to have everything ready for production in six months. Will that give you enough time?

Alex: Yeah, that should be OK. But I'd like to know exactly how much we can spend on all this. How much are you budgeting for our side of things?

PM: Well, I've given you a provisional budget of 50k for your team for all the development work. That's to include testing and production of a full range of samples. But I'll need you to give me full details of your exact costs.

Alex: Ah, no problem with that. I'll give you all the details once I get the specifications.

Unit 2   Decision page 22

Well, in this case we really had to move very quickly. There was no way that we could deliver products that had not been tested to our customers. So the priority was first to determine which solutions were feasible in the time we had available. That eliminated the option of building a separate testing plant, simply because there wasn't enough time to complete it. The three remaining options were all equally feasible. So then it became a question of choosing the solution that would be the most cost-effective. In fact, the one that was selected was 'offloading' testing to the factories that had excess capacity, and that was chosen mainly because it would be cheaper for the company and it would also be a solution that could be used systematically whenever the same problem occurred at any of the plants. I was the project manager and that was my job for the next six months. It was a lot of work co-ordinating all the different factors, but in the end it worked out fine and we still use the system today. For me, it taught me that the most obvious solutions are not, in fact, always the best. Because, of course, we could have just gone and bought testing machines and installed them directly.

Unit 3   Listening page 29

A ... so, here are the designs I've done so far – see any problems?

B Hmm, I'm not sure that I can. You've done a great job on these. How long will it take to finish them, do you think?

A That's the thing I'm worried about. Er ...

B Go on ... that's what we're here for.

A Well, I'm a bit stuck for time. I've got so much to do this week, I'm afraid I might not meet our deadline.

B I'm sure we can work this out. Maybe I could get some of the other stuff done and you can concentrate on these.

A Great – then I should be able to get these in on time.

B If anyone can do it, you can!

Unit 3   Decision page 30

Well, actually, I think it is pretty evident what the team leader should do in cases like this. Team leaders should be very cautious about judging a team's decision. If the proper process was followed and team members are behind the decisions and results, then the team leader should present the findings as just that: the team's decision. Of course, the parameters of the task should have been shared fully with the team at the beginning. This wasn't the case, but under the circumstances, the team offered seemingly practical ideas. In fact, you know what, presenting the team's ideas would have been a perfect example of leadership! Who knows, management may even have approved a budget for the team's suggestions.

Ideally, the leader should focus on the aims of the brief and provide resources to help the team achieve those aims, but should not influence the team's decision-making or, worse, make decisions for them.

Unit 4   Listening 1 page 34

Interviewer: What is an intranet?

Jennifer: An intranet is an area where people in a company can share information of all sorts, and it can be accessed by everybody within a company, however large that company is.

Int: How many staff regularly use the intranet?

Jennifer: It's very difficult to say because we don't actually see where the people who are using it come from, but from the number of hits we can average that at least 50 per cent of the company use it all the time.

Int: What are the most popular parts of the intranet?

Jennifer: I would say generally the most important bits that get used most of the time are the what's new section, er, maybe the special offers, definitely the staff directory and of course useful links giving access to all sorts of things outside the company.

Int: What are the biggest challenges in managing the intranet?

Jennifer: The biggest challenge is trying to keep the information current and trying not to overload the site with too much information. As our intranet has contributors from all over the different areas of the company, we don't want people to duplicate information, so we have to keep our eye on what goes on, so that we can continually weed out anything that's unnecessary.

Int: What are the main security issues for the intranet?

Jennifer: Well, it won't be possible for anybody outside a company to actually access an intranet site. However, of course there is always the possibility of people downloading information and emailing it to people, so we do have to make sure we don't put really sensitive information about our company on the intranet. Also, we don't put photographs of people there unless they give us their permission as there is a slight risk of someone actually picking up a photograph and using it for some purpose. These are very, very minor risks but we do take them into consideration.

Int: Who supplies the content for the intranet?

Jennifer: For our intranet site, we have content supplied by everyone within the company. Anyone can ask if they can have something on the intranet. We just have to edit it like we would a newspaper and try to keep certain things, some certain criteria, in our minds.

Int: How has the intranet's role developed since it began?

Jennifer: It's grown enormously. To begin with, intranet sites just used to give people very minor information, but it's rather like a magazine now and because people use it a lot, more information can go onto it, and people will want to access it more frequently, so it does just grow and grow.

Unit 4   Listening 2 page 38

1 Last week's meeting was very productive, wasn't it?
   Last week's meeting wasn't very productive, was it?

2 You wouldn't be able to help me with these calculations, would you?
   You'd be able to help me with these calculations, wouldn't you?

3 You aren't suggesting that we didn't give you all the information you needed, are you?
   You're suggesting that we didn't give you all the information you needed, aren't you?

4 But that doesn't mean that the project won't be successful in the long term, does it?
   But that means that the project won't be successful in the long term, doesn't it?

5 I'd love to have a copy of that chart you showed us. You couldn't give me one, could you?
   I'd love to have a copy of that chart you showed us. You'll give me one, won't you?

Unit 4   Listening 3 page 38

Interviewer: Gérard, what exactly is the difference between 'business intelligence' and 'industrial espionage'?

Gérard Desmarest: Well, the two terms are really very different because the first is entirely legal and the second is not. Business intelligence is the collection of information through any legal or 'open' source. So that could be through trade publications, business magazines, government organisations, specialist data sources, the internet or even just through straightforward observation. On the other hand, 'industrial espionage' is all about gathering intelligence by illegal methods. Now, there are various ways people can do that, by electronic surveillance, by stealing confidential information and, of course, by recruiting human agents from inside a business operation.

Int: How should businesses go about protecting their information?

GD: I'd say there are really two critical areas where businesses are particularly vulnerable; the first of those is through their information systems. It may be that a business hasn't protected its communication network properly. So it might not even know that critical files have been interfered with or have gone missing. So, protecting your information, how it is accessed and how it is exchanged – that's the first thing. On the human side, there are other dangers. People are not always honest and they may be prepared to communicate confidential information in exchange for something they want. You know, a competitor might try to influence or even hire a key member of your staff. So, you really need to have staff you can trust and that means being sure that what they are doing is in the best interests of the company. So, I'm afraid there are quite a lot of good reasons for companies to install software and systems to monitor the activities of their employees. It's sad to have to say that, but these days information is just too valuable.

Int: How would you advise an employee to be more aware of the danger of espionage?

GD: I would say that it's more a question of training than advising. I say that because most employees do not understand the techniques that outsiders can use to obtain information about a business. So, intelligence or security training can be very helpful because it's always easier for people to protect themselves once they know what they have to protect themselves against. You know, competitors can get a lot of useful information from employees just by asking the right questions at the right time. And an employee may not even realise that he or she is being manipulated. So, good, basic security training is definitely the first thing, and that's something that most companies don't provide because they don't know the risks that they are running.

Int: Can you give us an example of a company that you have advised and explain how you helped them?

GD: Well, I'm afraid I can't give you any names but, er, yes, I can answer that question in general terms. I mean, I've been involved in cases where we've been called into a company that had been the target of industrial espionage, and our job was to identify and locate the systems that had been installed. These were mostly quite sophisticated electronic devices which recorded telephone conversations and monitored meetings and then transmitted that information to outsiders. So, the first part of the job was to conduct a full security review and we did that at the weekend when there was nobody at the company. And then once we'd done that, well, we advised the company's information managers on what they had to do to make sure that it wouldn't happen again. But, er, obviously I can't discuss the exact details with you – in my profession we don't give away confidential information, we protect it!

Unit 4   Listening 4 page 39

1

A Head office say they want the sales information for all our subsidiaries as soon as possible.

B Well, so far I'm afraid I have only been able to get sales figures for Europe.

A Why didn't you tell me? Don't you realise how important this is?

B I'm sorry. I didn't know it was that urgent.

A Look. Could you just tell me when you'll have it ready by?

2

A Shall we go over these figures again before we send them to the accounts department?

B I don't think that's really necessary. They look pretty good to me.

A Well, I'm not so sure about that. I'd like to be certain that there are no major errors.

B I'm afraid I don't have the time to do that right now. Why don't you check them yourself?

3

A We still haven't found what's causing the system to fail like that. We've tried everything.

B That's too bad. It's already caused us a lot of delays.

A Yeah, I understand that. So, what would you advise me to do?

B I don't know. How about arranging a meeting with the people who installed the software?

A Good idea. I'll do just that.

4

A I have to make a presentation to the directors about how we can improve our information system.

B Well, there's plenty to say about that.

A I know. That's exactly the problem. If you were in my position, what would you say?

B I think I'd just focus on the plans for the new network. I'd show them that chart we prepared.

A Oh, right. Do you have any idea what we did with that?

B I have a copy on my computer. I'll send it to you.

Unit 4   Decision page 40

This isn't an isolated example by any means. DigitalVisions is facing exactly the sort of dilemma that many major corporations are finding themselves in today. And it's an extremely complex one with no easy solution. On the one hand, there is a law made by one country which happens to be the home of many multinational businesses. And corporations can't afford to ignore that law without taking considerable risks. But on the other hand, there is the whole question of whether or not a company can, or indeed should, impose a law on employees in another country when that law directly contradicts its own national labour legislation. So, it raises some difficult questions: Is a company entitled to know everything about its employees and their behaviour? How will it use such information? A lot of people are starting to say that, yes, companies should have that information. Indeed, some businesses probably already do have it. Remember that 75 per cent of companies in the US now have some sort of employee surveillance system – IT or camera. So, my feeling on this one is that it is a question that will evolve very quickly and that will be resolved at the highest levels of government. So, for me, the problem at DigitalVisions has to be solved over a period of time – they can't just impose a solution on their staff like this. I think they should definitely not install the hotline in countries where it meets with serious opposition. What they have to do first is to open negotiations with staff and their representatives and try to reach an agreement on how the hotline should be used.

Unit 5   Listening 1 page 42

a Siemens is producing a special range of fashion phones designed to be lifestyle accessories. One of these has two clear functions: it is a phone and, more importantly, it can be clipped onto a bag or item of clothing, which makes it a fashion statement as well.

b Another Siemens model features a large screen on a small device, which can be closed to protect the screen. When opened, it provides plenty of room for both display and keypad. It's called the Jackknife.

c Nokia has a new model where the telephone itself is a secondary function. This suggests that the mobile phone as a separate device could disappear altogether and be designed to perform specific tasks aimed at particular types of users. The primary function of this model is as a gaming console.

d   Sony Ericsson has pioneered a clever new shape in camera phones, seen in a new model which resembles a camera when closed. The device opens to the side to reveal a standard mobile phone keypad, and Sony based the controls on their digital camera. This is the Clamshell.

Unit 5   Listening 2 page 47

OK, let me start by saying that what we need to achieve is the creation of a corporate website which is an effective sales and marketing tool. The first thing we need to do is ask our information technology experts a few questions. And the answers we need from the IT staff, as you can see from this slide, concern the hardware we require and the time we need to spend maintaining the site. Now, while we're waiting for those answers, I suggest that the marketing department starts by preparing product descriptions and conducting an online survey. My view is that the online survey should be modelled on the questionnaires we used for our last market research. Finally, I want the communications department to organise regular meetings to keep everyone up-to-date and informed. Now, any questions?

Unit 6   Listening 1 page 54

1
Benetton is, of course, one of the big names in modern advertising and everyone remembers the series of shock campaigns that the company did with Oliviero Toscani in the 1990s. Now, that may have been a great way to build awareness of the Benetton company, but it certainly wasn't always a commercial success. So I think it's very interesting to see how they've changed their advertising in their new campaign. Of course, there's no direct connection between the animal in the picture and the clothes that Benetton sells, but this really is an ad that has great emotional impact. Benetton is associating its name with a cause – the protection of animals and nature – and that gives them a very good platform. This is more than just photography – it's art. It's the type of ad that people will want to put on their walls, and there's no better place for an advert than that.

2
Creativity is at the heart of advertising, which is why I've chosen this ad – you know, I think it's a great example of just that. At first sight, it just looks like a very straightforward shot of a group of young Maasai people, standing together out in the emptiness of the African plains. And you're almost left wondering what this advert could be for, because there's no obvious trace of anything connected with consumer society. But then when you look more closely, you realise that, in fact, the people have been positioned to form the outline of a Land Rover four-wheel drive vehicle – the Freelander Maasai. I think it's a very subtle ad because what it's saying to people is 'Look, this is the vehicle that the Maasai have chosen, and they've done that because they know it's a reflection of their own qualities as a tribe – strong, fearless, intrepid.' So for the target audience, this is an ad that's not only reassuring, it's also one that makes a very direct appeal to their sense of adventure.

Unit 6   Listening 2 page 55

1
Max Schling lived in New York. He opened a flower shop there. To publicise his business he ran an advert in The New York Times. It was in shorthand. Some bosses asked their secretaries to translate it. They told them that it said: 'Remember Max Schling Flowers.'

2
One of the best stories I ever heard about advertising is about Max Schling, who was a New York florist. Now this was back in the 1920s, and Max had just started his business and was looking for a good way to publicise it. And then one day he had this brilliant idea: he ran an ad in The New York Times – only it wasn't like any of the other ads in the paper because it was all in shorthand, which is an abbreviated language that people like secretaries use to take notes. Well, of course, none of the businessmen who'd bought the paper could read shorthand so they had no idea what the ad actually said. Guess what happened? As soon as they arrived at work they asked their secretaries to translate it. And what did it say? 'Remember Max Schling Flowers next time the boss wants to send flowers to his wife.' Now for me that was one smart advertisement! And in the end, Schling went on to become one of the most famous flower businesses in New York.

3
Remember that business trip that I was supposed to do? You know, for the International advertising festival. Well, you'll never believe this! Everything went just fine to begin with – I had a great flight out, the hotel was OK and the festival itself was really a great success. Anyway, to cut a long story short, when I was getting ready to leave, I put my passport and my tickets into the side pocket of my bag – just to be sure that I'd know exactly where they were. Well, I asked the receptionist to call for a taxi and sure enough ten minutes later this car drew up. I went over to talk to the driver and just then a second taxi arrived. And this driver then started shouting at the first driver and saying that I was *his* client. Well, in all the confusion, I wasn't paying attention to my bag and suddenly when I turned round to look for it, I saw that the second driver had taken it and was putting it into his car. And then he just jumped into his car and drove off, leaving me with no passport, no ticket and no money. What a nightmare!

Unit 7   Preview page 60

Marvin Hunt
I specialise in the area of employment law, but not just here in the UK. I work all over Europe and I deal with a whole range of legal issues arising out of employment. So, one week I could be advising a major corporation about their hiring policies and the next I could be involved in resolving a dispute between workers and employers. We've got a very challenging case coming up soon where a group of female employees is claiming that they were paid less than the male employees for the same work.

Louise Grainger

My training was in law and in life sciences. So my double background is a great help in my line of business, which is the environment. These days, companies are coming under a lot of pressure from lawyers and also from environmentalists who say that their operations may be causing damage to the environment or even creating health problems for some people. So my job is to help businesses to evaluate the risks that they face. At the moment I'm advising a petroleum company that is accused of polluting the local water supply.

Marsha Maspero

I'm in IP, which is our jargon for intellectual property. That refers to things like the brand names and the patented inventions that belong to an organisation. So we have a network of associates in countries around the world who give us specialist advice to help companies to protect their intellectual property in international markets. My own speciality is actually the entertainment industry, which means that I'm often working with people from the music and film industry. For instance, I've just finished defending a very famous client from the sports industry whose pictures were being used on a commercial website without his permission.

Samuel Chase

Product liability is where I work. All businesses are responsible for making sure that their products do not cause harm to the consumers who use them. What we do is advise companies when they have to deal with complaints. That could involve negotiating with other lawyers or actually defending the company in court. We have a big case at the moment where we're helping a pharmaceutical company to prepare a strategy to deal with litigation that may result from complaints about one of its best-selling drugs.

Unit 7 — Listening page 65

1

Monica: David, I think you know that we've been having a lot of problems with the Donsanto case. We're already behind schedule and at this rate we'll never be ready to present the case in court. Here's what I have in mind: I'd like you to take on responsibility for the whole case from now on.

David: That's out of the question! I'm in the middle of negotiations with the employees of Dextra Manufacturing about compensation so I don't see how I can take on a whole new case just like that! Besides, it's a lot of responsibility.

Monica: I'm sure we can find someone to replace you. That way you'd be completely free to deal with Donsanto. We would give you full support and you'd be able to choose the people you want to work with.

David: Well, if you give me an assistant and a budget to cover my expenses, I suppose I just might be interested. But I can't give you an answer right now – not before I've had a look at the files to see what's been done so far. Why don't you get those to me and then I'll be in a better position to give you my decision?

2

Harvey: Hi, Jane. Well, are you still interested in buying the laptop?

Jane: Not at that price. You know I can't afford that much. You're asking for five hundred and I could probably get a new one for less than eight. Why don't we say four?

Harvey: No way! You know it's worth more than that. It's only six months old and it's still under guarantee. And you won't have to buy any software – it's all installed.

Jane: Four hundred, that's my final offer. You can take it or leave it.

Harvey: Oh, well, that's too bad then.

3

Johanna: Hi, Rudy. You're just the person I was looking for.

Rudy: I don't like the sound of that! Don't tell me you're going to ask me to cover for you again!

Johanna: Sorry to ask you at such short notice, but what I'm proposing is that you cover for me at the project meeting on Friday and I'll make it up to you whenever you like.

Rudy: That suits me fine, actually, because I'm going to need you to cover for me at the end of the month. So, if you can do that, then you've got a deal.

Johanna: OK – done!

Unit 7 — Decision page 66

This is a classic dilemma. Here we have two companies that had actually both successfully launched their businesses in more or less the same sector. The similarities probably end there, too, because on the one hand you have Glow Industries, which is a start-up, and on the other you have an international organisation with connections to some very big players in the beauty business. So big money meets small money, if you like, because Glow by JLo has $100 million in annual revenue and Glow Industries just two or three million. The problem is that neither of the companies is in fact the first to register a trademark containing the word 'Glow' because other businesses are already selling products under similar names. And this is also where it gets even more complicated: because when Terri took legal action against Sweetface, they responded by buying a stake in one of the companies that was already using the name 'Glow' and then what they did was to counterattack, accusing Terri herself of stealing their name. But that generated a lot of negative publicity for Glow by JLo, and eventually the two sides reached a settlement. There are no details of exactly what that involved but Terri Williamson agreed to change the name of her products – so there is every reason to suppose that she received substantial compensation.

Unit 8 — Listening 1 page 68

The amazing thing about most successful brands is that very little can knock them off the top once they've become well established and they've achieved brand loyalty from their customers. I mean, certain big brands have survived scandals about sweatshops, they've continued to sell even though the sports teams they chose to promote them lost all their matches in one season! But the one thing that can *kill a* brand, and particularly a luxury brand, is if it loses its image of exclusivity. If you give too many retailers licences and let them sell at the price they see fit – well, then you're in trouble! You must never lose control of the pricing policy.

Unit 8   Listening 2 page 72

Interviewer: You used to be a brand asset manager and you've moved into the area of corporate identity. Could you tell us how corporate identity and brand asset management are linked?

Manager: I feel qualified to do both because a good corporate image, like a brand image, will separate and distinguish a company and its products and services from all others. A 'brand' in this case is the face of the company, the one that the public sees. When you have a face, you have a brand you own. So the identity, whether it be corporate identity, brand identity or both, should be the company's visual statement to the world about who and what the company is and what its products and services stand for.

Int: What is the biggest challenge companies face in establishing a clear brand identity?

Manager: There are many challenges, of course, but they must all be faced. Companies must understand who they are, what their product is and who their customers are – all of which lead to the key contributor of identity: finding the right price. Are they economical products at a good price, or expensive quality products? The price is a key distinguishing factor in terms of competitors. If there is no one in the market, then brand identity might not even matter, products might just happily survive without an identity.

Int: How do companies check the effectiveness of their corporate brand?

Manager: They can do a visual audit, which means conducting interviews and analyses on everything the company produces, like letterheads, business cards, vehicles, signage, packaging, ads and so on. This should be done every three to five years, ideally. All the visual materials need to say 'this is who we are and this is what our products stand for', year in, year out. The company name isn't more or less important than the brands they sell; in most cases the brands and corporate name are synonymous.

Int: You say 'in most cases'. When is this not the case?

Manager: Well, lots of big conglomerates with a variety of brands actually keep a low corporate profile, while the brands are in the forefront. People remember the products but not the firm that produces them. However, that doesn't mean that if the company is involved in some wrongdoing or if their identity gets tarnished, it won't have a negative effect on the brand. In the end, the corporate brand's reputation will affect the product brand's reputation, and vice versa.

Unit 8   Listening 3 page 73

Jack: As you can see on the slide here, we are going to redesign the interiors of all our directly operated stores in line with the new brand image of classic sobriety. This will reinforce the message of the media campaigns and should lead to a considerable increase in sales!

Catherine: Yes. It *is* a good idea, but I can't help wondering where the budget for this is going to come from.

Jack: Yes, I was going to come to that. We will of course have to cut the advertising budget, and I feel we should scrap the TV campaign altogether. A better-targeted print campaign supported by the new ...

Catherine: Hold on, what do you mean, scrap the TV campaign? Why didn't you tell me? We did so much research for that, you know, and that campaign will get us the extra sales we need. I'm sorry, but I ...

Jack: Look, don't take this personally – it isn't that your idea is bad, it's just that this is clearly the best way to ...

Unit 8   Decision page 74

This is a tricky situation indeed, though not unusual. Managing success in the luxury brand business is almost as difficult as getting to the top in the first place. With the sales of brands like Burberry increasing as they are, democratisation is inevitable. I mean, look at the CEO at Dior – he has tripled sales figures in six years and that shows it *is* possible to expand a brand and keep it exclusive. However, the Burberry case is a little more complicated as some of the new brand enthusiasts are famous for bad and even sometimes dangerous behaviour – a truly complicated dilemma. I think though, I would have to say they should embrace the new markets. The increased sales aren't doing them any harm! And it doesn't look like the alternative markets are repelling their target customers. Their website does note its 'broad appeal' in its 'About us' section, even though it only features people who look very wealthy and conventional. For the moment, they seem to be taking the 'wait and see' approach. I think they should fully exploit these new market opportunities while they last, but I guess they are too afraid of getting a downmarket image.

Unit 9   Listening 1 page 80

Interviewer: Why did you invest your money in textiles, such a difficult market?

Bradley Hopper: Yeah, I know, people thought I was crazy but, hey, I could never work with a product I didn't like. And it was clothes that I was interested in more than anything else. At first, I wanted to get into the designer end but that's even more difficult.

Int: Your investment has certainly paid off. Turnover of around a hundred million dollars, right?

BH: Yeah, it's been a very good year for us. But it took some time to get to this point, although I guess I knew we could do it. It's profit that drives me. I know I said I love great clothes and that, but what your first priority has to be is making money, you know what I mean. That is the key to success as far as I'm concerned.

Int: Can you relax now that you've established the brand?

BH: Well, not exactly. In my business you have to keep reinventing yourself, investing in design and marketing, and hope you get noticed by the best retail outlets. There is so much competition out there and they're all cutting costs in a very price-sensitive market. But it isn't being the cheapest that counts. What keeps me one step ahead is knowing where to cut costs and where to invest.

Int: And what is the next investment?

BH: Well, I'm proud to say we're planning to launch our first environmental product line this year, a T-shirt line made from 100 per cent grown-in-the-USA certified organic cotton. There's a huge market for that kind of environmentally friendly product.

Int: That sounds like an interesting development.

BH: Yes, but I may not be around to see it – I'm thinking of selling up and starting out as a venture capitalist, or rather a business angel. It's the excitement you get at the beginning of a venture that I'm after. And I prefer the image of angel because that would mean being more involved than just a venture capitalist, you know, and it's the hands-on part that really interests me.

Unit 9   Listening 2 page 81

Leader: ... OK, hold on, let's just sum up what has been decided so far and then if we are all agreed, we can continue to prioritise what's left on the list. We all agree that it is imperative to draw up criteria for the companies we want to trade in, right? Otherwise, we'll never get a comprehensive list together. Now, I know it would be useful to establish relationships with the CFOs of companies on our list, but we don't have to do that now. I'm afraid we can forget about a trip to Frankfurt – it just doesn't make sense, and we're going to recruit specialists for the job, anyway. Right, what next?

Team member: Well, maybe the next step should be to start the recruitment process ...

Unit 10   Listening 1 page 89

Interviewer: There's a lot of interest in renewable energies these days. Could you explain briefly what these are?

Mia Hansen: Well, when we talk about energy sources, we usually divide these into two very different categories: non-renewable and renewable. Non-renewable refers to all the energies that depend on using mineral or petroleum resources, which you can only use once. For example, if you use a barrel of oil to produce electricity or fuel, then that energy will never be replaced. On the other hand, renewable energies depend on natural forces like sunlight, which, of course, are unlimited. So, when you use renewable energy, you're not reducing the amount of that energy that is available, because it's constant – so the same quantity of energy will always be there in the future.

Int: Can you give us some examples of renewable energies?

MH: Of course, I mean ... I'm sure most people today are familiar with the wind towers or wind turbines that you can find in many places. Well, wind power is just one example of this, and like most renewable energies, or 'alternative energies' as they're often called, it originates from sunlight. The action of the sun on the atmosphere not only creates wind but it also generates heat, which makes water evaporate. So, almost all renewable energies rely on the sun. Other examples are solar power, of course, water and wave power, and also what we call biomass energy, which comes from plants and vegetable matter. But I should add that there are other renewable energies that do not depend on the sun, for instance, geothermal energy, which uses the heat that is under the surface of the earth, and tidal energy, which uses the gravitational effect of the moon.

Int: What's the future for alternative energy?

MH: I think it has a very important role to play in the future because, as I said, it uses energy sources that are abundant, so there's no danger of them disappearing like our traditional energy resources. But what's just as important is the fact that it's non-polluting – and you don't have to burn anything to produce power. And that means it doesn't produce gases that harm the environment and cause health problems. Unfortunately, there's no way you can suddenly switch to using only renewable energies – it's just not that simple.

Int: Why not?

MH: Well, for a number of reasons, actually. Cost is definitely one of those, because power generated from alternative energies is still relatively expensive. And then there's the fact that many of the technologies are experimental and we don't yet have the systems in place that will allow us to generate power cheaply from say, waves – though there's no doubt in my mind that we will have those soon. Yet another problem is with the nature of the energy sources themselves – the wind, for example, doesn't always blow so you have to compensate for variations in the amounts of energy that can be produced.

Int: So, what are governments doing to encourage the development of renewable energies?

MH: I think it's easier to take an example to explain this. If we look at the situation in the United Kingdom, we can see the sorts of problems that governments in many countries are facing. The main uses of energy in the UK at the moment are household consumption and transport. Then to a lesser degree you have industry and, lastly, services. If we just look at the first two – well, if you wanted to replace the energy that they consume with electricity from wind, then you'd have to build hundreds of thousands of wind turbines to do that! And today that's just not possible for both technical and environmental reasons. So, in fact, the UK government has set a fairly modest target, which is to have 25 per cent of its energy coming from renewable sources by 2025. But where will the rest come from? Well, that's the big question. Nuclear energy could be one solution, but nobody wants to live next to a nuclear power station. So at the moment there are no easy answers – renewable energy can help, but it won't provide a magic solution.

Unit 10   Listening 2 page 91

1 **A** Hi, Ray. I thought I'd give you a call to see how things are going on your side. Everything going smoothly?

   B I'd say we're doing OK, but we have hit a couple of snags recently.

   A Oh, really? Any idea what the problem is?

   B The engineers have found a problem with the power supply. It keeps cutting out and they don't know why.

   A Well, that doesn't sound too good. How can we sort this out, then?

B Why don't we have a video conference with the supplier? They should be able to come up with some suggestions.

2 A So, Don, can you give me an update on progress so far? No hitches?

B Nothing too serious, no. The next batch of samples should be ready by the end of the month.

A The end of the month! So, what's gone wrong? I thought we said they had to be ready for testing by the fifteenth.

B I know that's what we were aiming for. But we haven't received some of the precision tools we ordered.

A Let's hope they're here soon, but if the worst comes to the worst, we could extend the deadline. Why didn't you tell me about this before, though?

3 A Hi, Alan. So, how did it go?

B Not that well, actually.

A Really? Don't tell me that they're not going to sign the contract.

B Not just yet, that's for sure. They say they'll only sign if we give them a guarantee that we won't raise prices by more than two per cent a year.

A You can't be serious! There's no way we could agree to that, not with energy prices as high as they are. How do you suggest we deal with this?

B I don't know, but I think we'd better call head office first and see what they have to say.

Unit 11   Preview page 94

If you have a look at some recent examples of companies that have gone public or, at least, announced their intention of doing so, then you can see some quite distinct scenarios. For example, if we take Steven Spielberg's film production company, DreamWorks, it's pretty clear that the primary motivation is to allow the original investors to cash in their investment. On the other hand, in the case of a business like Virgin Blue, the IPO is obviously more directly tied in to the nature of the business – airlines require huge sums of capital to purchase aircraft, and getting that capital from the public rather than from a bank can be very tempting. Another case in point is Domino's Pizza, where the priorities are slightly different because the company is primarily interested in paying off some of its debt while also compensating some of its senior staff. But there are other reasons, of course, why a business might decide to go public.

Unit 11   Listening 1 page 96

I wouldn't say that the Google IPO was really all that successful even if they did raise $1.7 billion from the sale of almost 20 million stocks. Because you have to remember that initially the company had hoped that its IPO would bring in almost $3.7 billion and they were expecting to sell 26 million stocks on the market. So, if you compare the price they actually sold for, $85, with what the company had projected, which was between 108 and $135, then you can see that it didn't really work out that well. You know, I think the management team made quite a few mistakes and that's why they didn't make their target. Probably the most serious was with the timing of the IPO – it was set for

August and that's not the best time to get the financial community on board because it's right in the middle of the summer vacation. Secondly, there was the attitude concerning the disclosure of the company's plans. These were never published in sufficient detail and investors were left in some doubt about what the company was planning. Lastly, the actual process of the auction was complicated and, if anything, instead of simplifying things, it really made it more difficult for investors to buy the shares. However, having said that, I should add that for investors, the Google IPO was a really great opportunity: they could buy at a relatively low price and within a few days the shares had risen to $125.

Unit 11   Listening 2 page 99

As CEO of InnovaTex, I'd like to say a few words about the company before I go on to look at the specific details of our IPO. To sum up our company in a few words: InnovaTex is a young company in a vibrant growth sector. We have first-class products, a dedicated and talented staff and I think we have a great future ahead of us. I'll come back to all that later in this presentation. But now I'd just like to say how proud I am, not only of what we have already achieved but also of being chosen to lead the company at this critical moment in its history as we embark on our next journey. Today, we are about to begin that journey. And that brings me straight to my main message: I sincerely hope that as many of you as possible will be joining us; in other words, that you and your clients will be among our future stockholders!

In my presentation today, I'll be starting with who we are and then giving a review of our recent performance. I'll then move on to an analysis of the risks and the challenges that lie ahead. After that, I'll look at the capital and management structure and how it will be affected by the offering. And finally, I'll discuss the more practical details of the offering, such as the timing.

Unit 11   Decision page 100

Well, I think the whole Hi Wire story goes to show that it is not always that easy to get an IPO right. In this case, first of all, there is the question of how the IPO was organised, and that brings up two problems: the timing and the choice of the bank to manage the launch. For the timing, it was already clear that the internet boom was coming to an end, so the company was entering the market at the worst possible time. But the real problem was that they were doing that with their stocks priced too high – they hadn't reduced them at all. Now why they attempted to do that is also the result of the relationship between the company and its investment advisers. In this case they really weren't that compatible: on one hand, a traditional Wall Street investment bank with very conservative ideas about how to launch a public company and on the other, a young rule-breaking, risk-taking enterprise with very definite ideas. What happened? Well, basically, both sides had overvalued the company, they couldn't sign up enough investors and eventually they had to accept the fact that they couldn't go ahead with the IPO. So it was cancelled for the second time – now that didn't do either of their reputations any good. And remember, on Wall Street nobody ever forgets a failed IPO.

Competition is one of the most critical factors for any business, and knowing where you stand in relation to your competitors is crucial. And this has become a permanent preoccupation for a lot of businesses. But how do you find out? Well, there are various ways you can approach it, but one of the principal tools that's used is based on a theory developed by Michael Porter, a professor at the Harvard Business School. According to him, there are five fundamental forces that affect a company's competitive position. So, if we put this into the form of a diagram, then at the centre you'd have 'Competitive rivalry'. Then you'd put in the four forces or factors that are going to influence this. In the box right at the top you'd have 'Threat of entry'. Now this just means: what is the probability that other businesses will attempt to enter our sector? Then you have two other factors: 'Power of buyers' and 'Power of suppliers', let's say one on each side. This is pretty straightforward and it just refers to the power that both of these groups can exert. So, for example, if you are a company selling to a major distribution chain, then your buyers can impose certain conditions on you. The same is true for suppliers: if you depend on one source, then you don't have much room for manoeuvre. Lastly, there is 'Substitution' or 'Substitute products' – now, this is quite easy to understand, too: most products can be replaced by others, so, of course, the ideal situation is to have one which can't be. But that's not often the case.

In practice, Porter's theory is very helpful because it suggests a number of ways that businesses can build barriers to prevent other companies from entering into direct competition. Among these, there are four which I think are particularly important: differentiation – making your product or service unique; economies of scale – getting a cost advantage over your competition; distribution – having a network which gives you access to markets; and switching costs – making it prohibitively expensive for your customers to change to a rival product or service.

I think that the Honda corporation is a great example of a business that has successfully entered new markets by using a brilliant combination of quality engineering, efficient production and innovative design. The original company, The Honda Technical Research Institute, was set up in 1946 by Soichiro Honda and it was originally just a small domestic manufacturer of cycle engines. Their first commercial product came out one year later. This was the A Type, a small engine designed to be fitted to bicycles. But only ten years later they had already designed the Supercub, which was the first really successful mass-market motorcycle. This was one of the motorbikes that they introduced to the US market when they opened their first office there in 1959, and it was a huge success. It was followed by a whole range of new and exciting models that allowed Honda to take more than 60 per cent of the US market for motorcycles by 1966. But the company had by then started to move into a new sector, the automobile industry, and in 1963 its first car, the S 500, went on sale in Japan. Honda then repeated what it had done in the US

motorcycle markets, and after producing a series of revolutionary cars like the Civic and the Prelude, in 2001 its Accura model became the best-selling car in the US. They had literally taken the automobile market by storm. During the period from 1970 to 2000 Honda was also busy developing new activities in other industries, including robotics, generators and biotechnology, to mention just three. And they haven't stopped at that. One of their most significant moves was into aircraft engines, and it could well be that from now on we'll see the arrival of commercial aircraft under the Honda name. A prototype, the Honda Jet, has already flown and with 441 subsidiaries supporting the company's efforts around the world, Honda represents a threat that's impossible to ignore. So the sky is certainly no limit for them.

1

Lewis: Hi, Georgia. I just wanted to tell you that we've just finalised the prices for the next quarter. We reckon that we can reduce prices by five per cent max starting next month.

Georgia: You must be crazy, Lewis! I told you that our competitors are already at least ten per cent cheaper than we are and they're still bringing their prices down. There'll be a riot if I tell the sales staff that. Can't we find a better solution?

Lewis: Listen, Georgia, that's the way it is, so just tell them it's five per cent – whether they like it or not!

2

Steve: OK, Martin, so what we've decided to do is to introduce electronic sales tracking. That way, each salesperson will record all transactions, and the data will be centralised at head office.

Martin: That sounds fine, Steve. But how long will it take before the whole system is operational?

Steve: I'd like to have it up and running in two months.

Martin: Two months? That's not long. What are your views on finding the time to train everyone to use the system?

Steve: I don't know, er, but it should be possible to block a week in June and get everybody together then. Do you think that would work out?

Martin: Well, yes, I think it might be possible.

3

Greg: I hope I'm not interrupting you, Marta, but there's something I think we need to discuss.

Marta: Go ahead, Greg. What's the problem?

Greg: Well, I've received some complaints from your subordinates. They say you have been assigning too much extra work.

Marta: Listen, Greg, you know we're short-staffed at the moment so let's keep things in perspective. Especially if you won't let me hire any temporary staff. So why don't we just forget about it?

Greg: Forget about it? Look, I know we don't see eye to eye on this, but surely we need to do something!

This is one of the classic cola war stories and also a very interesting case for international marketing because it shows how easy it is for a company, even one like Coca-Cola, to get it wrong when they enter a new market. Parle, the owner of Thums Up, actually decided to sell its brand to Coca-Cola, and Coca-Cola imagined that in no time they would be able to get Indian customers to switch to their brands. But that's not what happened, and after several years of poor performance, Coca-Cola's managers realised that many of their target consumers actually preferred Thums Up. So they revamped the brand, and today Thums Up is the best-selling cola on the continent.

Unit 13   Listening 1 page 112

Frank

Our department specialises in advising and managing transactions for our corporate customers. These are usually businesses which need our specialist assistance with managing their capital. Now, that could involve arranging for a company to go public or issuing shares to enable a business to acquire another company. But it's not always like that because we also provide assistance to companies that are having problems and need to find new sources of capital. In cases like that, we work with our own specialists and put together a plan to raise capital but also to look at how the company can be reorganised.

Matt

In my department we specialise in emerging businesses. These are new companies which are entering markets with new products or services. My job is to identify the businesses that we think have development potential and arrange for investors to take a stake in the capital of the company. Then we advise the company in different ways. This could be about how to develop more effective marketing solutions or about how to find strategic partners to assist them in growing as fast as possible. And, of course, we can also assist them in preparing for a public offering of their shares.

Claudia

The bank's customers come to us when they are thinking of expanding their businesses or setting up in new markets. It's our job to estimate their chances of succeeding. We provide information concerning market trends, competition, etc. – anything we think they need to know – and we also give them our forecasts for the sector they are interested in. If we think the prospects are good, we advise our clients to go ahead with their projects, and we generally get involved in the strategic planning of the business, too.

Unit 13   Listening 2 page 115

Interviewer: Good morning, Mr Sanders, and welcome to the programme today.

Jeff Sanders: Good morning.

Int: Maybe I could start by asking why there is such huge media interest in this alliance.

JS: I think there is one main reason for that: Cazenove has

been in the City of London for 181 years and is one of the few British investment banks. People are bound to be interested in the future of such a firm.

Int: And how did the deal come about?

JS: Well, first of all, Chase bought Robert Fleming, another British investment bank, for £4.9 billion ($7.7 billion), and later bought JP Morgan itself for $36 billion. JP Morgan Chase is now paying £110 million to Cazenove for a half share of the investment-banking joint venture and putting in £50 million of capital and 70 of its staff.

Int: Why was JP Morgan Chase so keen to do a deal with Cazenove?

JS: Well, just look at the recent press comments: the media says that Cazenove is a uniquely wonderful institution that displays all of the virtues of the City of old and none of its vices, and that its client list is the envy of its rivals.

Int: How has the deal been received by those who are directly concerned?

JS: A spokesperson for JP Morgan says all of Cazenove's clients are delighted about it. It is a good deal for JP Morgan, but also for Cazenove's shareholders – and most of those are its employees, who will retain control of a large part of Cazenove's business. They will also see the release of another £230 million of capital from JP Morgan, with the prospect of a lot more in the future.

Int: So, what do you think JP Morgan's long-term plans are?

JS: After five years, JP Morgan will have the right to buy Cazenove out, and Cazenove will have the right to sell to the bank at a price they set independently. Though there are a few penalties involved, this means that it is almost certain that the US giant will end up with the lot.

Unit 13   Listening 3 page 117

1   **A** After looking at this from all sides, I think it's pretty clear that the time has come to expand into the eastern European markets. Don't you agree?

    B I don't think that's what we should do at all. I think it'd be much better to focus on the markets in southern Europe, where we already have a foothold, and consolidate our position there.

    A Well, all things considered, I'm absolutely convinced the right thing to do is to expand in the east.

    B Have you looked at the cost? Where will we get the money from?

    A I've already discussed the plan with our advisers and they say they can find us the partners we'll need. So that shouldn't be a problem. I would just like your support, that's all.

    B Well, I'm sorry but for me it's no.

    A Look, unless you're prepared to change your mind on this one, I'll just have to go ahead without you on the team.

2   **A** This is the situation: we have an investor who wants to buy into the company, and he's prepared to pay cash for 30 per cent of our stocks.

    B I'm not so sure that it would be a good idea to have another person making the big decisions.

    A Well, we need capital to expand, and this guy has already helped several other companies to go public in the hi-tech sector. We've all worked really hard together to get this far and this could be our big break. We're in this together, you know, and it really would be to our advantage.

B Yes, I suppose you're right. When can we meet up with him?

3 A It's in all our interests to take the bank to court – they should be made to pay us compensation for our losses.

B Our case is almost impossible to prove, and if we lose, think of all the bad publicity. I'm really against it.

C I'm sure we could prove it was the bank's fault. They did make inaccurate predictions about our performance, and that caused our share price to fall dramatically.

D All things considered, the most sensible thing would be to talk to our lawyers first and see what they have to say.

A They may advise another course of action, but you're right – that should be our first step.

Unit 14　Listening 1 page 122

Notice how the king uses 'we' straightaway: 'We few, we happy few'. This puts him in the position of a democratic leader from the beginning. He too is part of the team. It is very motivating for the team to feel the leader is part of it and working towards the same goals. They are, as he puts it so well, a 'band of brothers'. He makes them feel part of an exclusive club (the 'happy few'). Indeed they are privileged to be part of this team! They have been chosen especially, and others have been excluded – the 'gentlemen in England now a-bed'. And the people who really invest time and energy and make sacrifices – 'he to-day that sheds his blood with me' – will be rewarded. He tells them they will be remembered as heroes and become gentlemen. Now, if you put that in the context of a manager today motivating, let's say, his sales team, you have all the necessary elements. It's like saying: 'OK, guys, we have a difficult mission to complete but I wouldn't ask you if I didn't think you could do it – and there are big bonuses and promotions in it for us all if we succeed.'

Unit 14　Listening 2 page 125

1 A Did you get the information about the restructuring plan? I sent it to you yesterday.

B Yeah, I got it. But it's not going to be easy to get the message across. And some people are going to be very unhappy.

A I know that. But they have to understand that this affects all of us, and this is the only option we have.

2 A Looks like we have still got some serious problems with delivery. I don't know why we never seem to be able to get the goods to our customers on time.

B Well, one of the main problems is with the central warehouse. The automated system just isn't producing the results we expected.

A Look. We have to find a solution, and fast. Why don't you take charge of this? Identify the exact problem and then find some way to fix it.

B Great. I already have a pretty good idea of what needs to be done. I'll get on to it right away.

3 A You do realise that your department has failed to reach its targets, don't you?

B Yes, I'm aware of that. But I still think we did as well as we could under the circumstances.

A But this is the third time this has happened. So, look, I'm going to give you one last chance. OK?

4 A How many units are you expecting us to sell per month?

B I think that a ten per cent increase for each salesperson should be about right.

A Ten per cent! That's an awful lot.

B Well, I'm not saying that it will be easy. But I am offering a two per cent increase in commission to anyone who makes those numbers. I think that's fair, isn't it?

Unit 14　Decision page 126

Well, before I say anything else, I would just like to say that I agree with the consultants when they say that training is an excellent motivator. And I find the various options they propose very interesting. It's difficult to choose between them but I think it's really important to solve communication problems as soon as and whenever they occur. There is obviously a huge breakdown in communication here with the majority of the staff dissatisfied with how they are being managed! Therefore, I would send the managers on the course offered by the Future Management Consultancy as soon as possible. On the other hand, the employees wouldn't see the immediate benefit of this, so I think I would use the rest of the budget for one-day stress management courses at Key Associates or possibly the health and fitness courses at Top Health. The fitness courses would be seen to be a life enhancer for everyone, and staff would feel that their overall well-being was a cause for concern for the company.

Long term, I think it would be a very good thing to offer a full course in stress management as so many staff members complain of stress. Or it might be better to consider installing gym and training facilities, because having a health and fitness programme for all staff members is very important, particularly in the manufacturing sector – and it could eliminate a lot of stress into the bargain!

Unit 15　Listening 1 page 132

Managing director: As you can see from the figures, our market share has been falling by about ten per cent every year over the last five years. I know that I am partly to blame – I failed to see the need to adjust our pricing policy in line with the competition. We all hoped our customers would continue to pay for quality.

Consultant: Have you done any customer satisfaction surveys recently?

MD: Yes, it really was a revelation: you see, we have a policy of excellent customer service in our stores, but that costs a lot. We aim to make shopping a pleasant experience but it turns out, and this is the most interesting aspect, that people prefer the huge choice and cheaper goods they find in the hypermarket.

Consultant: Can you tell me what you think your options are now?

MD: Well, we are thinking of either selling out to the hypermarket – they have made us an offer, you know – or possibly trying to compete with them. That's where you come in. We feel we need a consultant to advise us on the best course of action. What do you think we should do?

Consultant: I'll have to do a full audit before I can answer that but my initial feeling is: don't sell. Let's look at the quality aspect a bit more and possibly even put up prices! My job is to turn what seems to be a disadvantage on its head and make it an advantage. It's a risk, but we may need to invest in a huge advertising campaign to attract customers back to the store – but it often pays off.

Unit 15   Listening 2 page 133

A I've just come from a meeting with the new consultant and he said that if we were outsourcing to them, we would have to have complete confidence.

B What does that mean exactly?

A Well, they need access to every type of information we have, and he suggested co-operating fully with their team. So, I told him we would.

B So they can tell us how to do our job!

A Look, the bottom line is the CEO wants us to give them our full co-operation and I recommend not judging the outcome just yet. And the consultant pointed out that they may make improvements around here.

B Or ruin us completely with their fees!

A Look, the CEO told us at a meeting last week that he would be giving promotions on the basis of their evaluation of each department. What he wants us to do is work with them, not against them – so let's do it!

Unit 15   Listening 3 page 133

Student A

Production manager: I'm glad to get a chance to speak to you before you prepare your final report. I promised to keep team members informed.

Consultant: No problem.

PM: So, what have you come up with so far?

Consultant: Well, the results of the customer satisfaction survey are pretty bad, I'm afraid. There were a lot of negative comments about delays, high prices and poor quality. This seemed to suggest that the production department just isn't profitable anymore.

PM: So, what are you saying?

Consultant: Well, to be honest, we were thinking of suggesting outsourcing production, but a little further research revealed that your main problem can be solved by changing suppliers. So, we're going to recommend changing to more competitive, efficient and cost-effective suppliers. Do you think there will be any resistance to a change like this?

PM: I'll explain the alternative, which is job losses, and there shouldn't be a problem!

Student B

Team manager: Hi, Terry, how are you?

Supplier: Fine, thanks.

TM: We have a big order to put in this month and it is pretty urgent.

Supplier: What kind of deadline are we looking at?

TM: Two to three weeks maximum.

Supplier: I don't think we could meet that deadline. I could make you a priority but it would mean a bit of a price increase. You'll have problems finding anyone else in the market with the same quality – it might be worth your while doing a deal with us on this one.

TM: Look, I'll be honest with you, I'll have to try to find someone else – a price increase won't be accepted in the present climate. I get the feeling our consultants are going to recommend outsourcing production if we don't become more cost efficient.

Unit 15   Decision page 134

This is indeed an interesting dilemma. Consultants have a confidentiality clause in their contracts, but obviously there is a limit to how much one should take responsibility for. This case is obviously pre-regulation and the Sarbanes-Oxley Act. In fact, it reminds me of the situation Sherron Watkins found herself in at Enron. Of course, she was an employee of the company and not of their auditors, but she faced a similar dilemma. She did not contact anyone from outside the company straightaway. However, she did write an anonymous memo to the CEO, to inform him that the company was involved in accounting fraud on a large scale. He later said that he wasn't aware of any irregularities before receiving the letter. She then met face to face with him, and an internal inquiry was opened. Her claims were dismissed but we know now that Enron was getting deeper and deeper into debt. She finally made the decision to go to the regulators with her story.

Her critics say she spoke out only when she was sure the company was going out of business and that she first sold off her stock options worth $17,000. This was minimal compared to other executives. However, I think she did achieve something, as she said herself: as a result, the 2002 Sarbanes-Oxley Act requires CEOs and CFOs to certify that financial accounts are true. If they're found to be lying, they face up to 20 years in gaol. Monetary fines don't do it: if you've made $100 million and you're fined $25 million, you're still *very* rich. But the idea of going to gaol scares these guys to death.